T0119144

Peter Riedemann's Hutterite Confession of Faith

Classics of the Radical Reformation

Classics of the Radical Reformation is an English-language series of Anabaptist and Free Church documents translated and annotated under the direction of the Institute of Mennonite Studies, which is the research agency of the Anabaptist Mennonite Biblical Seminaries, and published by Plough Publishing House.

1. *The Legacy of Michael Sattler.* Trans., ed. John Howard Yoder.

2. *The Writings of Pilgram Marpeck.* Trans., ed. William Klassen and Walter Klaassen.

3. *Anabaptism in Outline: Selected Primary Sources.* Trans., ed. Walter Klaassen.

4. *The Sources of Swiss Anabaptism: The Grebel Letters and Related Documents.* Ed. Leland Harder.

5. *Balthasar Hubmaier: Theologian of Anabaptism.* Ed. H. Wayne Pipkin and John Howard Yoder.

6. *The Writings of Dirk Philips.* Ed. Cornelius J. Dyck, William E. Keeney, and Alvin J. Beachy.

7. *The Anabaptist Writings of David Joris: 1535–1543.* Ed. Gary K. Waite.

8. *The Essential Carlstadt: Fifteen Tracts by Andreas Bodenstein.* Trans., ed. E. J. Furcha.

9. *Peter Riedemann's Hutterite Confession of Faith.* Ed. John J. Friesen.

10. Sources of South German/Austrian Anabaptism. Ed. C. Arnold Snyder, trans. Walter Klaassen, Frank Friesen, and Werner O. Packull.

11. *Confessions of Faith in the Anabaptist Tradition: 1527–1660.* Ed. Karl Koop.

12. *Jörg Maler's Kunstbuch: Writings of the Pilgram Marpeck Circle.* Ed. John D. Rempel.

13. *Later Writings of the Swiss Anabaptists: 1529–1592.* Ed. C. Arnold Snyder.

Peter Riedemann's Hutterite Confession of Faith

Translation of the 1565 German Edition of
*Confession of Our Religion, Teaching, and Faith
By the Brothers Who Are Known as the Hutterites*

Translated and edited by
John J. Friesen

PLOUGH PUBLISHING HOUSE

Published by Plough Publishing House
Walden, New York
Robertsbridge, England
Elsmore, Australia
www.plough.com

Plough produces books, a quarterly magazine, and Plough.com to encourage people and help them put their faith into action. We believe Jesus can transform the world and that his teachings and example apply to all aspects of life. At the same time, we seek common ground with all people regardless of their creed.

Plough is the publishing house of the Bruderhof, an international community of families and singles seeking to follow Jesus together. Members of the Bruderhof are committed to a way of radical discipleship in the spirit of the Sermon on the Mount. Inspired by the first church in Jerusalem (Acts 2 and 4), they renounce private property and share everything in common in a life of nonviolence, justice, and service to neighbors near and far. To learn more about the Bruderhof's faith, history, and daily life, see Bruderhof.com. (Views expressed by Plough authors are their own and do not necessarily reflect the position of the Bruderhof.)

This volume is a translation of the second edition, dated 1565, of
*Rechenschafft unserer Religion / Leer und Glaubens /
Von den Brüdern so man die Hutterischen Nen't ausgangen /*
Durch Peter Riedemann

This translation is based on the copy in the British Museum and the English translation by Kathleen E. Hasenberg, *Peter Rideman, Account of our Religion, Doctrine and Faith: Given by Peter Rideman of the Brothers Whom Men Call Hutterian* (London: Hodder and Stoughton in conjunction with Plough Publishing House, 1950).

Scripture quotations are translated directly from Riedemann's text and thus do not follow any one English version.

ISBN: 978-0-874-86272-0

Library of Congress Cataloging-in-Publication Data pending.

To the Hutterian Brethren Church,
which for five centuries has kept
the vision of communal living alive

Contents

Confession of Our Religion, Teaching, and Faith
By the Brothers Who Are Known as the Hutterites
Through Peter Riedemann

Abbreviations

In the notes, names of biblical books are abbreviated to first letters. Here are abbreviations for Apocryphal or Deuterocanonical books:

Bar.	Baruch	Rest of Esther	Additions to Esther
Bel.	Bel and the Dragon	Sir.	Sirach (Ecclesiasticus)
1-2 Esd.	1-2 Esdras	Song of Thr.	Prayer of Azariah and
Jth.	Judith		Song of the Three Jews
Let. Jer.	Letter of Jeremiah	Sus.	Susanna
1-4 Macc.	1-4 Maccabees	Tob.	Tobit
Pr. Man.	Prayer of Manasseh	Wisd. of Sol.	Wisdom of Solomon

Other sources:

Herald Press	Scottdale, Pa., and Waterloo, Ont.: Herald Press
ME	*The Mennonite Encyclopedia.* 5 vols. Herald Press, 1955-59, 1990.
ML	*Mennonitisches Lexikon.* Vols. 1-3: Frankfurt a. M. and Weierhof, 1913-42, 1958. Vol. 4: Karlsruhe: Heinrich Schneider, 1967.
MQR	*Mennonite Quarterly Review.* Goshen, Ind.

Preface to the New Edition

Peter Riedemann's Hutterite Confession of Faith is one of the most important documents of the sixteenth-century Anabaptist movement. Written during Riedemann's two-year imprisonment in Wolkersdorf in Hesse, Germany, from 1540 to 1542, it not only was a personal confession but also expressed the faith of the Hutterite communal group in Moravia. This community was the only Anabaptist communal group to survive the bitter persecutions in 1535. By the early 1540s, Hutterites were able to re-establish communities under the protection of sympathetic nobles.

When Riedemann left his place of imprisonment in Wolkersdorf and took up his mantle as spiritual leader of the Hutterites, the *Confession* quickly gained importance within the community. It was based on biblical principles, gave theological expression to the community's faith, followed the outline of the Apostles' Creed, and provided practical guidance for how to live in community. An indication of its importance is that it was the only document published by Hutterites in the sixteenth century.

The *Confession* survived the fierce persecutions in the Thirty Years' War (1618–48), when all Hutterite communities in Moravia (Czechia today) were destroyed, and again when the communities that survived in Hungary (Slovakia today) were also destroyed a few decades later. Wagonloads of Hutterite writings were confiscated by the Jesuits and government authorities, but the surviving remnant of Hutterites always managed to retain copies of the *Confession*. Following the migrations and calamities, the *Confession* was eventually taken to North America and remains a prized document in Hutterite communities.

The publication of Riedemann's *Confession* in English in 1950[1] made this important work more accessible to Hutterites, many of whom are now more conversant in English than in German. It also made this document available to English-reading students and scholars, thus broadening the use and influence of this work within academic circles.

Following its republication in 1999 as part of the Classics of the Radical Reformation series,[2] *Peter Riedemann's Hutterite Confession of Faith* was positively reviewed in several scholarly publications. It has also been cited more than three dozen times in academic journals. One of the most significant discussions of Riedemann's theology is in David Griffin's *The Word Became Flesh*.[3] In this "rapprochement" Griffin leans heavily on Riedemann's *Confession* as an expression of Anabaptist thinking.

Riedemann's Hutterite Confession of Faith has also received a positive reception by contemporary Hutterites. In 1997, two years before its publication, Arnold Hofer asked to see the translation. (At that time Hofer was a German teacher at Riverbend Community, Manitoba, and president of the Hutterian Education Committee; in 2017 he became elder of the Schmiedeleut Group I conference.) He indicated that Hutterites had been discussing the possibility of translating Riedemann's Confession into modern English and they were wondering if the translation that I had completed, and Herald Press was about to publish, could serve their communities' purposes. Hutterite leaders in various groups reviewed the translation and, after extensive discussions, decided to adopt it for their use.

When the *Confession* was printed in 1999, the Hutterites ordered more than 5,000 copies for distribution within their communities. They also produced expanded editions in hardcover and softcover that included a brief historical survey of Hutterite history written by Dora Maendel, Fairholme Community, Manitoba, a five-page historical timeline, and a translation of an epistle written by Peter Riedemann in 1540 while imprisoned in Wolkersdorf.

The English translation continues to play a formative role in Hutterite communities. Some communities provide a copy to young people for instruction prior to baptism. Others give a copy to newly married couples or to ministers at their election or ordination.

Arnold Hofer says he believes it is having a significant influence. He adds that the Bible index in the English translation helps ministers cross-reference the many places where the Hutterite *Lehren* and *Vorreden* (traditional sermons) refer to particular sections of Riedemann's *Confession*. Edward Kleinsasser, a minister in Crystal Spring Community, Manitoba, also says the English translation has played a role in a spiritual awakening among Hutterites. He, too, uses quotations from Riedemann's *Confession* to augment the *Lehren* and *Vorreden* when he preaches. Patrick Murphy, James Valley Community, Manitoba, says the *Confession* provides Hutterites with a communal understanding of the Christian faith, providing a strong alternative to the more individualistic mainline and evangelical religious vocabulary. All the Hutterite leaders with whom I spoke agree that the *Confession* remains essential for shaping their future.

Young-Pyo Jun, a Korean Anabaptist who studied at Canadian Mennonite Bible College (now Canadian Mennonite University) in the 1990s, has translated Riedemann's *Confession* into Korean; his translation was published in 2018.[4]

Supplementing this English translation, a number of books have been published about Riedemann's *Confession* and the sixteenth-century Hutterite communities in Moravia. In 1995, Werner Packull turned his attention to Hutterite studies and published *Hutterite Beginnings*.[5] Packull divides his study into two parts. In part 1, he discusses early Anabaptist communitarian experiments, and in part 2, he discusses the emergence of the Hutterites. In this study, Packull provides a more comprehensive and nuanced understanding of Anabaptist communitarian efforts.

In 2002, Martin Rothkegel published an essay in which he examines a manuscript found in the University Library of Breslau/ Wroclaw (Poland), written by Riedemann around 1549, which consists of his paraphrases of the Gospels of Mark, Luke, and Matthew.[6] Rothkegel discovered that Riedemann's paraphrases are similar to other paraphrases during his time and depend heavily on those of Erasmus. The aim of Riedemann's paraphrases, Rothkegel concludes, was to get at the spiritual meaning of the literal text. To accomplish this, Riedemann especially used etymology and allegory.

In 2003, Andrea Chudaska published her doctoral dissertation, which she wrote for Gottfried Seebass, professor at the University of Heidelberg and one of the foremost Anabaptist scholars in Europe. Chudaska's study, *Peter Riedemann*, provides an insightful discussion of Riedemann's life and thought and places his *Confession* into its social, political, and cultural context, including the regions of Silesia, central Germany, and Moravia.[7] Her book provides an excellent review of the primary and secondary literature related to Riedemann, includes a detailed outline of Riedemann's life based on a comprehensive use of sources, and helpfully discusses Riedemann's theology.

In 2006, Astrid von Schlachta published a survey of Hutterite history from the sixteenth to the twentieth centuries, explaining in the preface that her aim is "to purge the Hutterite story of myths and clichés that reflect only the euphoria and growth, and include the shadows of divisions and repeated conflicts."[8] She provides helpful context for the early Hutterite story but pays little specific attention to Riedemann and his writings.

In 2007, Werner O. Packull, building on his study in *Hutterite Beginnings*, published *Peter Riedemann*, a major study of the life and writings of Riedemann. In this work Packull provides a detailed account of Riedemann's life, including an analysis of the influences on his thought. He concludes with two chapters in which he discusses the *Confession*. In one chapter he deals with the theological section of the *Confession*, and in the other he treats the section that addresses practical living. In the latter chapter, Packull writes that "by giving particular community practices a confessional and biblical base, Riedemann's Confession gave a particular shape and definition to the subsequent Hutterite tradition," and this powerful influence was possible because the *Confession* "achieved a normative status in subsequent generations."[9]

An English translation of an earlier confession written by Riedemann when he was imprisoned in Gmunden from 1529 to 1532 was published by Plough in 1993 and again in 2016.[10] In 2010 the Hutterian Brethren Book Centre published this book in German.[11] This early work includes some of the themes that Riedemann later incorporated into the *Confession* of 1542. Central to this work is his weaving together of faith and love as key foci in the divine-human drama. This emphasis on faith and love seems to be written as a critique of Luther's emphasis on *sola fide* (by faith alone). For Riedemann, in order for faith to be genuine, it must be expressed in concrete actions of love toward neighbor.

Another recently published book that sheds light on Riedemann's era is Hauprecht Zapff's *Johannes Der Evangelist über alle Kapitel erklärt*.[12] Although this book doesn't mention Riedemann, it brings to light writings by Hutterites that hitherto have been largely unknown. This book is one example of the rich material Rothkegel has discovered in European archives near former Hutterite communities. These materials need to be researched more fully for content, methodology, and style. The result may be a fuller understanding of Riedemann, whose influence is still powerful centuries later.

In the meantime, it is gratifying that Plough is republishing *Peter Riedemann's Hutterite Confession of Faith* and thus helping to keep its message alive for future generations of readers, including students, scholars, and Hutterites.

John J. Friesen

Notes

1.   Peter Rideman, *Account of our Religion, Doctrine and Faith: Given by Peter Rideman of the Brothers Whom Men Call Hutterian*, translated by Kathleen E. Hasenberg (London: Hodder and Stoughton in conjunction with Plough Publishing House, 1950).

2.   Peter Riedemann, *Peter Riedemann's Hutterite Confession of Faith*, translated and edited by John J. Friesen (Waterloo, ON; Scottdale, PA: Herald Press, 1999).

3.   David Griffin, *The Word Became Flesh: A Rapprochement of Christian Natural Law and Radical Christological Ethics* (Eugene, OR: Wipf and Stock, 2016).

4.   후터라이터 신앙고백서 (Daejeon, South Korea: Daejanggan, 2018).

5.   Werner O. Packull, *Hutterite Beginnings: Communitarian Experiments during the Reformation* (Baltimore: Johns Hopkins University, 1995). In 2000 his book was translated into German by Astrid von Schlachta and published as *Die Anfaenge der Hutterer: Experiment in der Guetergemeinschaft waehrend der Reformationszeit* (Innsbruck, Austria: Wagner Verlag, 2000).

6.   Martin Rothkegel, "Learned in the School of David: Peter Riedemann's Paraphrases of the Gospels," *Commoners and Community, Essays in Honour of Werner O. Packull*, edited by C. Arnold Snyder (Kitchener, ON: Pandora, 2002).

7.   Andrea Chudaska, *Peter Riedemann: konfessionsbildendes Taeufertum im 16. Jahrhundert*, Quellen und Forschungen zur Reformationsgeschichte 76 (Heidelberg: Verein Fuer Reformationsgeschichte, Guetersloher Verlagshaus, 2003).

8. Astrid von Schlachta, *Die Hutterer zwischen Tyrol und Amerika: Eine Reise durch die Jahrhunderte* (Innsbruck, Austria: Universitaetsverlag Wagner, 2006); published in English translation as *From the Tyrol to North America: The Hutterite Story through the Centuries*, translated by Werner Packull and Karin Packull (Kitchener, ON: Pandora, 2008); quote from 13.

9. Werner O. Packull, *Peter Riedemann: Shaper of the Hutterite Tradition* (Kitchener, ON: Pandora, 2007); quotes from 161.

10. Peter Riedemann, *Love Is Like Fire: The Confession of an Anabaptist Prisoner; Written at Gmunden, Upper Austria between 1529 and 1532*, translated by Kathleen Hasenberg and edited by Emmy Barth Maendel (Walden, NY: Plough, 1993).

11. Peter Riedemann, *Liebe brennt wie Feuer: die Rechenschaft und Glaubensbekenntnis eines Täufers: geschrieben ins Gefängnis zu Gmunden, Oberösterreich im Jahre 1530* (MacGregor, MB: Hutterian Brethren Book Centre, 2010).

12. Hauprecht Zapff, *Johannes Der Evangelist über alle Kapitel erklärt: Ein täuferischer Bibelkommentar von 1597*, edited by Martin Rothkegel (MacGregor, MB: Hutterian Brethren Book Centre, 2017).

General Editor's Preface

In the last three decades there has been a change in understanding the origins, nature, and development of the Radical Reformation in general and of the Anabaptists in particular. Scholars have become aware of the diversity and variety of the Radical Reformers.

When primary source materials from the Radical Reformers are available and studied, one can grasp how early Anabaptists agreed or disagreed, came together or diverged. The Institute of Mennonite Studies has a vision to make such sources available in English in this series, Classics of the Radical Reformation (CRR).

Though scholarly, CRR editions are meant also for the wider audience of those interested in the Anabaptist and free church writers of the sixteenth century. The translations are intended to be true and polished, yet not excessively literal or wooden.

With this ninth volume in the series, we encounter a Radical Reformer whose work endures and continues to exercise substantial influence among present-day descendants of a radical and communal vision of discipleship. Peter Riedemann wrote this *Confession of Faith* and many letters and hymns. The *Confession* has served as the basic text for Hutterites from the sixteenth century up to the present day.

We are grateful to Professor John J. Friesen of Canadian Mennonite Bible College, Winnipeg, for making a new and readable translation of this pivotal document. Radical Reformation Christians from many denominations and manifestations of the body of Christ are grateful to have in hand this modern and readable translation. The introduction by the editor, a respected and capable historian, sets this book within the context of radical movements at the time of its origin.

—*H. Wayne Pipkin, General Editor, CRR*
Archbold, Ohio

Translator-Editor's Preface

Peter Riedemann's *Hutterite Confession of Faith* provides the theological grounding for the Hutterite understanding of economic communalism, and gives numerous practical examples of it. This *Confession* has guided the Hutterian communities from the sixteenth century to the present. While in prison in the early 1540s, Riedemann wrote this book for the Lutheran ruler, Philip of Hesse, to interpret the vision of a renewed community pursued by the Hutterites. He tried to overcome popular misconceptions about Anabaptists by presenting the Hutterite-Anabaptist beliefs and way of life. A copy of the *Confession* was taken to Moravia, and the Hutterites quickly accepted it as the definitive statement of their faith.

The *Confession* consists of two major parts. Early in the first part, Riedemann expounds the Hutterite view of various theological issues, using short, pithy sections of half a page to a couple of pages in length. This discussion is structured around the Apostles' Creed. He argues that the understanding of the faith and the church which he presents is the intended meaning of the Apostles' Creed and the Nicene and Chalcedonian creeds. Later in the first part, Riedemann explores implications of this faith for the life of the community. In the second part of the *Confession*, he deals with six issues more extensively.

The *Confession* is liberally supported by biblical quotations and allusions. The 1565 edition cites these Scriptures by book and chapter, in the page margins. Verse citations were added later. In this translation, amended references are in footnotes. Riedemann creatively weaves together a renewed reading of the Bible with the best in the tradition of the classical Christian creeds. Thereby he produces a powerful synthesis of Scripture and tradition. He builds a dynamic view of Christian community based on both tradition and the Bible.

In the *Confession*, Riedemann shows that his view of a faithful Christian community is not marginal or sectarian. He presents the Hutterite community as expressing the heart of the Scriptures and the best in the creedal tradition of the early church. The Introduction in this volume provides a new and comprehensive history of Peter Riedemann. It shows the range of influences that shaped his theology and were thus involved in the formation of the Hutterite community.

This volume is a fresh translation in modern English from the German edition of 1565. The Introduction includes a textual history of the book. The 1950 English translation prepared in England by Kathleen E. Hasenberg and the Society of Brothers was in an old English style and needed updating. When H. Wayne Pipkin, then associate director of the Institute of Mennonite Studies, asked me to undertake this project, I eagerly accepted because of my long-standing interest in Peter Riedemann and the Hutterites.

Many other attempts at expressing the Christian faith in communal living have failed, but the Hutterite communal experience has stood for centuries, despite periods of incredible persecution. The Anabaptist theology that inspired this long history of faithful discipleship deserves to be available to modern English readers. In addition, it is gratifying to see how Bruderhofers and Hutterites themselves want to use this English translation for instruction in their own communities. I believe that Riedemann's dynamic vision challenges all believers toward greater faithfulness to the Lord and to each other.

Numerous people need to be thanked. In this translation, Plough Publishing House of Farmington, Pennsylvania, generously made available to me the preliminary work they had done up to 1990 on a new translation. I benefited from their work even while studiously and conscientiously checking everything and retranslating from German. Winifred M. Hildel of the Plough Publishing House read the translation carefully and made numerous helpful suggestions.

Gratitude is also due my research assistant, Laura Braun, who laboriously checked biblical references for accuracy and put them in the manuscript. This assistance was made possible through a summer research grant provided by the Canadian Mennonite Bible College, Winnipeg. Dorothy, my wife, assisted with some translation nuances and offered support and encouragement during the whole process.

To H. Wayne Pipkin, General Editor of the CRR series, I owe special gratitude for extending to me the invitation to do this project, and for providing strong guidance, patience, and encouragement.

—*John J. Friesen*
  Winnipeg, Manitoba

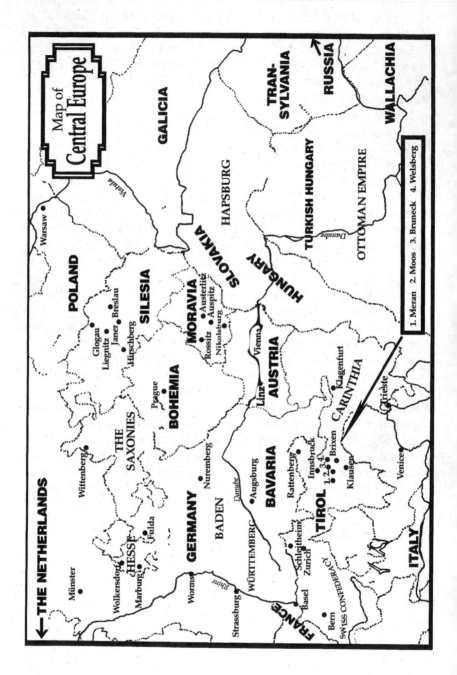

Map of
Central Europe

THE NETHERLANDS

Münster

Wolkersdorf
Marburg
HESSE
Fulda

Wittenberg

THE
SAXONIES

Warsaw

POLAND

Glogau
Liegnitz
Janer
Breslau
Hirschberg

SILESIA

GALICIA

Prague

BOHEMIA

MORAVIA
Kossitz
Auspitz
Austerlitz
Nikolsburg

SLOVAKIA

HAPSBURG

TRAN-
SYLVANIA

RUSSIA

WALLACHIA

Nuremberg

GERMANY

BADEN

Worms

Rhine

WÜRTEMBERG

Strassburg

FRANCE

Augsburg

Danube

BAVARIA

Rattenberg

Schleitheim
Zurich

Basel

SWISS CONFEDERACY

Bern

Innsbruck
1. 2. 3. 4.
Klausen

TIROL

Brixen

Linz

Vienna

AUSTRIA

HUNGARY

Klagenfurt

CARINTHIA

Trieste

Venice

ITALY

Vistula

Danube

TURKISH HUNGARY

OTTOMAN EMPIRE

1. Meran   2. Moos   3. Bruneck   4. Welsberg

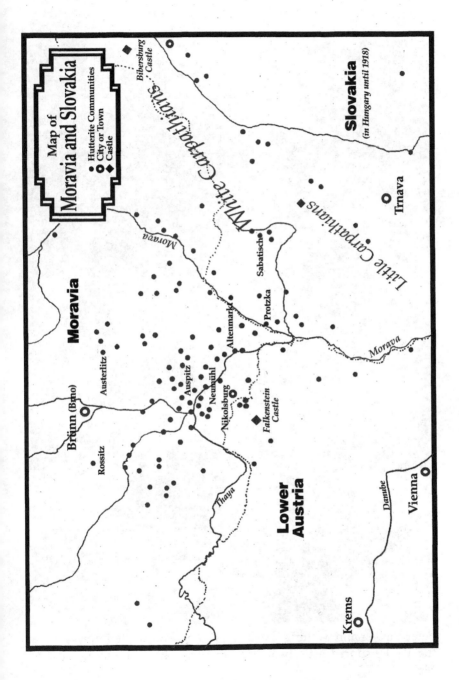

Map of
Moravia and Slovakia

Hutterite Communities •
City or Town ○
Castle ◆

Moravia

Brünn (Brno) ○

Austerlitz •

Rossitz •

Auspitz •

Neumühl •

Altenmarkt •

Nikolsburg ○

Falkenstein
Castle ◆

Thaya

Lower
Austria

Krems ○

Vienna ○

Danube

White Carpathians

Morava

Moravia

Little Carpathians

Bibersburg
Castle ◆

Sabatische •

Protzka •

Morava

Slovakia
(in Hungary until 1918)

Trnava ○

Peter Riedemann, writing the *Confession of Faith* while imprisoned at the Wolkersdorf Castle near Marburg in 1540-42. Painting by Ivan Moon, 1975.

Introduction

Labeled a heretic before his twenty-third birthday, young Peter Riedemann (1506-1556) had a burning desire for reform. He wandered far from his native home and was constantly in danger of being captured and executed by officials suspicious and fearful of Anabaptists. During his twenties and thirties, he was imprisoned for nearly nine years.

Riedemann developed a vision that went beyond the religious reform he wanted for the church. He also yearned to see economic, social, and political reform. His view of needed change was comprehensive, transforming all aspects of people's lives.

This leader did not see himself as a heretic, holding beliefs rejected by others; or a sectarian, starting a group as an alternative to the state church. He believed that his vision for reform expressed the heart of Christian tradition. Riedemann was trying to recapture the essence of historical Christianity as expressed in Scripture and in the great creeds of the church. He saw himself standing in a long line of true Christian teachers, leaders calling the church back to its historical basics. He was reforming the center, not the edges.

Riedemann was born in 1506 in Hirschberg (now Jelenia Góra, in southwest Poland), Silesia, about fifty kilometers southwest of Liegnitz (Legnica). He was a cobbler by trade. Little is known about his life before about age twenty-three. Practically all the available information is a brief note in the Hutterite *Chronicle*: in 1532 Riedemann was released from prison in Gmunden, Upper Austria.[1] Then he made his way to Anabaptist groups in Moravia, joining his vision for reform to their experience of communalism.

During his first brief stay in Moravia, he married. However, he spent little time at home in the next decade. From 1532 to 1542, Riedemann was mostly traveling as a missioner for the Hutterites. He tirelessly moved through Austrian and German states, promoting his vision for reform.[2] He spent almost six of those ten years in prison.

Three times Riedemann was imprisoned. He appeared on the historical scene in 1532, after a three-year prison term in Gmunden. Later, while on a missionary journey for the Hutterites, he spent more than four years in the Nuremberg prison. His last imprisonment (about two years) was in Hesse, at Marburg and then at Wolkersdorf, again while on a missionary journey. In prison, he wrote the *Confession of Faith,* in which he expressed his and the Hutterite community's powerful vision.[3] There he also received the call to take up leadership in the Hutterite communities in Moravia.

During his Gmunden imprisonment (1529-32), Riedemann composed a meditation, his *First Confession,* available in English as *Love Is Like Fire.*[4] In many respects it was a forerunner of his *Confession of Faith,* the subject of this volume. He wrote this later *Confession* during his imprisonment in Hesse (1540-42),[5] before he accepted the invitation from the Hutterite communities in Moravia to serve as their leader.[6] For fourteen years he served as a spiritual leader to the Hutterites, guiding their communities through a period of intense persecution. He lived to see the beginning of the era when Hutterites were relatively tolerated.[7] He died in 1556 in a Hutterite community at Protzka (Broczko, now Brodsko), Slovakia, then part of Hungary.[8]

Riedemann's inspiring letters, forty-six hymns, and the *Confession of Faith* helped set the direction for Hutterite communities through the centuries.[9] The German edition of Riedemann's *Confession* is still used by Hutterites in western Canada and United States as their theological guide. The Bruderhofs in eastern United States and England also use the *Confession.*

Fascinating questions arise about the setting of Riedemann's early life. From what background did he come? Where and when did he become Anabaptist? Who influenced his formative years? What helped to shape his *Confession of Faith?*[10]

During recent decades, studies have established that Anabaptism was not solidly uniform. In the sixteenth century, numerous Anabaptist movements were appearing at about the same time in various parts of Europe, largely within what was once the Holy Roman Empire.[11] Anabaptist groups overlapped, made contact with each other, shared ideas, and disagreed with each other. There were considerable similarities. Yet the various groups had different basic characteristics, starting points, and theological emphases.

Research has identified at least five major circles of Anabaptism: Swiss-South German, Central German, Tirolean-Moravian, Dutch, and the Marpeck circle.[12] Each grouping has its own traits. Some of these groups can be further subdivided.

Which circle most influenced the theology in Riedemann's *Confession of Faith*? Was his teaching shaped by the humanist biblicism of the Swiss-South German Anabaptism of Grebel, Manz, and Sattler? By the mysticism[13] and chiliasm[14] of the Central German Anabaptism of Hut and Denck, developed in the locale of the Peasants' Revolt? By Marpeck or Hubmaier, who were less separatist than most Anabaptists and willing to see Christians as rulers or civil officers? What role did Tirolean-Moravian Anabaptism play in his theology? How did the spiritualism of Melchior Hoffmann and the Münsterite experiment of Dutch Anabaptism influence his thinking?

Silesia: Riedemann's Early Life and Influences

The Hutterites' own extensive history book, *Die älteste Chronik der Hutterischen Brüder* (The oldest chronicle of the Hutterite brothers: *Chronicle*), begins the story of Riedemann with his imprisonment in Gmunden, at age twenty-three. Then it traces his travels and ideas as they developed from that point.[15] Since Riedemann was born in Hirschberg, it is fitting to begin with Silesia in reviewing his life and thought. Likely his earliest views of Christian reform were given shape in Silesia.[16]

The majority of the people in lower Silesia, where Hirschberg was located, were Germans whose ancestors had settled in the area in the thirteenth century. Most of the upper classes were German. The principal city was Breslau (now Wroclaw, Poland). Liegnitz was one of the more important cities in the northern part of Silesia. Hirschberg was within the political jurisdiction of Liegnitz. Local rulers in Silesia had considerable autonomy and were frequently at war with each other. In 1527, Ferdinand I, Hapsburg ruler in Vienna, gained political control of Silesia and imposed a measure of peace on the region.[17] He was staunchly Catholic, and his firm grip on the region made religious reform difficult.

The reform in Silesia was led by Caspar Schwenckfeld (b. 1489). He was of noble birth and educated in various universities of Europe.

He had traveled, as usual for a nobleman's son, and was a man of grace, manners, culture, and self-confidence. Though aware of humanism, he was not a humanist. He had no specific training in law, theology, or any other discipline.[18] A courtier among the local nobles, he came to the court of Duke Frederick II of Liegnitz by 1521.[19]

Schwenckfeld had converted to religious reform in 1519. Though he admired Luther at this early stage, his reform was not specifically Lutheran.[20] Various reform impulses appeared among lay people in Silesia, including anti-clericalism (criticism of clergy, church leaders) and a desire to raise the moral level of the church. After Schwenckfeld was appointed to the court at Liegnitz, he served as midwife to the duke's conversion to reform[21] and promoted religious reform in the regions in and around Liegnitz.[22]

At first Schwenckfeld believed that his reform ideas were in agreement with Luther's. However, by 1524 he began to notice differences. To try to resolve them, he made three trips to Wittenberg in the mid-1520s to confer with Luther. To his surprise, Luther rebuffed him. Schwenckfeld then began to chart a separate path. He felt his reform was a middle way between Luther and the Catholics.[23]

The two main issues which separated Luther and Schwenckfeld were the interpretation of the eucharist[24] (the Lord's Supper) and the lack of moral improvement in regions of Lutheran reform. During the middle and latter 1520s, Luther was placing increasing emphasis on the "real presence" of Christ's body in the eucharist (Matt. 26:26). This led to Luther's abortive discussions with Zwingli at Marburg in 1529. On moral reform, Luther's main concern was to overcome a theology of works-righteousness and develop a theology of grace. He saw salvation as a gift of God, not earned by humans. This theology became known as *sola fideism* (salvation by faith alone), but it was not producing the moral results which Schwenckfeld believed ought to accompany religious reform.

In contrast to Luther, Schwenckfeld emphasized that "it is Christ himself by his inner Word who directs the faithful to the Middle Way."[25] Schwenckfeld developed a spiritual theology. He preached that the transforming power of the inner word was more important than external forms. For Schwenckfeld, sanctification was an increasingly central concern. On the other hand, Luther in 1525 was engaged in a sharp debate over free will with Erasmus, then at Basel. He saw all issues from the perspective of protecting salvation as a gift of God and a work by God.[26] Fallen humans are thus powerless to do anything good in the sight of God and must wait for God to bestow salvation on them. Luther thought Schwenckfeld's view of sanctification strayed dangerously close to human works-righteousness.

From 1524 to 1526, Schwenckfeld was engaged in two difficult struggles. There was increasing tension between himself and the Lutheran reformers in Silesia.[27] The center of the Lutheran reform was Breslau, and Liegnitz was the center of the reform led by Schwenckfeld. Schwenckfeld's other struggle was with Roman Catholicism, which was vigorously resisting church reform in Silesia.

Meanwhile, the German Peasants' Revolt of 1524 to 1525 developed. These uprisings largely bypassed Silesia, convulsing the lands to the east and west. However, the effects were keenly felt in Silesia. The Catholic Church charged that Schwenckfeld's reforms "provided occasion and encouragement to insurrection and social upheaval."[28]

Schwenckfeld became engaged in increasingly difficult religious conflicts. In a 1526 circular letter, he recommended that the Lord's Supper be suspended until conflict between Catholics and Lutherans halted. That move further isolated him from the Lutheran camp.[29]

In this setting, the Silesian Anabaptist movement developed. It is largely shrouded in obscurity because it had no defining event, nor did it produce a continuing community in Silesia. In addition, the initial years of reform in Silesia produced no sharp lines separating Lutheran, Schwenckfeldian, and Anabaptist groups.

Sometime after 1525, distinctions began to develop between the various reform groups. In the emerging Anabaptist movement in Silesia, the leaders who made their mark were mostly from other countries. A number of native Silesians who became active in the Anabaptist movement are best known for later activities in the Hutterite and Gabrielite communities in Moravia and Slovakia. Two local Anabaptists, in addition to Peter Riedemann, were Bärthl Riedmair[30] and Caspar Braitmichel.[31] Riedmair and Braitmichel eventually made their way to Moravia, likely as part of the Gabriel Ascherham group, and both eventually joined the Hutterites. Probably late in life, Braitmichel began the great Hutterite Chronicle and carried it to 1542. He ceased because of failing eyesight and died in 1573.[32]

Balthasar Hubmaier, from near Augsburg, had contact with the Anabaptist movement in Silesia. While in Nikolsburg, Moravia, he dedicated his second book on *Freedom of the Will* to Frederick II, duke of Liegnitz.[33] However, there is no evidence that Hubmaier's writing on free will had a major influence on Anabaptism in Silesia.

Hans Hut was also connected with Anabaptism in Silesia. It is not clear whether Hans Hut ever came to Silesia.[34] His chiliasm and interim peace ethic (until Christ returns) do not seem to have figured prominently in the theology of the Silesian Anabaptist movement.

In late 1527 and early 1528, a number of Anabaptists arrived in Liegnitz, largely because of its reputation for tolerance. One was the Swiss Anabaptist printer Froschauer. He was fleeing from Emperor Ferdinand I and was attracted to the University of Liegnitz, established in 1525.[35] Shortly after he arrived, Froschauer gave up his Anabaptist beliefs and joined the Schwenkfelder movement. This conversion shows the ease with which people moved from one group to the other in the Silesian reform movements of that time.

In 1528 two other Anabaptists arrived in Silesia: Oswald Glaidt and Andreas Fischer. Fischer's exact birth date and place of origin are not known, though recent research suggests that he may have originated in Austria or in a southern German state.[36] He perhaps became Anabaptist in an area influenced by Hans Hut's theology.

When Glaidt and Fischer arrived in Silesia, they preached in the countryside and won many people to Anabaptism. They may have linked with local Anabaptist groups. Glaidt and Fischer emphasized adult baptism, likely in the tradition of Hans Hut: baptism only after teaching and belief, and not before age thirty.[37]

Glaidt appears to have been pacifist. It is not clear that Fischer was pacifist; a few years later in Moravia, he sided with the *Schwertler* (sword-bearers) and was willing to be protected by the nobility.[38] Both Glaidt and Fischer seem to have taught communalism and sharing of goods, though not in the strict form later practiced by Hutterites in Moravia.[39] The evidence suggests that Glaidt was more eschatological[40] in his theology than Fischer. Yet neither made chiliasm a key issue in their teaching while in Silesia.[41]

Glaidt and Fischer's disagreement with Schwenckfeld did not focus on these issues, however, but on whether the Sabbath ought to be observed by Christians.[42] In late 1528 and early 1529, Glaidt and Fischer wrote articles promoting the view that "one has a duty to celebrate the Sabbath, Saturday, because it is the word, will, and commandment of God (Exod. 20)."[43] Their documents have been lost, but Schwenckfeld's reply is extant. Since Schwenckfeld quoted them extensively, it is possible to reconstruct their Sabbatarian arguments.[44]

Glaidt and Fischer asserted that observing Sunday as the day of rest was a pattern initiated by the popes. They saw Sunday observance as a human invention, to be discarded as the church was being reformed. Christ had superseded the priestly or ritual law, but the moral law still applied to Christians. The Ten Commandments were the center of the moral law and should be totally kept. Therefore, the Sabbath and not Sunday ought to be the day of rest.[45] Their Sabbatarianism may have been influenced by Hans Hut, who in his eschatological thinking favored the number seven. On the other hand, it may also have been based on a biblical restitutionism and developed by people within the Anabaptist movement in Silesia.[46]

About the same time, another Anabaptist arrived in Silesia. Gabriel Ascherham, a furrier from Bavaria, was a spiritualist in the tradition of Hans Denck. He placed more emphasis on the inner Spirit of God than on the written Word, and stressed the spiritual meaning of ceremonies more than their particular outer form. He wrote a book entitled *Unterschied göttlicher und menschlicher Weisheit* (Distinction between divine and human wisdom), which emphasizes "baptism of the Holy Spirit to such a degree that the external observance of water baptism becomes almost superfluous, and the disputes about infant and believers baptism irrelevant."[47] He had also gone on missionary journeys with Hans Hut. Ascherham was active in the Breslau, Glogau, and Glatz areas of Silesia, finding many Anabaptists there.[48]

Another Anabaptist leader in Silesia was Clemens Adler. Some think Adler was a Swiss Anabaptist; others believe he came from the Anabaptist communities in Moravia. He may even have been native to Silesia.[49] It is not clear when he appeared as an Anabaptist in Silesia. He seems to have been active in areas to the south of Liegnitz, around Schweidnitz, Glatz, and Jauer.[50] Adler was an advocate of moral reform and of changes in the practice of the eucharist.[51] He was willing to take dramatic action to bring about change. On one occasion he came into the church in Glatz and ordered the priest to be silent so he could speak. Adler was forced out of the church. Undaunted, he held a service outdoors. Adler was captured, imprisoned, released, and continued preaching on a nearby estate. The issue he addressed at this time was the proper form and interpretation of the eucharist.[52]

His writings show his concern that the gospel message be appropriated inwardly and not merely outwardly, with just a show of obedience to the written Word.[53] Adler was a strong proponent of peace, forgiveness, and not retaliating against evil. He believed evil had to be met with suffering.[54] He made a strong case for community of goods.[55] He also advocated not swearing the oath, which he discussed in the context of making a commitment to God.[56] Commitments to God were required, and oaths forbidden.

Adler argued that the Sabbath was given in the old covenant as an external sign of what God requires of his believers: "They should leave their evil works, and with their thoughts, words and deeds not do anything which is against God."[57] He said it was not important to keep the actual Sabbath (on Saturday) according to the Mosaic Law.

He also addressed the significance of the Law. Although salvation can only be attained through Christ and not through the Law, the Law shows humans what they ought to do and not do. So the Law becomes a witness to eternal life.[58] Adler did not include a lengthy section on adult baptism but did make references to it and assumed it as part of the Christian life.[59]

Adler left for Moravia and may have been gone for some time. In 1533 he was again active in the Glogau region of Silesia. He was arrested and executed, possibly in 1533. The history and travels of Adler and Riedemann show that they might have met in Silesia or Moravia. Adler might have been in Silesia as early as 1525, introducing Anabaptism to the Schweidnitz area.[60] There is a remarkable overlap of ideas in the writings of Adler and Riedemann.

By 1528 numerous Anabaptists were in various regions of Silesia. They gave attention to issues of baptism, peace, communalism, and the end-time. Yet the Sabbath and the eucharist were debated most vigorously and publicly. Earlier historians saw Sabbatarianism as evidence of Judaizing. Later interpreters have taken Sabbatarianism as evidence of spiritualism, especially a spiritualism that resulted when Hut's predictions about the end-time failed to materialize.[61]

On August 1, 1528, Emperor Ferdinand I issued a decree that "the religion in the region (Silesia) be returned to its pristine state."[62] The death penalty was prescribed for anyone questioning the "real presence," and for anyone "who rejected child baptism and engaged in rebaptism."[63] This decree resulted in the emigration of a large number of Anabaptists from Silesia.[64] Gabriel Ascherham led a group to Moravia, perhaps as many as two thousand believers.

In the face of this threat from the emperor, Duke Frederick II of

Liegnitz decided to abandon Schwenckfeld and to ally his region with Luther's reform. The Reichstag in 1526 had allowed nobles to decide whether their people would be Roman Catholic or Lutheran. In 1529, Schwenckfeld left for Strassburg (French: Strasbourg). A year and a half later, on March 15, 1530, the emperor ordered Duke Frederick II to expel Anabaptists, and more of them fled then.[65] During that expulsion, Andreas Fischer left for Nikolsburg in Moravia.[66]

Since Peter Riedemann was imprisoned in Gmunden in 1529, he might have fled Silesia after the emperor's decree of August 1528. Perhaps he traveled with some of the groups who left for Moravia. No concrete evidence has appeared to date his departure from Silesia, or to identify the route he took from Silesia to Gmunden.

Gmunden: First Imprisonment

Riedemann was imprisoned in Gmunden from 1529 to 1532. Apparently he arrived in the Linz area of Upper Austria in 1529, was drawn into the local Anabaptist group under the leadership of Wolfgang Brandhuber, and was ordained Servant of the Word.[67] He was captured and imprisoned, not in Linz, the capital city of Upper Austria, but in Gmunden, on the banks of the Traunsee. In prison, he was "subjected to great pain, hunger, and mistreatment."[68] After Riedemann was released from prison in 1532, he briefly visited the Anabaptist group in Linz, then traveled to Moravia.

The Anabaptism that Riedemann met in Linz and Gmunden of Austria was partly shaped by the legacy of Hans Hut.[69] Hut had been active in Upper Austria. His ideas were evident locally,[70] such as an emphasis on the nearness of Christ's second coming and a belief in suffering as a confirmation of faithfulness.[71]

However, Wolfgang Brandhuber was likely the major influence on Riedemann in the Linz-Gmunden area. Brandhuber was the leader of the Linz congregation when Riedemann arrived in 1529. Brandhuber's influence extended all over Upper Austria, where he founded congregations. His reputation extended even into the Tirol (Tyrol).[72] Daniel Liechty claims that "Wolfgang Brandhuber led the Linz congregation in a characteristically Hutian manner."[73]

In his letters, however, Brandhuber shows little evidence of influence from Hut. Chiliasm did not much interest him. He emphasized a faith based upon Scripture and a spiritual life of patient suffering and mutual sharing, rejecting worldly grandeur. His views on sharing material possessions, though not expressing the full extent of communalism which the Hutterites later adopted in Moravia, did emphasize that "all things that serve to honor God should be held in common."[74] Brandhuber also argued that war and vengeance do not fit a true Christian faith.[75] These ideas have little in common with Hut's main theological emphases. They are, however, similar to the ideas which become prominent in Riedemann's *Confession of Faith*.

During Riedemann's imprisonment in Gmunden, he wrote a treatise known as his *First Confession*.[76] It is much shorter than his later *Confession of Faith*, and the organization is different, but the methodology and approach to issues is similar. His discussion in the *First Confession* consists largely of weaving together quotations and allusions from Scripture. The treatise consists of three sections.

In the first section, he begins with a long discussion of God's love for humans. He argues that God calls people to love God and each other. He rejects war and violence. He discusses faith in terms of God's call and human response, carefully avoiding any reference to Luther's theology of faith as initiated solely by God without human participation. He makes the case for missions and adult baptism.

In the second section, he follows the principal affirmations of the Apostles' Creed, thus prefiguring the structure of the *Confession of Faith*. The discussion falls into three parts: affirmations of faith in God, Christ, and the Holy Spirit. On God, Riedemann emphasizes that people are created good. He appears to be rejecting Luther's emphasis on the total depravity of humanity. On Christ, he includes lengthy comment on the Lord's Supper or the mass, and he rejects both Catholic and Lutheran views. He submits "that as Christ in the breaking of the bread had given his body to be broken for our salvation, so those who break the bread in the Lord's Supper commit themselves to give their bodies in love for God's sake, and to serve each other, even unto death in persecution."[77] Then he describes the Holy Spirit as comforter, enabler, and protector of the poor.[78]

The third and shortest section of the *First Confession* outlines seven pillars on which the house of God is built: fear of God, God's wisdom, God's knowledge, God's counsel, God's power, God's surpassing wisdom, and God as friend.

In Riedemann's *First Confession*, there is no hint of the chiliasm of Hut, nor of a spiritualism which places the inspiration of the Spirit over the witness of the written word of Scripture. He wrote while under the influence of Brandhuber, and his ideas seem consistent with Brandhuber's. The main issues Riedemann presents in the treatise are similar to his thought in the later *Confession of Faith*. Brandhuber may be the source of some of the ideas, since he also emphasized love, missions, adult baptism, peace, and sharing of material goods.[79] Yet many teachings in the *First Confession* were also current in Anabaptist groups in Silesia before 1529. Thus Riedemann could have developed some of them in his native region. Dependence on Hans Hut's ideas seems slight, except for the emphasis on missions, which was pervasive among Anabaptists anyhow.

Toward the end of 1532, Riedemann was released from prison and went to Austerlitz, Moravia.[80] There he joined communalist Anabaptists led by Jakob Wiedemann and Philip Jäger. They had been part of the Nikolsburg Anabaptists but had separated from them in 1528.[81] The Hutterite *Chronicle* states that the communalists left because the Nikolsburg group was not pacifist and was willing to use the sword, having the spirit of Münster, and was called Sabbatarian.[82] The nonresistant communalists were called *Stäbler* (staff-bearers).

In its terse style, the *Chronicle* describes the 1528 departure of the communalists from Nikolsburg (now Mikulov). "These men then spread out a cloak in front of the people, and each laid his possessions on it with a willing heart—without being forced—so that the needy might be supported in accordance with the teaching of the prophets and apostles. Isa. 23:18; Acts 2:44-45; 4:34-35; 5:1-11."[83]

The communalist group of about two hundred adults led by Wiedemann and Jäger went to Austerlitz. There the lords Kaunitz gave them lodging. When they negotiated with the lords, they stated that, because of their faith in God, they would not pay war taxes.[84]

In 1529, the Austerlitz group seems to have adopted a church order as its own constitution. The order may have originated with Schiemer or Schlaffer in the Linz-Gmunden area, to which Riedemann came in 1529, or with the Anabaptists who emigrated from the Tirol in 1529.[85]

Also in 1529, Jakob Hutter first came on the scene in Moravia. He had become Anabaptist in the Tirol, possibly at Klagenfurt.[86] Because of severe persecution in the Tirol, the local Anabaptists sent Hutter and Simon Schützinger to see if Moravia would provide a haven for Tirolean Anabaptists. According to the Hutterite writings, Hutter and

Schützinger, in the name of the Anabaptists in the Tirol, "united in peace with the church at Austerlitz."[87] They thus recognized that this group was a place of refuge for their persecuted fellow believers in the Tirol; they also seem to have either acknowledged or created unity in the group. Perhaps there had been internal tensions.

At this time other Anabaptist groups were also in Moravia. In 1528, Gabriel Ascherham and a group of Anabaptists from Silesia settled in Rossitz (now Rosice), near Austerlitz. Some members of Ascherham's group may have settled in Rossitz in 1527.[88] This group from Silesia was also communalist; some of them had settled in Rossitz before the communalists left Nikolsburg to settle in Austerlitz. In 1529 more Anabaptists fled from Silesia and joined Ascherham's group, which might have had up to two thousand Silesian refugees.

In 1528, Anabaptists from Hesse and the Palatinate arrived in Moravia under the leadership of Philipp Plener, a Swabian.[89] They initially settled with the Gabriel Ascherham group. However, tensions soon arose between the two leaders, Gabriel Ascherham and Philipp Plener. In 1529, the Philippites moved to Auspitz, between the Austerlitz and Nikolsburg communities.[90] The Philippites were also communalists, and their community continued to be augmented by new arrivals from south and central German regions.[91] Thus by 1529, there were three major communalist groups in Moravia: one led by Ascherham at Rossitz, another by Wiedemann and Jäger at Austerlitz, and the third by Philipp Plener at Auspitz.

An event which had major implications for Anabaptism in Moravia was the division in Austerlitz on January 8, 1531.[92] The unity within the Austerlitz group, acknowledged by Hutter in 1529, did not last. Factions developed. A number of people, among them Wilhelm Reublin and George Zaunring, opposed the leadership of Jakob Wiedemann; they accused him of mismanagement and acting like an absolute ruler.[93] Hence, in the dead of winter, part of the Austerlitz group decided to leave for Auspitz, perhaps 350 persons out of about 600. They were led by Reublin and Zaunring.[94] Most of the people who left had apparently come from the Tirol. They did not unite with the Philippite group already at Auspitz.

Since Jakob Hutter and Simon Schützinger were respected, they were invited by both groups to come to Moravia and mediate between them.[95] In 1531, Hutter and Schützinger came from the Tirol, investigated the situation, and decided Wiedemann was at fault.

Wiedemann refused to accept the decision, and the division could not be repaired. Hutter and Schützinger also found Reublin unacceptable for leadership in the Auspitz group because "he was not wholeheartedly practicing apostolic communalism."[96] Before Hutter and Schützinger left, they appointed Zaunring as leader of the Tirolean group in Auspitz.[97] Remarkably, the group at Auspitz gave Hutter and Schützinger authority to make these leadership changes.

The new group at Auspitz, desperately poor financially and with many ill people, had to endure further internal conflict. Within the year, Zaunring was found to have administered discipline more leniently to his wife than to other members of the group. The resulting conflict led to Zaunring's dismissal from leadership. Again Hutter and Schützinger came from the Tirol to settle matters in Auspitz.[98]

It was decided that Schützinger would remain with the Auspitz group as its leader. Hutter and Schützinger also made another major organizational change. The *Chronicle* does not supply reasons but simply states that Hutter and Schützinger formed a loose federation of the Gabrielites at Rossitz, the Philippites at Auspitz, and the Tiroleans at Auspitz.[99] Gabriel Ascherham, the Silesian, was apparently appointed senior bishop (*Vorsteher*) of the three affiliated groups.[100]

Arrival in Moravia

Riedemann arrived in Moravia in late 1532, shortly after the Auspitz Tirolean community members had been robbed, beaten, and raped by a group of marauding soldiers.[101] Riedemann chose to come to the Auspitz Tirolean group of communalists, though nearby was also a group of communalists from Silesia. While there, he married an Anabaptist sister, Katharine, called Treindl, and he was appointed Servant of the Word (*Diener des Wortes*).[102] He was with the Auspitz Tiroleans for less than a year and then was sent to Franconia.

Tirolean Anabaptism: Formation and Background

Before following Riedemann to Franconia, we recognize forces that shaped the Tirolean Anabaptist movement, with which Riedemann identified in Moravia. Anabaptism in the Tirol was inspired and influenced by a remarkable number of people. As in other Anabaptist areas, Anabaptism in the Tirol was interwoven with social and economic upheavals. One of the earliest reform leaders there was Michael Gaismair.[103] He was not an Anabaptist but came to prominence during the Peasants' Revolt in the Tirolean Brixen area in 1525. The uprising in which he became a leader expressed a mixture of religious, social, and political concerns, as did such revolts in many other areas in the Holy Roman Empire during the same years.

Gaismair was secretary to the vice-regent of the Tirol and secretary to the bishop of Brixen. In May of 1525, he was likely involved in drawing up the sixty-two Meran Articles, addressing areas of political, religious, and social abuse.[104] Miners and peasants of the area presented the articles to the diets of Meran and Innsbruck.[105] Among other things, they called for reform on the basis of "the equality of man."[106] The officials rejected this attempt at reform.

In late 1525 and early 1526, Gaismair became more radical. He visited Zwingli and drew up plans for military action. To free the Tirol from tyrannical rule, he hoped he would receive military assistance from various Swiss cantons, as well as from France and Venice.[107] He wrote a new constitution (*Landesordnung*) for the Tirol. It called for abolishing the power of the nobility and radically equalizing all people, including burgers and peasants, even to the point of destroying walled cities.[108]

In the summer of 1526, Gaismair assembled an army to free the Tirolean land. Faced with overwhelming odds, he and his peasant army retreated to the region of Venice. They asked for protection and offered their military services to Venice.[109] Gaismair's hoped-for assistance from Venice, the king of France, and the Swiss cantons came to nothing. Gaismair lived in Venetian territory until 1532, when an acquaintance assassinated him in hope of collecting a reward which the Council of Innsbruck had offered for Gaismair's death.[110]

No clear connection has been established between this armed attempt to create an independent mountain territory modeled after the Swiss cantons, and the Anabaptist movement which arose shortly afterward.[111] Gaismair's planned reforms for the peasants and miners in the Tirol provides the context, however, for later Anabaptist reforms.[112] Many needs for reform expressed in the Gaismair events continued in the Tirol for years. Some concerns were given new shape in the Anabaptist reforms, especially among the communalists.

The first official record of Anabaptism in the Tirol is in early 1527. On January 2, 1527, Ferdinand I of Austria, brother of the emperor

Charles V, issued a warning against unauthorized preachers (*Winkelprediger*) in the Puster Valley of the Tirol.[113] In April of the same year, Ferdinand I sent another edict to the authorities throughout the Tirol, noting that Anabaptists had appeared in many regions. The officials were to be diligent in suppressing them.[114] He called them rebels and charged them with provoking disturbances and spilling blood.[115] In the summer of 1527, Ferdinand I issued more mandates against Anabaptists in the Tirol, noting that they were also questioning Christ's presence in the elements of the mass.[116]

The founder of the Anabaptist movement in the Tirol cannot be determined with certainty. It does not appear that the movement began with just one person or in one locale. It is possible, however, to identify Anabaptists present in the Tirol after the movement had begun. Two Anabaptist missioners active in the Tirol in the fall of 1527 were Leonhard Schiemer and Hans Schlaffer.

Schiemer, a former Franciscan friar, made his way to Nikolsburg in Moravia in early 1527 and debated with Hubmaier over the use of the sword (allowed by Hubmaier).[117] Leaving Nikolsburg, he went to Vienna, where he had conversations with Hut about his beliefs.[118] Finding Hut's ideas biblical, he requested rebaptism by Oswald Glaidt in the spring of 1527.[119] Schiemer was active in the Inn Valley of the Tirol for only about six months. He was arrested in Rattenberg on November 25, 1527, and beheaded there on January 14, 1528.[120]

Schlaffer, a former priest, had met Hans Hut in Nikolsburg.[121] He also met and was influenced by a number of other Anabaptists, including Denck, Ludwig Hätzer, Jakob Wiedemann, Glaidt, and Brandhuber.[122] From September to December 1527, Schlaffer was active in the Inn Valley, meeting Anabaptist cells already in existence and preaching to people not yet converted to the Anabaptist movement. He was captured December 5, 1527, and beheaded on February 4, 1528, at Schwaz, a town about ten miles from Rattenberg.[123]

In his correspondence, Schiemer's ideas show some influence from Denck and Hut.[124] In a manner similar to Denck's, he acknowledged his deep sinfulness and dependence upon God's grace for salvation. He taught that God had left a threefold witness of himself on earth in the spirit, water, and blood; this is similar to Hut's threefold view of baptism. There is, however, little evidence of Hut's eschatological views, and Schiemer does not refer to communalism.

Hans Schlaffer's theology shows less influence from either Hut or Denck. He strongly defends adult baptism but does not discuss the threefold view of baptism that Hut emphasized: water, spirit, and martyrdom (blood).[125] Schlaffer distances himself from Hut's preoccupation with the nearing end-time and coming judgment.[126] He emphasizes a life of discipleship and faithfulness to God.[127] His concept of discipleship is expressed in his views that Christ is the "exemplar" for the Christian, and that justification brings a transformation of one's mode of living.[128] He warns against undue concern and speculation about "secret things"—likely meaning end-time speculation. He says God will reveal such events in his own time.[129] Schlaffer also strongly rejects accusations that adult baptism is a cover for revolution; he says he knows of no plans for revolution among people in his circles.[130] His writings show little evidence of communalism.

Georg Cajacob (Blaurock), a priest and a native of Chur, arrived in the Tirol after being expelled from a number of Swiss regions, including Zurich and Bern. In a recent study, Packull suggests that Blaurock likely visited the South Tirol twice, once between May and September of 1527, and again during the spring of 1529.[131] When he entered the South Tirol the second time, a number of new Anabaptist leaders had emerged, including Jakob Hutter. In July 1529, Blaurock was captured. He was tortured, and on September 6, 1529, he was burned at the stake in Klausen.[132]

Blaurock participated in founding the Zurich Anabaptist movement. He was the first to receive rebaptism by the hands of Conrad Grebel, in the home of Felix Manz's mother on January 21, 1525. An impulsive missioner for Anabaptism, he would even interrupt a church service and take the pulpit himself. He believed in the importance of Scripture, adult baptism, improvement of life, and the church as a body of believers united by faith in Christ. There is no evidence that he advocated community of goods.[133] Though Blaurock seems to have been an important Anabaptist figure in the Tirol, his influence was brief. He seems not to have contributed anything specific to the communalism of the Tirolean Anabaptists who left for Moravia.

Another Anabaptist native to the Tirol was Pilgram Marpeck. He was a member of the Upper Council as well as a mining magistrate in the city of Rattenberg, on the Inn River.[134] On January 28, 1528, Marpeck abruptly resigned his position as mining magistrate two weeks after Schiemer was executed at Rattenberg, and one week before Schlaffer was beheaded in Schwaz.[135] Marpeck seems to have left Rattenberg shortly thereafter, appearing in Strassburg in September of the same year, where he purchased citizenship.[136]

Marpeck was a moderate Anabaptist. He opposed the spiritualism of Schwenckfeld[137] but was equally opposed to the biblical literalism he saw in the Swiss Anabaptists. He thought such mechanical adherence to the written Word misinterpreted signs and figures in Scripture and caused unnecessary divisions in the church.[138] Marpeck rejected violence, yet he did not reject government office; he held such offices in Rattenberg and later in Strassburg and Augsburg. He believed in sharing with the needy but did not advocate community of goods. He was a strong advocate of adult baptism and believed the state had no right to determine matters of faith.[138] One finds little of the chiliasm of Hut in his writings.

None of the Anabaptist leaders in the Tirol noted thus far placed emphasis on communalism. They did not show the kind of theological sophistication and dependence upon the church's creedal tradition evident in the theological sections of Riedemann's two *Confessions*.

Jakob Hutter was the Anabaptist leader in the Tirol most influential in shaping the group in Moravia which Riedemann joined. Hutter (hatmaker), born in the Puster Valley of the Tirol, in the hamlet of Moos (now in Italy), received some education in nearby Bruneck (Brunico) and studied hatmaking in nearby Prags, in the Tirol. He likely came in contact with Anabaptism at Klagenfurt. In the first clear reference to Hutter as an Anabaptist, he barely eluded capture when a group of believers was surprised in Welsberg.[140] How long he had been an Anabaptist is not known, but some scholars have concluded that he was one as early as 1526.[141] He became a leader in the Anabaptist community of Spittall in Carinthia.[142] He also led a congregation in Welsberg in the Puster Valley.

Specific influences on Hutter are difficult to identify. His communalism and views on church reform speak to some of the issues of economic injustice and inequality raised by the revolt of Gaismair. Even though there is no direct historical connection between Gaismair's revolt and Hutter's reform, Hutter perhaps was a partisan of Gaismair.[143] Before Hutter was converted to pacifism, he might have been associated with the military revolts in the Tirol.

Persecution of Anabaptists in the Tirol was intense, so Hutter and

Simon Schützinger traveled to Moravia in 1529 to see whether it would be a safe refuge for persecuted Anabaptists from the Tirol.[144] From 1529 to 1535, Hutter was promoting the Anabaptist movement in the Tirol or was in Moravia settling disputes and organizing the Tirolean Anabaptist communalists.

The few extant letters by Hutter provide some insight into his thinking.[145] He expressed a strong sense of being led by God. He believed his view of communalism was God's vision for all of humanity. Hutter held that salvation is made available through faith in Christ.[146] He wrote his letters of comfort and encouragement with a strong sense of living in an evil world in which the faithful are persecuted.[147] Repeatedly, he called on believers to live in such a way "that their walk and life may be faultless, and that their life and walk not be a hindrance to Christ."[148]

Hutter's communalism became the vision of the Tirolean group in Moravia. Riedemann identified with this communalism during his brief stay in Moravia. The Tirolean Anabaptists in Moravia became Riedemann's home community for the rest of his life.

Missioner to Franconia

In 1533 Riedemann and Six Braitfus were sent as missioners (*Sendboten*) to Franconia to replace Zaunring. Zaunring, after he had repented from his lapses in leadership, had been sent as a missioner to Franconia; in 1533 he was executed in Bamberg, Upper Franconia.[149] Shortly after Riedemann arrived in Franconia with Six Braitfus, the two were captured. Braitfus was whipped and expelled, but Riedemann was imprisoned for more than four years in the city tower of Nuremberg.[150]

How did those four years influence Riedemann? His imprisonment was not particularly severe. He was allowed to write letters, so it can be assumed that he had some contact with local Anabaptists, both personally and by letter. His correspondence also shows that he maintained contact with the Hutterite communities in Moravia.

The city council of the free city of Nuremberg had a relatively lenient policy regarding Anabaptists, compared with other governments in the region in the mid-1530s.[151] During the early 1520s, the city council had decided to side with the Lutheran reform, though there were also Catholics and Zwinglians in the city.[152] The council vigorously combated Anabaptism, yet only one Anabaptist was executed: Wolfgang Vogel, a former Catholic priest, on March 26, 1527.[153]

A year later the Nuremburg city council protested the emperor's order to execute without trial all persons suspected of being Anabaptists. In July 1528, the city council decided to expel Anabaptists who would not recant.[154] Later the council demanded that those who were being exiled must promise never to return to Nuremberg. Braitfus was immediately expelled, and Riedemann was sent away after four years and ten weeks in prison.

At Nuremberg in Franconia, Riedemann had entered a region in which most of the local Anabaptists were common people. In the country, the majority were peasants. In the towns, Anabaptists were artisans and members of guilds; they included weavers, painters, smiths, printers, and a few former priests.[155] The Tirolean communalists at Auspitz in Moravia had contact with this area and had been sending missioners there, as shown by the activity of Zaunring.

The local Anabaptist movement in Franconia had been shaped under the influence of the Peasants' Revolt.[156] Thomas Müntzer, one of the principal leaders of the peasants, spent time in Nuremberg in late 1524.[157] In 1525 the Peasants' Revolt broke out in Franconia, in the area near Nuremberg. Even though the peasants had the support of some local nobles and priests, they were brutally crushed.[158]

After the collapse of that revolt, Anabaptism in Franconia developed in two directions. One form was led by Hans Hut, the other by Hans Denck. Hans Hut became Anabaptist some time after the failed Peasants' Revolt. He developed an Anabaptism influenced by Müntzer's mysticism and apocalypticism,[159] but without his agenda for social and economic reform through violent revolution. Instead of violence, Hut advocated an interim peace ethic, pacifism until the end of the age, which he believed was near and would bring sudden and violent war between believers and unbelievers. In that war, believers would unsheathe their swords and fight on the side of God's forces to defeat and destroy the evil ones.

Though Hans Denck was also a mystic, his theology was quite different from Hut's.[160] He was not involved in the Peasants' Revolt, nor was he interested in speculations about the end-times.[161] He is probably best known for one statement: "No one may truly know Christ except one who follows him in life."[162] That view of discipleship was part of his overarching theme about the love of God. As God loves humans, so humans are to love each other. In his theology, salvation and discipleship are woven into one theological fabric. His mysticism caused him to de-emphasize outer forms in favor of the Spirit within. Instead of the outer form of baptism, he stressed inner baptism. Instead of the literal (mechanically interpreted) word of Scripture, he emphasized the spirit of the written Word.

The spirit of Hut's and Denck's Anabaptism lived on in Franconia until 1533, when Peter Riedemann arrived in Nuremberg. Yet the legacy of Hans Hut was more prominent. Hut's chiliasm had been transformed into a new Anabaptism much more peaceful and not involved in end-time speculations. Despite persistent persecution, the Hutian Anabaptist movement had survived. The Nuremberg group had repeatedly reconstituted itself, frequently with refugees from other areas.[163]

Riedemann remained in prison in Nuremberg for four years. Little is known about his stay, except that he was imprisoned in the city tower. In July 1537, upon his promise that he would not preach in Nuremberg, he was released from prison. On the way back to Moravia, he visited some Philippite members in Upper Austria.[164]

The Philippites complained to Riedemann about the treatment they had received at the hands of the Hutterites in Auspitz, which had influenced them to leave the Hutterites. Riedemann did not immediately side with one or the other group. He indicated that he was willing to listen to the Philippites, but he wanted to speak to the Hutterites before taking any action.[165]

In Moravia

In September 1537, Riedemann and two Philippite members arrived at the Tirolean Hutterian communities in Moravia. Although Hans Amon was the *Vorsteher* (chief leader) at this time, Riedemann met with Leonhard Lanzenstiel and heard his account of the reasons for the conflict between the Hutterians on one side and the Gabrielites and the Philippites on the other. Subsequently, he also met with the followers of Philipp Plener and Gabriel Ascherham to hear their views of reasons for the conflict and division.[166]

During Riedemann's discussions with Lanzenstiel, Peter Hüter, Gabriel Ascherham's assistant, arrived and confessed that he had been wrong in the conflict. Apparently that confession convinced

Riedemann that the Hutterites had been right, and the Gabrielites and Philippites wrong. In following years, Riedemann used personal intercession and letter in trying to convince the Gabrielites and Philippites to rejoin the Hutterites. Initially he had limited success, but eventually he convinced many to rejoin the Hutterites.[167]

Riedemann had discovered that the Anabaptist situation in Moravia in 1537 was quite different from what it had been in 1533. Because of severe persecution of Anabaptists in the Tirol, Jakob Hutter and others had moved to Moravia in August 1533, and his arrival had far-reaching consequences. It led to what the Hutterites called "the great split (*die grosse Zerspaltung*)." Hutter soon met with leaders of the three federated communalist groups: Gabriel Ascherham of the Silesian group at Rossitz, Philipp Plener of the South German group at Auspitz, and Simon Schützinger of the Tirolean group, also at Auspitz. The three men seem to have had about equal authority in a federated relationship, with Ascherham exercising some overall leadership.[168] Hutter's arrival this time, in contrast to the other three times, was not in response to an invitation or a leadership crisis.

In a major speech, Hutter made a case for his becoming an equal leader with the others, claiming he had been appointed by God.[169] The three leaders resisted Hutter. Schützinger was the boldest in trying to silence Hutter in the Tirolean group. In the leadership struggle between Hutter and Schützinger, Hutter proved that Schützinger had been secretly hoarding money and thus had compromised his commitment to communalism. The Tirolean group deposed Schützinger and selected Hutter as leader.[170] Plener and Ascherham supported Schützinger and resisted Hutter's attempt to take over leadership of their groups.

In harsh discussions, Hutter and the Tiroleans condemned both Plener and Ascherham. At first Plener and Ascherham apparently retained most of their followers.[171] This division was a blow to the communalist movement in Moravia and yet also seemed to consolidate it. Hutter's stricter interpretation of communalism required full and unconditional financial participation. That became the pattern for the Hutterite faction of the communalists.

Hutter felt the need to justify his actions, so he sent a long letter to the Anabaptists in the Tirol, explaining why the split occurred.[172] He saw the conflict largely in terms of a larger battle between the forces of good and evil. The other three leaders had allied themselves with evil, which was why they had been deposed by the congregations.[173] In this conflict, the final arbiters were the congregations. Leaders were leaders only if they could persuade the members of their point of view.

The second major development in Moravia during Riedemann's imprisonment in Nuremberg was the persecution in 1535. In 1534 and 1535, the princes in Europe were horrified at the Anabaptist uprising in Münster in Westphalia. At the Moravian diet in the spring of 1535, Ferdinand I, eastern emperor in Vienna, ordered the nobles in Moravia to expel all Anabaptists from their lands. He believed, as did most of the nobility of Europe, that all Anabaptists were as threatening as those at Münster. The local nobles who had given refuge to the communalists at Rossitz and Auspitz were forced to expel them.[174]

The persecution was severe. Men, women, and children were scattered in the forests. A price was placed upon Jakob Hutter's head. The suffering became so intense that in 1535 the Tirolean communalists in Moravia finally asked Hutter to leave, since the authorities seemed primarily intent on capturing him.[175] All three communal groups suffered in the persecution. Most of the Hutterites scattered in the countryside in Moravia for the duration of the crisis. When persecution subsided in 1536, they regrouped in Auspitz.[176]

In the worst of the suffering, Philipp Plener left his group to look for refuge. Then he sent his people a message to scatter and find refuge wherever they could.[177] Most of the Philippites settled in Upper Austria and in various South German states.[179] Some Philippites, however, joined the Hutterites after the persecution subsided, and later Riedemann persuaded others to join the Hutterites.[179]

During the crisis, the major portion of the Gabrielite group from Rossitz left for Silesia under the leadership of Gabriel Ascherham. Their communal structure disintegrated, however, likely due to Ascherham's problematic leadership.[180] Some Gabrielites returned to Moravia and joined the Hutterites after the persecution had abated. Others joined under the encouragement of Riedemann after 1545, following the death of Ascherham.

Thus when Riedemann returned to the Hutterite community in Moravia in 1537, the Hutterite community was the major communal Anabaptist group in Moravia. It was led by Hans Amon, who had been selected as *Vorsteher* when Hutter left for the Tirol in 1535.[181]

During the two years that Riedemann was in Moravia, from 1537 to 1539, he related to scattered groups of Philippites. In 1537 he sent a lengthy letter to the groups in Upper Austria.[182] Members of those groups seem to have left Moravia before the great division in 1533, and he reminded them of the faith that they had shared. At the heart of true faith, he reminded them, is living in community and giving up private property.[183]

Early in 1538, Riedemann visited the scattered Philippite groups. He encouraged and organized them, establishing leaders in the various locations.[184] Later in 1538, he sent them and other Philippite groups a letter. Again he defended Jakob Hutter's case in the great division in 1533 and showed why the leadership of the Philippite and Gabrielite groups had been wrong. He repeatedly argued that Gabriel Ascherham and Philipp Plener had not been consistent enough in communal sharing.

Missioner to Hesse

In 1539 the Hutterite communities in Moravia received a request from Anabaptists in Hesse for help; they decided to send Peter Riedemann.[185] On the way to Hesse, Riedemann detoured through Upper Austria, again visiting scattered Anabaptist groups. He made a special effort to relate to the Philippites.

Riedemann also stopped to visit a group of Anabaptists in Lauingen, Swabia, who had come from Moravia.[186] A person who claimed to be inspired by the Spirit of God had deposed the leaders of the congregation, which was waiting for new leadership. In a letter to Hans Amon, leader of the Hutterites in Moravia, Riedemann expressed his concern about the group and noted that he had left them before they had resolved their problem.[187] He also met with a former Philippite group which by then had ceased communal living.

In Hesse, Riedemann became involved in settling problems within the local Anabaptist group. He wrote a long letter to Hans Amon, describing the tangled situation with which he had to work.[188] Riedemann reported that there was dissension in the group, and the group did not have confidence in its leader, Matthias. He noted that many Anabaptists were returning to the state church.

Riedemann initiated discussions which resulted in a split in the group. According to Riedemann, only about forty people joined him, including the troublesome leader Matthias.[189] Riedemann described Matthias as "self-willed and obstinate."[190] Riedemann asked Matthias to go to Moravia to learn about communal living and proper leadership, but he refused. In a letter to Amon, Riedemann asked Amon to make a decision about the leadership situation in Hesse.

As Riedemann discovered, Anabaptism in Hesse was in a critical state. What had once been a large, flourishing movement had become a small group, struggling and demoralized, racked by inner dissension. What had happened in Hesse to create this situation?

The first Anabaptist group in Hesse was formed as the result of the preaching of Hans Hut. Hut had started Anabaptist cells consisting primarily of former members of the Peasants' Revolt.[191] A leader of this Hut-type Anabaptism was Melchior Rinck. In 1533 a group of Hutian Anabaptists in Sorga, Hesse, was captured and brought to trial. They were found guilty of being Anabaptist. Philip, ruler of Hesse, had a lenient policy toward Anabaptists and expelled them instead of executing them as demanded by imperial law. Zaunring, a Hutterite missioner, invited the Sorga group to join the Hutterites in Moravia. They accepted this invitation. Riedemann may have met the group of refugees from Hesse, since he spent time in Moravia in 1533.

Another and perhaps a more important group of Anabaptists arose in Hesse under influence of Melchior Hoffmann. Hoffmann, who began his career as a Lutheran preacher, was the founder of Anabaptism in the Netherlands. In the early 1530s, on one of his trips from the Netherlands to Strassburg, he stopped in Hesse and started an Anabaptist group. The local leaders who continued Melchiorite Anabaptism in Hesse were Peter Tasch and Georg Schnabel.[192]

The Melchiorite Anabaptists in Hesse carried the burden of the Münsterite episode of 1534-35. Some of them were arrested in 1536. After being in prison for about two years, they presented a confession to Prince Philip. They attempted to distance themselves from the Münsterite movement by pledging obedience to the government and even promising to obey a call to arms. They disavowed polygamy[193] and rejected community of goods. Their main concern, though, was that the church be truly reformed. They believed that members of the church should live holy lives, and that ethical standards should be enforced through church discipline.[194]

In late 1538, Prince Philip arranged a discussion with this group of Melchiorite Anabaptists. Philip promised to reform the Hesse church more fully by improving the education of church members and by introducing church discipline. So Peter Tasch and many of the Melchiorite Anabaptists drew up a confession, presented it to Philip in December of 1538, and returned to the state church.[195]

When some Anabaptists in Hesse invited Riedemann to visit them, it was probably because so many others had left the Anabaptists. Those who remained Anabaptist in Hesse were few. They felt demoralized, and they lacked a sense of vision and direction. In Riedemann's first visit, he gathered Anabaptists interested in communalism, and in that group he primarily addressed issues of leadership.

Brief Return to Moravia

Riedemann remained in Hesse less than a year. In autumn 1539, Riedemann returned to Steinebrunn in Austria. He arrived "the week after St. Nicholas Day" (Dec. 6), just after the authorities had captured the Hutterite men in the community.[196] About 150 Hutterite men had been taken to the Falkenstein Castle.[197] Riedemann found only the grieving women and children. He apparently remained with the community for a while during this difficult time.

Missioner to Hesse Again

In early 1540, Riedemann was again sent to Hesse by the Hutterite community.[198] On the way he visited various groups in Upper and Lower Austria, the Tirol, Swabia, and Württemberg.[199] Riedemann took along a letter from Hans Amon to the Anabaptists in Hesse.[200] In the letter Amon chided the Anabaptists in Hesse for turning against the communities in Moravia. He acknowledged that there were different groups of Anabaptists in Hesse and admitted that they were involved in a struggle concerning their direction. Amon likely received his information about Hesse from Riedemann.

Shortly after arriving in Hesse, Riedemann was captured.[201] He was first kept in chains in a dungeon in Marburg.[202] Later he was transferred to the nearby castle at Wolkersdorf, where his imprisonment was less harsh and restrictive. Philip, the ruler of Hesse and one of the major Lutheran princes, did not execute Anabaptists. Instead, he tried to win them back by argument and discussion. Riedemann benefited from this leniency. During the imprisonment, Riedemann wrote a number of letters to the communities in Moravia.[203]

Riedemann's most important accomplishment during his imprisonment in Hesse was composing his *Confession of Faith*.[204] He wrote the *Confession* primarily to inform Prince Philip about the beliefs of Riedemann and the communalist Anabaptists whom he represented in Hesse.[205] A copy of the *Confession* was taken to the Hutterite communities in Moravia and was "quickly accepted by the Hutterites as the definitive statement of their faith."[206]

In 1540, possibly during the time when Riedemann was in prison in Hesse, Matthias recanted and joined the state church.[207] Perhaps he later joined the Anabaptists again.

Leader of Hutterites in Moravia

Hans Amon, leader of the Hutterites in Moravia, died in 1542. Leonhard Lanzenstiel was chosen to replace him, but he felt inadequate to take on the leadership by himself and invited Riedemann to join him as leader of the Hutterites.[208] After about two years of rather lenient imprisonment, Riedemann escaped and returned to Moravia to take up leadership with Lanzenstiel. Lanzenstiel led in the practical and administrative areas of the community, and Riedemann gave pastoral guidance. Riedemann continued as a leader until December 1556, when he died in the community of Protzka.[209]

Riedemann's career as leader of the Hutterite communities in Moravia falls into three distinct periods: 1542-47, with relative toleration even though Anabaptists were still outlawed; 1547-53, with severe persecution; and 1553-56, with a return to toleration and the beginning of the "golden age" of Hutterite development.[210]

From 1542 until 1547, the Hutterites experienced relative prosperity.[211] Hutterites, especially those sent out on missionary assignments, were being captured, tortured, and executed, but the communities in Moravia were mostly allowed to exist in peace.[212] During those years Riedemann, in addition to general duties as leader, worked to bring about reconciliation with the Gabrielites who had moved to Silesia. After Gabriel Ascherham's death in 1545, Riedemann persuaded many Gabrielites in Silesia to move to Moravia and join the Hutterites.[213]

Already in 1545 the Moravian princes were trying to restrict the economic communalism of the Hutterites, likely hoping to limit their growth.[214] By 1547 the Protestant John Frederick of Saxony had been defeated, and Philip of Hesse had surrendered to the Catholic rulers. Leading the Holy Roman Empire were Emperor Charles V and his brother Ferdinand I, who ruled in Vienna. They were staunchly Catholic and attempted to eradicate religious reform in their domains.[215] For a few years, they had hope of destroying the Lutheran and all other reforms. This brought a new and severe period of persecution upon the Hutterites in Moravia. The *Chronicle* vividly describes the 1548 capture and torture of Hans Greckenhofer and Hans Mändel.[216] They escaped.

The arrests were a sign of things to come. Hutterites were threatened with hanging if they did not comply with orders to recant their faith and join the Catholic Church.[217] They were expelled from Moravia, so they settled among Hutterites already in Slovakia, then part of Hungary. Next, Hutterites were ordered to leave that country as well.[218] Women and children were chased out of homes with hardly a moment's notice, sometimes with food still on the table.[219] Some had to spend nights in the snow and under hedges. Others dug holes and tunnels in the ground and hid in underground mazes for several years.[220] Hutterites lost most of their property. Many left possessions with neighbors while they were on the run, but even those "friends" helped themselves to whatever they wanted.[221] Left without protection, the Hutterites were beaten, robbed, and violated.[222]

Some Hutterites could not stand the pressure and left communal living to return to the state church. The *Chronicle* is harsh in its judgment of them, claiming that they were lax, superficial, chaff, impure, unable and unwilling to suffer for God's sake.[223] Those who returned to the state church were accused of preferring the pleasures of sin and the world, and of letting the favor of the devil win them over, instead of bearing the shame of Christ.[224] No allowance was made for the harsh persecution they suffered. The Hutterite writers of the *Chronicle* simply expected everyone to stand firm.

Finally in the early 1550s, the severest persecution ended. In 1553 the Moravian nobles reasserted their independence from the emperor. Hutterites were again allowed to establish communities in Moravia and Hungary.[225] They continued to send missioners to various regions of Europe. That resulted in the capture and execution of many missionary Hutterites, as recorded in the *Chronicle*.[226]

The *Chronicle* does not give details of Riedemann's activities during the years of persecution, nor in the few years of relative toleration until his death in 1556. Hutterite historians, however, treated him with great respect. In their view, his contribution was important for the eventual survival of the Hutterites.

The *Chronicle* records that he composed one last hymn on his deathbed, which begins, "From death's bonds Christ redeemed us, from the devil's might he freed us."[227] After years of personal suffering and imprisonment; of comforting many who were suffering, imprisoned, or mourning; and of leading Hutterites for fourteen difficult years—Riedemann died in 1556 in the relative peace and quiet of the community in Protzka.[228]

We return to the question with which this study began. What were the formative influences on Riedemann? The historical survey shows that Riedemann had close contact with most of the major streams of sixteenth-century Anabaptism. He likely began his life as an Anabaptist within the spiritualist, Sabbatarian reform movement in Silesia. He came into contact with another form of spiritualist Anabaptism in Gmunden, a style likely influenced by Hut and Denck, yet with its own characteristics. He joined the communalists in Moravia who were being shaped by concerns in the Tirol. With its social, economic, and religious reforms, the Tirol created a stream of Anabaptism which differed from other major branches of Anabaptism on economic issues.

For much of his early life as an Anabaptist, Riedemann moved in areas influenced by the chiliasm and apocalypticism of Hans Hut. Some interpreters see Riedemann as transposing Hut's end-time speculations into peaceful communalist forms. However, his ideas are so different from Hut's at so many points that Riedemann may also be seen as offering a major alternative to Hut's theology. Riedemann had contact with Dutch Melchiorite Anabaptists in Hesse. But for Riedemann, the Melchiorites in Hesse were compromisers, since many of them had returned to the state church.

Despite Riedemann's wide range of contacts with various Anabaptist groups, this historical survey has shown that his thinking drew most heavily upon Anabaptism from the Tirol. In the *Confession of Faith*, he encourages communalism, pacifism, and separation from the larger society, the world. These are themes characteristic of Jakob Hutter and other Tirolean Anabaptists who migrated to Moravia.

In Riedemann's theology, as expressed in the *Confession of Faith*, the central motif is communalism, the concept and practice of community of goods. In developing communalism, Riedemann drew together the spiritualism of Schwenckfeld and Denck, the biblicism held by most Anabaptists whom he met, and Michael Gaismair's vision for economic and social reform, but adapted to peaceful ways.

Textual History of Riedemann's *Confession of Faith*

The first edition of the *Confession of Faith* was likely printed between 1543 and 1545 in connection with a presentation to the princes of Moravia, to explain and defend the Hutterites' beliefs.[229] Its original title was *Rechenschafft unserer Religion / Leer und Glaubens*. (An account of our religion, teaching, and faith.)[230] Under the title appeared the initials for Peter Riedemann: "P. R." The following was added in handwriting in the Zurich copy: "Von uns Brüd'n So man dj Hutterischen nen't Ausgange" (By us brothers who are known as the Hutterites). The use of initials instead of name lets the writer fade into the background, reinforcing his claim to be spelling out the beliefs of the community. Perhaps he also had future safety in mind.

In addition, the title page includes most of 1 Peter 3:15: "Seit alle zeit vrbüetig yederman zur verantwortung / dem der Grund fordert der hoffnu'g die inn euch ist. 1 Pet. 3." (Always be ready to make a defense to anyone who demands from you an accounting for the hope that is in you.)[231] This verse justifies the book: Riedemann gives an account or confession of the Hutterites' faith and hope.

Two or three copies of the first edition (ca. 1545) are extant, one in the Zentralbibliothek in Zurich,[232] one in the City Library of Wroclaw (formerly Breslau, Poland),[233] and one in the Vienna Nationalbibliothek.[234] The extant copies of this edition list no date and no publisher. Perhaps it was prepared by a traveling printer. It consists of a pocket-size version of 288 leaves.[235]

The *Confession of Faith* was printed in a second edition in 1565, by Philips Vollanndt, with the same title: *Rechenschafft unserer Religion / Leer und Glaubens*. On the title page, now as a subtitle, its origin is again attributed to the Hutterite community: *Von den Brüdern so man die Hutterischen Nen't ausgangen*. Here it says "by the brothers" rather than "by us brothers." Since this 1565 edition was printed after

Riedemann's death in 1556, the writer is named on the title page: "Durch Peter Ryedeman" (through Peter Riedemann). The use of "through" is a reminder that he wrote for the community, which has approved the *Confession*. The title page also quotes 1 Peter 3:15. Several copies of this second edition are extant: in the Austrian Nationalbibliothek in Vienna, in the British Museum, in the Library of the University of Chicago, and at a Bruderhof in Montana.[236]

Four modern editions of Riedemann's *Confession of Faith* have been published.[237] In 1902 the Hutterites in North America published an edition in Berne, Indiana, using the University of Chicago copy of the second edition. This edition was corrected and reprinted in 1962. In 1938 the Society of Brothers (Bruderhof communities) produced a new edition of the *Confession of Faith*, using the copy in the British Museum. In 1950 the Society of Brothers published the first English translation, by Kathleen E. Hasenberg, entitled *Confession of Faith: Account of Our Religion, Doctrine and Faith*. In addition to these four, there is a rare 1870 reprint of the *Confession of Faith* in the *Mitteilungen aus dem Antiquariat von S. Calvary.*[238]

Riedemann did not generally supply Scripture references in the first edition. Marginal references were added in the 1565 edition, citing the Bible by book and chapter, without giving verse divisions (which Robert Estienne [Stephanus] had introduced in the New Testament in 1551). The 1565 edition identified location in the chapter with letters: *a, b, c,* or *d.* The 1902 edition included biblical references in the text, without specifying verse numbers. The first to offer marginal verse references was the 1938 edition, published by the Cotswold Bruderhof in England, through the "Publishing House of the Hutterian Brethren in the U.S.A., Canada, and England." The 1950 translation (reprinted in 1970) put Bible references in endnotes.

This fresh English translation is based on the copy of the 1565 (second) edition in the British Museum. Amended biblical references are provided here in footnotes and in a Scripture index.

Overview of the *Confession of Faith*

Peter Riedemann, a simple cobbler, wrote the *Confession of Faith*. The book expresses Riedemann's personal views; more significantly, it also sums up the beliefs of the Hutterite communalists centered in

Moravia. This *Confession* was quickly approved by the Hutterite community, to be their official statement.

The *Confession of Faith* consists of two parts. The first has ninety short sections about theology and ethics, beginning with God and ending with "the life, conduct, and adornment of Christians." The second part provides six longer discussions on how the people of God should be separated from the world. He deals with the church, grace, the Supper of Christ, swearing, and governmental authority. In each section Riedemann argues a particular theological view or ethical admonition.

The *Confession of Faith* is thoroughly based on Scripture. Each section refers to the Bible, alludes to it, or quotes directly from various parts of Scripture and the Apocrypha.[239] In the sequence of editions, references were clarified, and citation methods were developed. Biblical imagery is prominent throughout the *Confession*. Riedemann skillfully weaves his material into one harmonious whole.

The first part of the *Confession* has at least 1,432 biblical references, plus allusions. There are at least 320 references to the Old Testament, 55 to the Apocrypha, primarily to Wisdom and Sirach (Ecclesiasticus), and 1,057 to the New Testament. Among references to the New Testament, 390 cite the Gospels, and 667 call on other books in the New Testament, chiefly Paul's epistles.

Like Hans Denck and Pilgram Marpeck, Riedemann stresses that the literal word of Scripture must be interpreted through the Holy Spirit, not in a rigid or mechanical fashion (1 Cor. 2:10-16, cited in "Concerning Oaths"). The written Word is truly understood only through the living Word, the word of the gospel.

A second characteristic of the *Confession* is that a large portion of the first part (29 of 90 sections) is organized around the Apostles' Creed. Thus Riedemann bases his *Confession* not only on the Bible but also on tradition. Following exposition of the Apostles' Creed, 32 sections deal with related classical theological themes, such as faith, original sin, law, baptism, and the Lord's Supper. The last third (29 sections) of the first part deals with practical concerns of community living, such as warfare, taxation, making swords, and trade.

By using the Apostles' Creed as an outline, Riedemann was able briefly to address classical theological themes. His *Confession* is theologically more comprehensive than, for example, the articles of *Brotherly Union*, called the *Schleitheim Confession*, drawn up by Swiss and South German Anabaptists in 1527 at Schleitheim, Switzerland. Riedemann's *Confession* is an example of an Anabaptist community in dialogue with the wider Christian theological tradition.

In the first sections of the *Confession*, Riedemann affirms the Trinity: Father, Son, and Holy Spirit. Riedemann thus separates himself from the anti-trinitarian movements of the sixteenth century and demonstrates his orthodox view of the Trinity. In describing the relationships of Father, Son, and Holy Spirit to each other, Riedemann emphasizes that they are equal, not subordinate to one another, yet also one. Thus he avoids the charge of being Arian (subordinating the Son).[240] He affirms that though there are three names, there is "yet one substance, one nature, one essence" ("We Confess the Holy Spirit"). In speaking of God's oneness, he does not shy away from using the key theological term in the Nicene Creed: "of one substance" (*homoousios*). He also uses metaphors of fire, heat, and light to describe the threeness as well as the essential oneness of God.

In his discussion of God, Riedemann uses a mixture of biblical references and traditional creedal terms. He says that the Son proceeds from the Father, the Son was with the Father in the beginning, the Son is in the Father as the Father is in the Son, the Son and the Father are one nature and one strength, and the Son is the only begotten one of the Father. On the Holy Spirit, he uses the term included in the Western version of the Nicene Creed, that the Holy Spirit "proceeds" from both Father and Son ("We Confess the Holy Spirit").

The Christology section is brief. Yet the emphasis is so consistent with the Christology of the Creed of Chalcedon that it appears he was consciously affirming an orthodox Christology. He declares that Christ became incarnate, fully human and in the flesh, and yet also remained fully divine. Since Christ was fully divine, he was able to provide salvation and overcome death; because he was fully human, through him we can become "God's anointed."

In these early sections, Riedemann shows that the Hutterites' belief is based on the Bible, and that it is consistent with the traditional terminology and concepts of the Apostles' Creed and the Nicene and Chalcedonian creeds. Throughout the discussion, he uses both biblical and traditional creedal terminology.

He provides a unique and creative application of the Trinity by rooting communalism in the Trinity:

Community means that those who have this fellowship hold all things in common, no one having anything for oneself, but each sharing all things with the others. Just so, the Father has nothing for himself, but everything he has, he has with the Son. Likewise, the Son has nothing for himself, but all he has, he has with the Father and with all who have fellowship with him. ("Community of Saints")

Riedemann correctly notes that in the traditional view of the Trinity, the three persons share all characteristics and are seen as equal in all respects. He argues that if the church is really a holy community, it should exhibit the same characteristics: all members should share all things with each other and each be equal with the others. Riedemann lays a theological and trinitarian foundation for communal sharing.

He closes his comments on the Apostles' Creed with a lengthy discussion of the church. He describes it as "an assembly of the children of God," "the foundation and ground of truth," "a community gathered by God through his Spirit," and "a community of saints because they have fellowship in holy things." His emphasis is on the church as gathered, created by God, holy, and in character consistent with the character of God. The church is not basically defined by separation from the world but by relationship to Christ and God.

In the 32 sections following the Apostles' Creed, Riedemann deals with other theological affirmations. The key is his section on faith. Faith, he says, is not merely empty words from people who profess Christ and then live to suit themselves. Faith is a real divine power which renews people and makes them like God in character. This lays the foundation for the sections on faithful living. He ties faith and discipleship together and reaffirms this connection in the section on "Doctrine." He insists that teaching exists to produce fruit.

Riedemann also addresses the issues of original sin and free will, issues over which Luther and Erasmus had a major controversy.[241] He agrees with the view traditional since Augustine, that all people inherit sin from Adam, and that this inherited, original sin is the cause of both physical and eternal death. Riedemann differs from Luther's view of grace by arguing that Christ's death and resurrection have freed people from eternal death if they respond to God in faith. Like Erasmus, he holds that Christ has given people who believe in him the ability to respond to God and thus lead changed lives.

Response to God in faith, he is quick to point out, is not a good deed for which we humans deserve merit, but a gift from God, given through Christ. Yet in Christ, people *can* turn to God in faith and be changed. After Christ's death and resurrection, eternal death is the result of unbelief and not of inherited punishment. Thus children need not be baptized, since until they reach the age of accountability, they will not be punished. This discussion of faith lays the foundation for the possibility and necessity of Christians being faithful to God in their daily life in the community. Sanctification, the theological theme which Schwenckfeld tried unsuccessfully to incorporate into the reform in Silesia, is prominent in Riedemann's theology.

In the last 29 sections of the first part, Riedemann expounds various aspects of community living. Few of these issues are simply individual ethics. For Riedemann, ethics or discipleship is *community* ethics. Being Christian is developing an ethic by which the whole community will live. Thus the character of the community is shaped by the character of God, and the character of the individual is shaped by the character of the community to which people commit themselves. Issues of warfare, adultery, innkeeping, making swords, and taxation—these are not matters for the individual to decide separately; they are issues the community decides.

The last half of the *Confession* consists of six sections which elaborate issues already introduced in the first half of the book. Here Riedemann treats the church as the people of God separated from the world, the community and how it should be built up, the covenant of grace, the Supper of Christ, swearing, and governmental authority.

In these sections there is greater emphasis on themes of separation than in the first half of the *Confession*. In the first half, Riedemann was apparently more concerned to identify the areas of agreement between Hutterite beliefs and orthodox Christian beliefs. The first half consists of bridge-building. In the second half of the *Confession*, sharper distinctions are drawn, especially distinctions between the true church and the false church, or the world.

Riedemann concludes the *Confession* with a reminder that he is writing in the German state of Hesse and that his aim is to reveal the truth so that "all the children of God may walk in the truth."

Dates for Riedemann and Hutterite Origins

1506	Peter Riedemann born at Hirschberg, Silesia; then learns trade of cobbler.
1517	Luther nails his 95 theses to castle church door in Wittenberg (Oct. 31).
1519-20	Zwingli begins church reform in Zurich.
1524-25	Peasants' Revolt, with social concerns, led in the Tirol by Michael Gaismair.
1524-29	Caspar Schwenckfeld leads church reform in Silesia, Riedemann's area.
1525	Grebel, Manz, and Blaurock rebaptized in Zurich (Jan. 21). Bolt Eberli, first Anabaptist martyr (May 29, 1525); Felix Manz, second (Jan. 5, 1527).
1526	Anabaptists increase and are penalized. Conrad Grebel dies of the plague.
1526-28	Balthasar Hubmaier attracts many Anabaptists to Nikolsburg; is executed.
1527	Anabaptists adopt *Schleitheim Confession* (Feb. 24), by Michael Sattler.
1527-28	Many Anabaptists arriving in Silesia, fleeing persecution.
1528	Anabaptists outlawed in Silesia; many leave for Nikolsburg area of Moravia. Hubmaier's "sword-bearer" Anabaptists stay at Nikolsburg but soon disband. "Staff-bearer" communalists go to Austerlitz, led by Wiedemann and Jäger. Gabriel Ascherham communalists from Silesia to Rossitz, near Austerlitz. Philipp Plener communal Anabaptists from Hesse and Palatinate to Moravia.
1529	Blaurock, Hutter's predecessor, burned at the stake in the Tirol (Sept. 6). Philippites move to Auspitz, between Austerlitz and Nikolsburg. Jakob Hutter (hatmaker), Anabaptist from the Tirol, visits Moravia.
1529-32	Riedemann, 23, in prison at Gmunden, the Tirol; writes *First Confession*.
1530	More Anabaptists expelled from Silesia, including Andreas Fischer.
1531	Division in Austerlitz community; some leave for Auspitz. Federation of two communities at Auspitz and one at Rossitz, with Ascherham as *Vorsteher*.
1532	Riedemann joins communalist Anabaptists at Austerlitz; marries Katherine.
1532-35	Münsterite Anabaptists practice community of goods but become fanatic.
1533-37	Riedemann as missioner to Franconia; imprisoned four years at Nuremberg.
1533	Hutter and more Tirolean Anabaptists move to Moravia, fleeing persecution. Hutter calls for stricter communalism, exposes inconsistencies of leaders, becomes *Vorsteher* of federated colonies. In this "great split," some leave.
1535	Severe persecution of communal Anabaptists in Moravia; Hutter leaves.
1535-42	Hans Amon follows Hutter as *Vorsteher* (chief leader) of the Hutterites.
1536	Hutter as missioner, burned at the stake at Innsbruck, Austria (Feb. 25).
1537-39	Riedemann discovers conflict in Moravia; works with Hutterites for unity.
1539	Riedemann as missioner to Hesse; visits grieving Hutterites in Austria.
1540-42	Riedemann, again missioner to Hesse, writes *Confession of Faith* in prison.
1542-65	Leonhard Lanzenstiel as *Vorsteher* of Hutterites, assisted by Riedemann.
1542-47	Hutterites in Moravia enjoy relative toleration.
1543-45	*Confession of Faith*, first ed., presented to princes of Moravia; 2d ed., 1565.
1547-53	Riedemann guides the Hutterites through severe persecution.
1553-56	Riedemann helps lead Hutterites into a "golden age," under toleration.
1556	Riedemann dies peacefully at Protzka, Hungary (now Brodsko, Slovakia).
1560s	Caspar Braitmichel carries the Hutterite *Chronicle* to 1542.
1561	Hutterites make only known reply to 1557 Lutheran attack on Anabaptists.
1565-78	Peter Walpot as *Vorsteher* of about 30,000 Hutterites during their "golden age," with about 100 *Haushaben* (*Bruderhöfe*, farm colonies) in Moravia and Slovakia. Schools and crafts well developed. Books and letters written.
1592	Golden period yielding to Counter-Reformation persecution and decline of Hutterites. Those not converting to Catholicism ordered to leave Moravia.
1601	Claus Braidl in long letter defends community of goods on biblical grounds.
1618-48	Thirty Years' War drives Hutterites from Moravia, to refuge in Slovakia.
1639-62	Andreas Ehrenpreis at Sabatisch, Slovakia, restoring communal discipline.

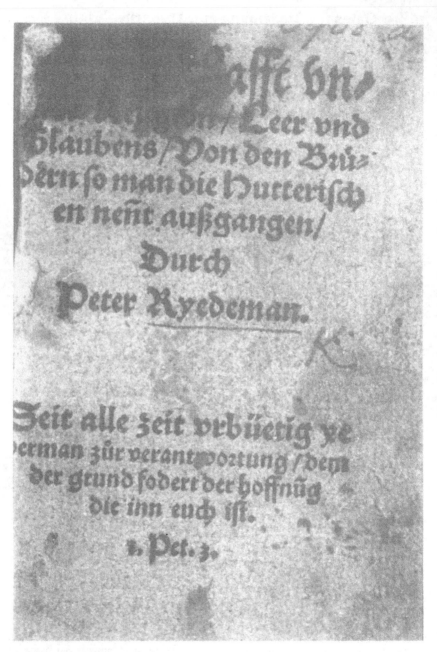

...asft vn~
...Leer vnd
Glaubens / Von den Brü~
dern so man die Hutterisch
en nent. außgangen /
Durch
Peter Ryedeman.

Seit alle zeit vrbütig ye
derman zür verantwortung / dem
der grund fodert der hoffnüg
die inn euch ist.
1. Pet. 3.

Title page of the 1565 edition. British Museum.

52

Confession of Our Religion, Teaching, and Faith

By the Brothers Who Are Known as the Hutterites

Through
Peter Riedemann

Always be ready to make a defense
to anyone who demands from you
an accounting for the hope that is in you.
—1 Peter 3:15

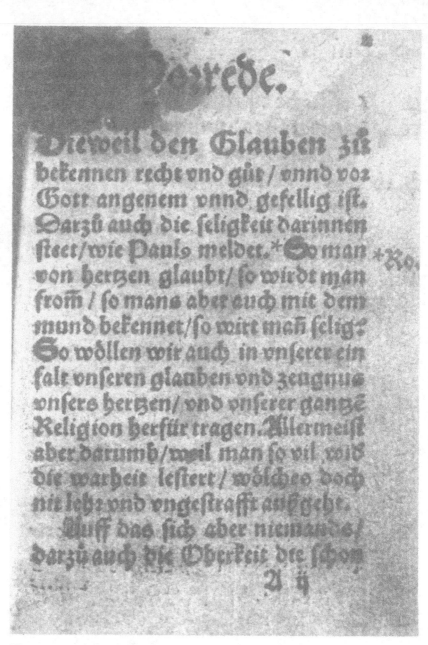

First page of the Preface, from the 1565 edition. British Museum.

Preface

Confessing our faith is good and acceptable before God and also contributes to our salvation, as Paul declares, "If one believes with the heart, one becomes righteous; if one also confesses with the lips, one becomes saved."[1] Therefore, in our simple manner we want to confess our faith, the testimony of our heart, and our entire religion. Above all, we want to make this confession because there is so much blasphemy against the truth, which will not go unheeded or unpunished.

We want to give an account of our faith, our teachings, and our way of life as much in sequence as possible. We do this so that no one, not even the authorities, who perhaps at the instigation of others have already laid their hands upon the Lord's peaceful people, may bring further guilt upon themselves by violating the apple of the Lord's eye.[2] Through this account we believe everyone will be able to recognize that we are not heretics and seducers,[3] as we are blasphemously called. We have not deserted the church that is in Christ Jesus, nor have we founded another sect outside the church. On the contrary, we have drawn near to the church and committed ourselves utterly to serve God and Christ with a blameless conscience within the church.

First, we want to consider the twelve principal articles of the Christian faith, which include the unlimited power of the Father, the righteousness of the Son, the forgiveness of the Holy Spirit, and that the church is accepted by God through Christ and gathered by the Holy Spirit. We shall consider what the church and the fellowship of believers is, what faith is and where it comes from, what we believe and teach about God, and what idolatry is. Further, we shall tell how God created people in his image, what the image of God is, and how people turned away from this and fell into sin, which led to their death.

---

[1] Rom. 10:10.   [2] Zech. 2:8.   [3] Promoting beliefs rejected by others.

We also want to show what sin and original sin is, and to what extent sin harms and destroys. Following this, we want to tell how one finds God and his grace again in Christ. We shall speak of remorse and repentance, the nature of true repentance, and how the truly repentant person is again grafted into Christ. We want to discuss God's covenant, including the old covenant, the law and the new covenant, the gospel, infant baptism, and certain reasons given by those who baptize infants. Next we will speak of the true baptism of Christ and of his church, how one baptizes, and who should baptize and teach. Then we will also speak about elections and diversity of offices in the church.

We furthermore wish to speak of the misuse of the Lord's Supper and how Christ intended it to be observed. Community of goods should likewise not be forgotten. We want to speak of separation from the world, marriage and adultery, government, war, taxes, swearing an oath, and making clothes.

Following those topics, we will discuss whether a Christian can go to court or sit in judgment. We will speak about oath-taking, greeting, shaking hands, and embracing. Next we will discuss praying, singing, fasting, celebrating, buying and selling, innkeeping, and excessive drinking. Then we want to speak of meetings, the education of children, exclusion from and reacceptance into the church, and finally, the whole dress, conduct, and adornment of Christians.

In all this we do our utmost to have a blameless conscience before God and people. We should like, insofar as it is in our power, to attract and persuade everyone to renounce their ungodly nature and turn with all their hearts to God and his Christ.[1] May almighty God grant his blessing and bring to pass the deliberation of his servants to his glory.

We must now confess that we have not received all this from any human being but from the Lord in heaven, from whom comes every good and perfect gift.[2] Therefore, we give the honor to him, for it is his alone. Whoever resists is resisting the gifts of God. As for ourselves, we cannot work against the truth but only for the truth, by which we mean to stand firm to the end, with God's help and to his glory. Amen.

---

[1] Titus 2:12.   [2] James 1:17.

PART 1

Now Follows the Confession of Our Faith, Teaching, and Way of Life

The Apostles' Creed

We Confess God

First, we confess that there is one God, who has being in himself and through himself, and who has neither beginning nor end. He possesses all power in heaven, on earth, and in the abyss. For this reason the word *God* is fitting and due to him alone. Although there are others called "gods," that is, "the mighty ones,"[1] there is but one God and mighty Power over them all. God is so much greater than all other powers, and there is no power except that which proceeds from him, or is bestowed or given by him.

So great is God's power that he has brought into being and given shape to everything that exists.[2] Even today, all things owe their existence to God. As they have come into being through him, so they also have their end in him. Thus, all other gods or mighty powers ought truly to be ashamed and terrified before him, tremble and bow down, and honor him alone. His hand is strong. He shatters and creates again, humbles and exalts, kills and brings to life whom he will.[3] Therefore, he alone is rightly named God and given honor. He himself says, "Hear, O Israel, the Lord your God is one."[4] Again he says, "I am the Lord your God,[5] and beside me there is no other."[6] Thus we acknowledge one God.

Our one great God, because he is so great, is in all places at once, and he fills everything in heaven and on earth with his glory.[7] This divine glory, unlimited power, and Godhead may be recognized in what he has created.[8] When the day dawns, which is a work of his hands, it gives light to every place. Air fills and pervades the whole Creation and is in all places at once.[9] Even so, and still more, the

---

[1] 1 Cor. 8:5. [2] Gen. 1:1-2:1. [3] Deut. 32:39. [4] Deut. 6:4. [5] Deut. 4:35.
[6] Isa. 43:11. [7] Isa. 6:3; Ps. 33:6-7. [8] Rom. 1:20. [9] Gen. 1:1-10.

Creator shows himself faithfully and well in everything he has made, in each thing according to its nature.

Therefore, this one, eternal, almighty God is the one, eternal, and unchanging truth, which has being in itself and remains eternally unchanged.[1] This truth pours itself into believing souls. It transforms us[2] so that we may live by it, and so our words and deeds may testify to the truth within us.[3]

The Almighty Father

God, who is eternal truth, is the enemy of all falsehood and deceit, the enemy of all that has a feigned, purely outward appearance. Therefore, he will not be named Father by those who are disobedient and do not believe his word.[4] "If I am your Father," says Scripture, "where is the honor which is due me?"[5] In another place Scripture says, "This perverse and crooked generation has lost his favor, and they are not his children on account of their sin."[6]

God, who is a Spirit, desires to be worshiped and honored in spirit and in truth.[7] They who do not have the same spirit can neither honor nor worship him,[8] as David shows in these words: "To the wicked God says, 'Why do you take my covenant in your mouth and declare my law, seeing you hate discipline, and cast my word behind you?' "[9] From this it is clear that God will not be worshiped and honored by the unbelieving, the unjust, or the sinful, nor will he hear their prayer.[10]

Moreover, all who continue in sin and yet name God as Father, say what is not true. As already said, they are not God's children on account of their sins.[11] Whoever untruthfully calls God "Father," reviles and abuses God who is truth, and from whom no lie can come.[12] The [Jewish leaders] did this when they said, "We have one Father, God." Christ answered them, "If God were your Father, you would love me, for I came from God. I did not come of my own accord, but because he sent me. Why do you not understand my message? Because you will not listen to my word, you are of your father, the devil, and you want to fulfil his evil desires. He was a murderer from the beginning and never was rooted in the truth."[13] Those who

---

[1] John 14:1-14. [2] Wisd. of Sol. 7:7. [3] 2 John 1:4-6. [4] John 8:39-47. [5] Mal. 1:6. [6] Deut. 32:5. [7] John 4:24. [8] Rom. 8:1-8. [9] Ps. 50:16-17. [10] John 9:30-41. [11] Deut. 32:5. [12] 1 John 2:18-24. [13] John 8:41-44.

have not given themselves to God as a child cannot truthfully name God as a Father.

Therefore, the Father, in grace and fatherly love and constancy, sends his Son from heaven to bring us back to be his children, and to lead us to our true inheritance. When he came, he gave to all who received him and still receive him, power to become children of God.[1] He teaches these, and not the world, to call him "Father" when he says, "When you want to pray, do not babble as the heathen and unbelievers do. They think they will be heard for their many words. Do not be like them. Your Father knows what you need before you ask him. Pray, then, like this, 'Our Father who art in heaven.' "[2]

As has been said, Christ is teaching not the world but the disciples to call God "Father." Christ has chosen them from the world.[3] They are to call God "Father" not only with their lips but with sincere hearts in deed and in truth. They show with their whole lives that they are his obedient children. He says further of them, "I do not say I will pray to the Father on your behalf, for the Father himself loves you because you have loved me and have believed that I came from God."[4]

Our Father

We confess that God is our Father because in his grace he has accepted and chosen us through Christ to be his own.[5] For this reason, too, he sent his Word from heaven and made us alive again, for we were dead through the disease of sin.[6] He has given us a new birth to an imperishable hope,[7] grafted us into his divine nature,[8] and after we believed the gospel, sealed us with his promised Spirit.[9] This Spirit now accomplishes everything in us, eradicating and destroying the sin that we have by nature so that what is good, true, and holy, which he brings with him and plants in us, may take root and bear fruit.

Thus, this same Holy Spirit of God assures us through his very real power in us that we are God's children.[10] Through the Spirit, we may well dare with joy and certainty to call him "Father" and approach and cry to him with confidence for all our needs, since we know that he loves us.[11] In Christ, God has given us everything.[12] His ear is open for our cry, and he is attentive to grant our prayer.[13]

---

[1] John 1:12. [2] Matt. 6:7-13. [3] John 15:16-20. [4] John 16:26-27. [5] 1 Pet. 2:6-10.
[6] Eph. 2:1-13. [7] 1 Pet. 1:3-5. [8] 2 Pet. 1:3-4. [9] Eph. 1:13-23. [10] Rom. 8:11-17.
[11] John 16:25-33. [12] Rom. 8:26-34. [13] 1 Pet. 3:8-12.

Because we have experienced God's fatherly grace, we have given ourselves to be obedient to his will, as children to our Father. We do this so that he may use all our members according to his will and satisfaction. As obedient children, willingly and attentively, we want to endure and suffer his work in us. That means letting God take charge of our whole life, controlling all our members, including heart, lips, eyes, ears, hands, and feet. Then not we but he, the Lord, will accomplish everything in us.[1] He cares for us as a father for his children and showers us abundantly with all good things. Truly God is our Father, and we are his children.[2]

Who Has Made Heaven and Earth

We confess that God has created heaven and earth and everything in them out of nothing, for his honor and glory.[3] Because God was one and alone, there was no one else to know him. This was not sufficient for his glory and divinity, since he could be praised by no one.

In order, therefore, that God's glory, majesty, and divinity might be seen, known, and praised, he created heaven and earth and everything in them.[4] He made heaven his throne[5] but gave the earth with all that adorns it to people, making them rulers over it so that they might learn to know the Creator and Overseer. Paul confirms this when he says that if one observes them carefully, God's everlasting power and divinity are visible in his works from the time of the Creation of the world.[6] Thus it is evident that all of God's creatures, whatever they may be, are given to teach and to lead people to God.

As soon as people became perverse and turned away from God, the Creation also became perverted for them, so that what had formerly served for people's benefit now, on the contrary, served for their harm. As the wise teacher says, "Honey, milk, butter, oil, wheat, corn, flour, bread, cakes, gold, silver, bronze, and iron are all made for the benefit of believers. For the unbelievers and sinners, however, all of these are changed and transformed into evil."[7]

Thus, though Creation should lead the unbeliever to God, it does the opposite and leads the unbeliever away from God. Creation, however, reveals that it is not Creation itself but people's evil will and

---

[1] Gal. 2:17-21. [2] 2 Cor. 6:14-18. [3] Gen. 1:1-10. [4] Gen. 1. [5] Isa. 66:1.
[6] Rom. 1:20. [7] Sir. 39:26-27.

unjust acquisition and use of Creation by which they have become corrupted and made worthless. It is written, "Those people who have no knowledge of God are vain and arrogant and have not wanted to acknowledge the Eternal One on the basis of the good things that are visible. By observing Creation, they have not perceived nor acknowledged the Creator."[1]

Creation, from which we all can learn, is the first book written by God's own hand and given to us. It is a book that all people without exception can read: poor or rich, powerful or humble, noble or common, educated or uneducated. All created things point to obedience to God, for they all obey him and bear their fruit in season according to his bidding. Therefore, those who break God's commandments and admonitions have no excuse. They have known there is a God, yet they have not served or thanked him as God but have run after useless things.

By doing this, their foolish hearts have become blind, so that thinking themselves wise, they have become fools and have changed the manifestation of God's incorruptible glory into something earthly or human.[2] Therefore, we fully believe that everything made and created by God for his honor,[3] but used by humans to dishonor and shame him, will be a witness against those selfsame people at the last judgment. God's judgment will surely come upon them, and they will receive what they deserve.

We Believe in God, Our Almighty Father

After looking around in every direction, we found everything to be weak and powerless, without counsel or help. Only in the one eternal and almighty God did we find strength, power, glory, and overflowing goodness. God can indeed help, protect, and advise us. So we have clung to God and entrusted ourselves to him in order to receive of his strength. In this way, in part at least, we become free of our weakness and live for his righteousness.[4] We now believe confidently that in him we have every good gift, even eternal life itself,[5] for we have him who is eternal life.[6] Because we find all this in him, we believe in him alone and give him our heart in complete confidence.

---

[1] Wisd. of Sol. 13:1-3.　[2] Rom. 1:20-32.　[3] Gen. 1:25-31.　[4] 1 Pet. 2:21-25.
[5] James 1:9-20.　[6] Rev. 21:1-6.

Leaving everything else, we cleave to him and depend on him with such absolute certainty that we can acknowledge that everything we have comes from God.

Since God's nature and character is eternal life, he has made us partakers and sharers of himself by sealing our faith with his Holy Spirit, which is the security of our inheritance. Through his grace, for which we praise him, we experience his works in us, and this makes us certain of all his promises.[1] We firmly believe that he who cannot speak lies will fulfill these promises as surely as if they were already fulfilled.[2] Therefore we say with Paul, "Who can separate us from the love of God? Shall misery, fear, persecution, famine, nakedness, danger, imprisonment, or the sword separate us?"[3] The Scripture tells us, "For your sake we are killed all the day long; we are regarded as sheep for the slaughter."[4] "Nevertheless, in all things we are more than conquerors through him who loved us. I am certain that neither death nor life nor anything created shall separate us from the love of God."[5]

It is not that we of ourselves are so strong. We confidently believe that the power and strength we have found in God has overcome death, the world, sin, and the devil. That power will keep us faithful and immovable to the end, to God's glory.

We Also Confess Jesus Christ, God's Only Begotten Son

We acknowledge that God is one.[6] Since God is truth, apart from him there is no one who, in and of himself, remains unchanged in clarity and lives forever.[7] Truth is his name in all eternity.[8] Therefore, we acknowledge also his Son, who is the Word that was with God in the beginning and formed the world with God.[9] It is through him that all things were created, continue to exist, and shall be completed.[10] Thus, we have the Father and the Son, not two, however, but one God, for the Son is not without the Father, nor the Father without the Son. They are not two but one, the Son in the Father, and the Father in the Son.[11]

---

[1] Eph. 1:13-23.　[2] Heb. 6:10-16.　[3] Rom. 8:35-39.　[4] Ps. 44:22.　[5] Rom. 8:35-39.
[6] Deut. 6:4.　[7] Deut. 4:29-39.　[8] 1 John 14:1-14.　[9] 1 John 1:1-2.　[10] 1 Col. 1:16-22.
[11] John 14:15-24.

Jesus

This Word proceeded from the Father so that the harm caused by Adam's transgression could be healed and the Fall restored.[1] Jesus took upon himself human nature and character and became flesh,[2] so that as death came through a human, so resurrection from the dead and salvation should also come through a human.[3]

Since salvation is in Jesus alone,[4] he brought his true name with him. This is the name given him by the angel before he was conceived in his mother's womb, namely, "Jesus," that is, Savior.[5] He is the Savior who has robbed death of its power, torn its bond and snare asunder, and set us, his people, free.[6]

Christ

Because death, which could not be overpowered by the force of any hero, giant, or human strength, held such unassailable sway over us, a power other than human strength was needed. Therefore the Word, that is God himself,[7] although he took upon himself human nature, did not relinquish the power through which all things were created in order that through him death might be overcome.

Although the Word put on a human body and human nature,[8] yet the divine nature remained completely in him. As Paul testifies, "In him dwells all the fullness of the Godhead bodily and in essence."[9] Hence, he is also named "Christ" or the anointed of God, as is written of him, "The Spirit of the Lord is upon me; therefore, he has anointed me and sent me to proclaim the gospel."[10] He alone has the power to overcome death, to give life to whom he will,[11] and to share of his fullness with whom and in whatever measure he desires.[12] Those who receive from him become through him Christians or "God's anointed ones." Failing this, they have the name in vain.

Only Begotten

Jesus is the only begotten Son of the Father. He has come as a light into the world to illuminate the darkness which imprisoned and covered us.[13] In Scripture we read, "The people who sat in darkness

[1] Gen. 3:6-11. [2] John 1:14. [3] 1 Cor. 15:20-28. [4] Acts 4:12. [5] Luke 2:21.
[6] Isa. 25:6-8; Hos. 13:14; 1 Cor. 15:51-58; Heb. 2:12-18. [7] John 1:1. [8] John 1:14.
[9] Col. 2:9. [10] Isa. 61:1-2; Luke 4:18-19. [11] John 5:21. [12] John 1:16. [13] John 1:1-13.

have seen a great light, and upon those who sat in the shadow of death, a great light has dawned."[1] Christ testifies of himself, "I am the light of the world; whoever believes in me shall not walk in darkness, but shall have the light of life."[2]

He is the only begotten one, because in agreement with the Father, he came from him, being as different from the Creation as the name he has inherited is superior to that of the angels.[3] He is the unparalleled power of God by means of which his holy angels and all his other creatures were formed. From the Father, therefore, he has the birthright of the firstborn so that every knee should bow and every tongue confess that he is Lord, to the glory of God the Father.[4]

Son

Since the Word proceeded from the Truth and was spoken by the Truth, it is called the Son; but the Truth which spoke is the Father, the one from whom the Word came. The Word came from God,[5] yet it remained in him,[6] for he is everywhere, filling the earth with his breadth, and with his height reaching up to heaven. A word spoken by a man becomes severed from him because he is weak, but the word that proceeds from God remains in him for ever and ever because of God's strength. It can in no way break away from him. Thus the Word and the Truth, or the Son and the Father, are one.[7]

Though there are two names, there is one power and one essence,[8] upholding all things.[9] Through him we all live and move and have our being, and without his strength no one can exist.[10] The Son is the brightness of the Father's glory and the image of his nature. He is the one who has now taken us captive into his obedience and leads us in his way. He instructs us by his nature, manner, and character, so that he may become increasingly more known to all people.[11]

We Confess That Christ Is Lord

We know that no one can call Jesus Lord except through the Holy Spirit.[12] We also know that all those who confess him in truth to be Lord must be children of his Spirit, that is, must have his Spirit.

---

[1] Isa. 9:2; Matt. 4:12-16. [2] John 8:12. [3] Heb. 1:1-4. [4] Phil. 2:5-11. [5] John 8:36-47. [6] John 14:1-11. [7] John 16:12-15. [8] John 1:9-14. [9] Col. 1:12-15. [10] Acts 17:24-28. [11] Heb. 1:3. [12] 1 Cor. 12:3.

Since we experience his grace, which has been given us by God through him, we also confess him to be Lord. He is truly Lord because all power is given him by the Father, not only in heaven, but also on earth and under the earth.[1] For this reason all unclean spirits fear him and tremble in his presence.[2] He has overcome them, bound them, and taken away their power. Christ has delivered us, their prey, who were held captive in death, and set us free.[3]

No one may truthfully ascribe such glory and honor to Christ unless he has experienced this victory in himself. This means that Christ has overcome the devil in him too, has torn away his snare (his sin), set him free, and reconciled him with God.[4] Whoever confesses Christ on a different basis does not speak the truth but either labors under a delusion, pretends to have faith, or speaks from hearsay. They do not confess Christ as Lord.[5]

In the text mentioned above, Paul said that no one may call Christ "Lord" except through the Holy Spirit. The person in whom Christ is to become victorious must wholeheartedly surrender himself to Christ. That person must stand firm and allow Christ's work to be done in him. However, when this does not happen, Christ does not work in a person, and such a person remains in sin forever.

Our Lord

We confess Christ to be our Lord, because he himself bought us with his own blood to be his possession.[6] By his death he became victor over the devil, liberated us from the bonds of the evil one, and reconciled us with God the Father.[7] He made us a royal priesthood for himself and for his Father.[8] He also made us his dwelling place[9] and has now begun his work in us. Thus the sin from which he redeemed us, even if it stirs within us, may not take control of us, continue to destroy us, or lead us to death.[10]

Christ is rightly our Lord since he controls us and uses our members according to his will. He reveals himself by living and doing everything in us. We have completely surrendered ourselves to him, patiently and humbly submitting to his work and to his will in us.

Paul says, "When you submit to someone in obedience, you

---

[1] Matt. 28:18. [2] Heb. 2:12-16. [3] Mark 5:1-13. [4] 1 John 2:1-6. [5] 1 Cor. 12:3.
[6] 1 Pet. 1:13-21. [7] 2 Cor. 5:18-21. [8] 1 Pet. 2:9-12. [9] 2 Cor. 6:14-16. [10] John 8:24-32.

become that person's servant." [1] Such obedience to our Lord is not to be achieved by human effort, but is the work of God. God be praised that we are able to find this work within ourselves.[2] So in the strength of the same Spirit, we call him "Lord" in truth, and that rightly so, since he himself says, "You call me Master and Lord, and you are right, for so I am."[3]

Conceived of the Holy Spirit

As the time of compassion drew near when God wanted to fulfill his promise and have mercy on the lost human race, he sent his Word, who was in and with God in the beginning.[4] By means of his messenger Gabriel, he sent the Word to a virgin whom he had previously chosen.[5] As soon as she believed, she was sealed with the Holy Spirit.[6] Then she was told, "Power from on high will overshadow you, and the Holy Spirit will come down from above into you. Therefore, the Holy One who is to be born of you shall be called the Son of God."[7]

The Holy Spirit worked together with her faith so that the Word she believed took human nature from her and became a living fruit.[8] In this way what God had undertaken to do was fulfilled, and it was revealed how, and through what means, God wanted to send his Christ into the world.[9]

Sin was brought into the world by Adam[10] and was passed on to all his descendants.[11] They had been commanded by God to multiply by mingling the seed of man and woman.[12] Hence, it was necessary that he who was to do away with this sin[13] should have a different origin from the human one. We were conceived in the weakness of the flesh, but Christ was conceived in the power of God.

Through the union of the Holy Spirit with Mary's faith, the Word was conceived and became human.[14] He did not bring his human nature with him from heaven but received it from Mary. Therefore, Paul distinguishes the two natures of Christ in this way: "He was a descendant of David according to the flesh, and was powerfully declared to be the Son of God according to the Spirit, the one who sanctifies, from the time he was raised from the dead."[15]

---

[1] Rom. 6:16-18.   [2] 2 Cor. 3:3-6.   [3] John 13:13.   [4] John 1:1-2.   [5] Luke 1:26-28.
[6] Eph. 1:13.   [7] Luke 1:28-35.   [8] Heb. 2:11-16.   [9] Gen. 3:15; 12:1-3; Isa. 7:14-16.
[10] Gen. 3:6.   [11] Rom. 5:12-14.   [12] Gen. 1:28.   [13] 1 John 3:1-6.   [14] Luke 1:34-38.
[15] Rom. 1:1-4.

Since Jesus Christ entered the world in a different way from other children of Adam, he is likewise a different human being, different in that he led and completed his life in the power of God without any inclination to sin.[1] His power is so much greater than ours and far surpasses even that of the angels, and the fullness of the Godhead dwells in him.[2] Therefore, God laid upon him our weakness.[3] It is written, "For God made him who knew no sin to be sin for us, that we, being freed from sin, might live for righteousness." For this reason he was sent into the world.[4]

Born of the Virgin Mary

Thus we confess that Mary conceived and bore her child without loss of her virginity,[5] and that during and after his birth, she was as much a virgin as she was before, her virginity completely intact. She bore the Savior of the world,[6] a comfort and hope to all believers, and a glory to God the Father.[7] Christ was not someone invented and imaginary but a genuine and real person,[8] who was tempted and tested in all things, yet without sin.[9]

Suffered Under the Power of Pilate, Crucified, Died, and Buried

We believe that after Christ had finished the task for which the Father sent him, that is, to proclaim the Father's name[10] and to teach people repentance and faith in God,[11] he was given into the hands of sinners, according to the plan of God. After greatly humiliating and torturing him, these sinners put him to the most disgraceful death, namely, crucifixion.[12]

With Peter we confess that he was put to death in the flesh,[13] that is, insofar as he was descended from David[14] and born of Mary. He was made alive in the Spirit.[15] We believe that it was not the divine but the human nature of Christ that died. The divine nature, inasmuch as it had come from heaven and had withdrawn from him, forsook the hu-

---

[1] 2 Cor. 5:21; Heb. 4:14-15.　[2] Col. 2:9.　[3] Isa. 53:1-5; 1 Pet. 2:21-24.　[4] 2 Cor. 5:18-21; 1 Pet. 2:24.　[5] Isa. 7:14.　[6] Matt. 1:18-25; Luke 2:8-11; John 4:42.　[7] Luke 3:2-6.　[8] Phil. 2:5-8; Heb. 2:17-18.　[9] Heb. 4:15.　[10] John 17:20-26.　[11] Matt. 4:12-17.　[12] Matt. 27:27-56; Mark 15:16-41; Luke 23:24-49; John 19:1-37.　[13] 1 Pet. 3:18.　[14] Rom. 1:3.　[15] Luke 2:4-7.

man nature so that the Scripture might be fulfilled, "For a little while you made him suffer the absence of God and crowned him again with glory and honor."[1] The apostle says the same: "In Jesus we see one who, for a little while, suffered the absence of angels or of God, and is now crowned with glory and honor. Through the grace of God he tasted death for us all."[2]

Since our transgressions and sins so moved the Father that he laid them upon his Son and gave him up to die[3] for them, we confess that our sins have crucified him. Therefore, all who still continue in sin do not cease to crucify and mock the Son of God.[4] He came to take away our sin and destroy the work of the devil.[5] Those who do not allow their sin to be taken from them, but remain in it forever, mock his coming into the world and consider the blood of God's revelation to be unholy. To them, Christ's suffering and death are no comfort but a cause of eternal judgment.[6]

Again, he was taken down from the cross and laid in a grave[7] that his own word might be fulfilled: "Unless a grain of wheat falls into the ground and dies, it remains alone; but if it falls into the ground and dies, it brings forth much fruit."[8] He was laid in the earth and rose again, so that all who have fallen asleep and lie in the earth may through him rise and come forth. As the Scriptures tell us, "The hour is coming in which all who are in the grave shall hear his voice and shall come forth-those who have done good to the resurrection of life, and those who have done evil to the resurrection of judgment and condemnation."[9]

Descended into Hell

In order that he might fulfill all things,[10] we confess that Christ went down to the lowest parts of the earth, that is, to the place of captivity where those are kept who formerly did not believe the word spoken to them. Christ proclaimed to those spirits that the word of salvation had now been sent.[11] God had previously planned this word of salvation[12] and had promised it to humanity,[13] so that all who believed it in their hearts should be set free. Now, in accordance with

---

[1] Ps. 8:5. [2] Heb. 2:5-10. [3] Isa. 53:4-5. [4] Heb. 6:4-6. [5] 1 John 3:5-8. [6] Heb. 10:26-31. [7] Matt. 27:57-61; Mark 15:42-47; Luke 23:50-55; John 19:38-42. [8] John 12:24-26. [9] John 5:28-29. [10] Eph. 4:8-10. [11] 1 Pet. 3:18-21. [12] 1 Pet. 1:3-5. [13] Gen. 3:14-15; 12:1-4.

the Father's promise, Christ through his death had destroyed the power of death, hell, and the devil, which for so long had betrayed humans and led them astray.[1]

On the Third Day Arose from the Dead

We confess that after Christ had destroyed death's power through his own death,[2] he rose from the dead through the power of the Father. He became the firstborn of those who are to inherit salvation,[3] for death could not hold him. As David says of him, "I have always set the Lord before me; because he is at my right hand, I shall not be moved. Therefore, my heart is glad and my tongue rejoices, for my flesh also shall rest in the hope that you will not leave my soul in hell, neither will you suffer your Holy One to see corruption."[4]

Thus we confess that Christ is risen from the dead, and that he died and rose again in order to be Lord of the dead and of the living.[5] After he had overcome the devil and death and had risen again,[6] he was given power, might, and royal status by the Father.[7] As he himself says, "All power is given me in heaven and on earth."[8]

After his resurrection he was seen for several days by his disciples, those already chosen to be his witnesses,[9] and he ate and drank with them.[10] He also gave them the command to gather his bride, the church, to proclaim repentance and the forgiveness of sins to all nations,[11] and in his name to bring about the obedience that comes through faith.[12]

Ascended into Heaven,
Seated at the Right Hand of His Almighty Father

We confess also that Christ ascended above all heavens[13] and is seated at the right hand of the Father's might, power, strength, and glory.[14] This glory he, the Word, had from the Father before the foundation of the world was laid,[15] but set it aside when he came into the world as a poor and lowly servant. Paul tells us this with these words:

---

[1] Heb. 2:14-15.　[2] Isa. 25:6-9; Hos. 13:14; 1 Cor. 15:53-58.　[3] Acts 2:33-39.
[4] Ps. 16:8-11.　[5] Rom. 14:9.　[6] Heb. 2:14-15.　[7] Dan. 7:27-28.　[8] Matt. 28:18.　[9] Luke 24:13-35; John 20:1-17; 21:1-7; 1 Cor. 15:3-9.　[10] Acts 10:37-43.　[11] Matt. 28:18-20; Mark 16:15-16.　[12] Rom. 1:1-5; 16:17-20.　[13] Eph. 4:7-8.　[14] Acts 7:55-56.　[15] John 17:1-5.

"He did not think it robbery to be God's equal, but leaving behind his glory, he took upon himself the form of a servant, and even in appearance became like any other person."[1]

When Christ had finished his task, he said, "Glorify me again, O Father, with the glory I had with you before the world was made."[2] That is to say, the Word had stripped himself of radiant glory, had become human, and had taken human nature upon himself. The weakness of this human nature has died, and Christ now lives and reigns in the strength of God from eternity to eternity.[3]

Christ has received power and birthright from the Father; for as the Father has eternal life in himself, so also the Son has the same in himself. Moreover, he desires to give it to whomever he will, that is, to all those who believe in his name. As it is written,[4] "This is the will of the Father, who has sent me that everyone who sees the Son and believes in him, should not be lost but have eternal life."[5]

Christ now sits at the right hand of the power of God and knows our weakness, and he, although sinless, was tempted in every way. Thus he is our advocate, mediator, and reconciler, representing us before the Father.[6] John testifies, "We have an advocate before God, Jesus Christ, who is just; he is the atonement for our sins, and not for ours only, but for the whole world."[7] Truly we are comforted, assured of hope, and protected in all our misery and tribulation, because we know that not only in this world do we hope in Christ.[8]

From There He Will Come to Judge the Living and the Dead

We confess that the Father has entrusted judgment to the Son.[9] His coming will be terrifying; with flaming fire he will take vengeance on everything ungodly and on all human wrongdoing.[10] He will reward with honor and praise and with an imperishable nature those who seek eternal life, by patiently continuing to do good.[11] He whom the Father has given the power to judge says,[12] "I judge no one,[13] but the word that I have spoken will judge you on the day of reckoning."[14] This word will justify no one except the one who

---

[1] Phil. 2:5-8. [2] John 17:1-5. [3] John 1:14; Luke 2:1-12; Heb. 2:14-18. [4] John 5:21-29. [5] John 6:38-40. [6] Heb. 5:1-2; 1 Tim. 2:3-5. [7] 1 John 2:1-2. [8] 1 Cor. 15:12-20. [9] John 5:22. [10] 2 Thess. 1:6-10. [11] Rom. 2:1-8. [12] John 5:22. [13] John 8:15. [14] John 12:46-48.

has surrendered to it wholeheartedly, and who in this life has allowed the word to be a judge and guide. Whoever has not heeded the word will, however, be condemned.[1]

That is why we say that when the last trumpet sounds and the Son of Man in his glory comes from heaven with his holy angels,[2] and those who are in their graves rise[3] to meet him, the sentence of each one is already passed.[4] Christ says, "Whoever does not believe is condemned already."[5] A place for the unbeliever is also already prepared, since he has presented to us the story of the last judgment. When the Son of Man comes in all his glory with his holy angels, he will sit upon his glorious throne, with all nations gathered before him. He will separate them as a shepherd separates the sheep from the goats, the sheep on his right hand, but the goats on his left.[6]

So we see clearly enough that each one is already judged and sentenced, the devout to life and the godless to death.[7] It remains only for Christ to pronounce this sentence and to show each his place, as these words indicate: "Come, you blessed of my Father, inherit the kingdom prepared for you from the beginning. I was hungry, thirsty, naked, a stranger, sick, and in prison, and you came to my aid." But to the others he says, "Depart from me, you cursed, into eternal fire, prepared from the beginning for the devil and his angels; for I was in need of your help, and you did not minister to me."[8]

As Daniel says, "The court sat, and the books were opened."[9] After him, John testifies that the dead were judged from what was written in these books and sentenced according to their works.[10] So we truly believe that all our words and deeds, good or evil, are recorded before God and his Son as though written in a book. When the time comes, God will open his secret book and show to each all their deeds.[11] Paul says, "The day of the Lord will clarify all things, and then each will know why he is to be blessed or condemned."[12]

We Also Believe in Jesus Christ, His Only Son, Our Lord

We believe in Jesus Christ, in whom our whole salvation and redemption rests. He has stilled the Father's wrath, as we see from

---

[1] Mark 16:15-16. [2] 1 Thess. 4:16-17. [3] John 5:28-29. [4] 2 Thess. 1:6-7. [5] John 3:18. [6] Matt. 25:31-40. [7] John 5:28-29. [8] Matt. 25:34-46. [9] Dan. 7:26. [10] Rev. 20:11-15. [11] Matt. 10:19-22; Mark 4:22-23; Luke 8:17-18; 12:2-3. [12] 1 Cor. 3:12-15.

Paul's words, "In Christ, God was reconciling the world[1] with himself and not holding their sins against them."[2] Thus, through him we are reconciled to God. There is no other name through which we can attain salvation than the name of Jesus Christ of Nazareth.[3]

In the first place, we believe that we have salvation in Christ. We believe that Christ has redeemed us from the might and snare of the devil, in which we were held captive, for he has robbed the devil of his power and overwhelmed him.[4] The devil's snares are the sins in which we were imprisoned. By sinning we were serving the devil until Christ came to dwell in us by faith. Then through Christ's strength and work in us,[5] our sin was weakened, quenched, put to death, and taken away from us,[6] so that we could live for righteousness.[7] Christ is the one who brings about this righteousness in us, because without him we can do nothing.[8]

The Lord is truly our Redeemer. He works in us and has taken away those sins from which we could not otherwise ever be freed.[9] We served them long, but now, even if they do still stir in our members, they cannot rule over us any longer.[10] Whoever continues in sin and is held captive by it, while saying Christ has redeemed him, is like a prisoner who lies bound hand and foot, yet claims to be free. Who would not call that foolish? Whoever professes to be free and is in fact bound, wants still less to become free.[11] So too, he who says that Christ has redeemed him from sin[12] and yet continues to live sinfully, shows little wish to become free. Rather, as already indicated, through coming to us, he has freed us from sin in order that we may become servants of righteousness.

Many people, especially Lutherans, say that Christ is their righteousness and goodness even though they still lead abominable and impure lives. To speak like this is to give lip service to God, but to be far removed from him in their hearts.[13] It leads people away from Christ rather than toward him, because in this manner people are prevented from striving for true righteousness, which is only in Christ. They continue in their sins for ever and ever.

We confess that Christ is our righteousness and goodness, because he himself demonstrates and accomplishes in us the justifi-

---

[1] 1 John 1:1-2.   [2] 2 Cor. 5:19.   [3] Acts 4:12.   [4] Heb. 2:12-15.   [5] Eph. 3:14-17.
[6] 1 John 3:5-6.   [7] 1 Pet. 2:21-25.   [8] John 15:1-5.   [9] 1 Cor. 15:51-57.   [10] Rom. 6:8-18.
[11] John 8:31-34.   [12] Rom. 8:1-4.   [13] Isa. 29:13-14; Matt. 15:1-9.

cation and goodness that makes us beloved of God and pleasing to him.[1] We have no goodness apart from what he alone has worked in us,[2] although many denounce us, saying that we seek to be justified through our own deeds. We deny this, for we know that all our deeds, as far as they are our deeds, are nothing but sin and unrighteousness.[3] Insofar as the deeds are done in us by Christ,[4] they are true, just, good, pleasing to God, and loved by God. We are not ashamed to proclaim and declare this, because the angel said to Tobias, "It is good to keep silent about the king's secret, but it is honorable to reveal and to proclaim God's works."[5]

Through his actual strength and activity, Christ leads us to be partakers of his nature, character, and being.[6] This is a goodness that saves and leads to God.[7] Christ is our righteousness and goodness. He is our life; we ourselves do not live, but Christ lives in us.[8] Christ is our resurrection, our salvation, and our all in all. We also believe that Christ's incarnation[9] means that we can be transformed. His suffering and death are salvation and life for us. In Christ we truly have everything.[10]

We Confess the Holy Spirit

The power, essence, and nature of the Godhead are illustrated in Creation and recognized by us as the work of God's hand.[11] For example, when a word is spoken, a breath is exhaled. From both the speaker and the spoken word, a living breath or wind blows, and the sound of a voice goes forth. In the same way the Holy Spirit comes from the Father and the Son, or from the Truth and the Word. Just as the Son or the Word proceeds from the Father[12] and yet remains in him, so the Holy Spirit proceeds from both and remains in both for ever and ever.

Thus we acknowledge the Holy Spirit who, with the Father and the Son, is God. The names are three, but there is only one God,[13] bounteous to all who call to him in trust. Just as fire, heat, and light are three names and yet one substance, one nature, one essence; so are God the Father, Son, and Holy Spirit three names and yet only one

---

[1] John 15:1-10.   [2] Phil. 3:8-14.   [3] Rom. 14:23.   [4] John 16:13.   [5] Tob. 12:6-7.
[6] 2 Pet. 1:3-8.   [7] John 15:1-11.   [8] Gal. 2:16-20.   [9] Luke 2:1-12; *incarnation* means Christ fully human, in the flesh.   [10] Phil. 3:8-11.   [11] Rom. 1:20.   [12] John 8:25-38.
[13] Exod. 20:2-5; Deut. 5:6-10; 6:4-5.

being. As fire, heat, and light do not separate from each other (for where one is, there are all three; and where one is lacking, none is present), so it is with the Father, Son, and Holy Spirit. Where one of them is, there are all three;[1] but whoever lacks one, lacks all three.[2] One cannot take heat and light away from fire and still have fire. Much less can one take the Son and the Holy Spirit from the Father.

Just as breath lends voice to the word and gives it shape and sound, so also breath, wind, and Spirit of God make the Word alive and active within us[3] and lead us into all truth.[4] This is the power of God, doing, working, and perfecting everything; establishing it all; uniting, comforting, teaching, and instructing. All of the Spirit's work in us assures us that we are God's children.[5]

We Believe in the Holy Spirit

We believe that in the Holy Spirit we have all comfort, delight, and fruitfulness, and that he confirms, strengthens, and accomplishes all things. He also teaches and guides us,[6] assures us that we are children of God,[7] and makes us one with him, so that through his work, we are made part of the divine nature and character.[8] We experience his work within us in truth and power in the renewing of our hearts. God be praised!

In God we have absolute certainty that he has drawn our heart to him and made it his dwelling place. He has cut every sin, and lust to sin, out of our heart[9] and removed everything detestable. He has caused our hearts to cling to his Word, to seek, love, and listen to it diligently, and not only listen to it, but hold onto it and follow it faithfully.[10] We believe that all this is the work of the Holy Spirit in us.[11]

The Spirit Gathers One Holy, Christian Church

We confess that God through Christ has chosen and accepted a people for himself, a people without stain, wrinkle, or fault, but pure and holy[12] as he himself is holy.[13] Such a community or church is gathered together by the Holy Spirit, who from then on orders and con-

---

[1] John 14:15-24.   [2] 1 John 2:22-24.   [3] Heb. 4:12.   [4] John 16:13.   [5] Rom. 8:10-14.
[6] John 16:13-15.   [7] Rom. 8:10-16.   [8] 2 Pet. 1:3-4.   [9] Col. 2:8-12.   [10] 1 John 5:1-4.
[11] 1 Cor. 12:1-11.   [12] Eph. 5:26-27.   [13] 1 Pet. 1:13-16.

trols everything in the church.[1] The Spirit leads all the church members to be of one mind and to have one aim,[2] that they might think only like Jesus Christ, and be eager to do his will.[3] They are to cling to Christ as a bride to her bridegroom, and indeed strive to be one body with him,[4] one plant, one tree, yielding one kind of fruit.[5] Paul writes in his letter to the Romans, "Those who are led by the Spirit of God are children of God. . . . The same Spirit assures us that we are children of God."[6]

The church is an assembly of the children of God, as it is written, "You are the temple of the living God."[7] In God's Word we read, "I will dwell in them and walk in them; I will be their God, and they shall be my people."[8] Again it is written, "Therefore come out from among them and be separate, says the Lord, and touch no unclean thing. I will receive you and will be your Father, and you shall be my sons and daughters."[9] The children of God, however, become his children through the unifying Spirit.[10] Thus it is evident that the church is gathered through the Holy Spirit; the church has its being and continues to exist through the Spirit. There are no churches apart from those which the Holy Spirit gathers and builds.

A congregation made up of sinners-prostitutes, adulterers, rioters, and drunkards; covetous, selfish, and vain people; liars in word and deed-is no church of God. Such people do not belong to him.[11] As Paul says, "Anyone who does not have the Spirit of Christ, does not belong to him."[12] Not only is their assembly no church of Christ, but none of them can be in the church unless they repent of their sins. David says, "The sinner shall not stand in the congregation of the righteous."[13] Later, John says, "By no means shall anyone enter the church who is untruthful or unclean, but only those who are written in the Lamb's book of life.[14] Outside are dogs, sorcerers, the sexually immoral, idolaters, murderers, and whoever loves and practices a lie."[15]

What the Church Is

The church of Christ is a foundation and a basis of truth. It is a lamp, a star of light, and a lantern of righteousness,[16] in which the light

---

[1] Luke 24:45-49; Acts 1:1-8; 2:1-13. [2] Acts 2:14-21; 4:31-37. [3] 1 Cor. 2:10-16; Phil. 2:1-8. [4] Rom. 12:1-5. [5] 1 Cor. 12:1-11. [6] Rom. 8:11-17. [7] 2 Cor. 6:16-18. [8] Lev. 26:9-13. [9] Isa. 52:4-12. [10] Rom. 8:11-17. [11] Rev. 21:7-8. [12] Rom. 8:9. [13] Ps. 1:5-6. [14] Rev. 21:27. [15] Rev. 22:10-17. [16] 1 Tim. 3:14-16.

of grace is held up to the whole world,[1] so that its darkness, unbelief, and blindness may be illuminated, and people may learn to see and know the way of life.[2] So we see that the church of Christ is, in the first place, like a lantern completely filled with light, the light of Christ, which is then shed abroad to others.[3]

As the lantern of Christ has been made bright and clear by the light of the knowledge of God, so its radiance shines out into the distance to give light to those who still walk in darkness.[4] Christ himself commanded this when he said, "Let your light shine before others, that they may see your good works, and praise God, the Father in heaven."[5] Now this can take place only through the strength of the Spirit of Christ working within us.

Just as a light, in accordance with its own nature, sends out a beam to give light to people, so also the divine light, wherever it has been lit in a person, sends forth its divine ray according to its nature.[6] The nature of this light, however, is genuine divine righteousness, holiness, and truth. It sheds its light abroad more brightly and clearly than the sun to enlighten all people.[7]

The church of Christ is a pillar and foundation of truth and continues to be that.[8] Truth itself is expressed, confirmed, and put into action in the church by the Holy Spirit. Thus, whoever endures and submits to the working of the Spirit of Christ, is a member of this church.[9] Whoever does not want this and allows sin to rule over them, does not belong to the church.[10]

How One Is Led to the Church

The church of Christ is a foundation and basis of truth,[11] and the truth is built upon or entrusted to the church. No one may come to the church, much less become a member,[12] unless that person lives and walks in the truth, that is, in God, and has the truth in oneself.[13] That person must allow only the truth to rule, guide, and carry on its work within him so that it streams out from him like a light.

As we have said, however, God gathers his church through his Spirit. The church cannot be gathered in any other way. Therefore, those who are to call others to the church must have the same Spirit.

---

[1] Matt. 5:13-20. [2] Eph. 3:14-21. [3] Matt. 5:14-15. [4] Mark 4:14-25; Luke 8:9-21; 22:31-32. [5] Matt. 5:14-16. [6] Luke 11:33-36. [7] Eph. 3:14-21. [8] 1 Tim. 3:14-16.
[9] Rom. 8:6-14. [10] Ps. 1:4-6; 1 John 3:1-6. [11] 1 Tim. 3:14-16. [12] Ps. 1:4-6. [13] John 15:1-10.

That is why Christ, when he wished to send his disciples to gather his church, commanded them not to depart from Jerusalem until they were endued with power from on high, power to do this work.[1] He told them in what way and by what means they should gather the church, namely, with Word and sign.[2]

The covenant of God's grace is a covenant of the knowledge of God. Scripture tells us, "All shall know me, from the least to the greatest."[3] It is God's will to call people to this covenant, and to reveal and make himself known to them through his words. For as soon as we believe the Word with all our heart, it is God's will to seal it within us with his Spirit.[4] His Spirit will lead us into all truth and reveal everything to us.[5]

However, since Christ will not send out his disciples before they have received the grace of the Holy Spirit,[6] it is quite clear that he will not allow his Word or his signs to be treated lightly or carelessly. They should be used in the Spirit of Christ, not according to our human way of thinking.[7] When the Word is spoken in the Spirit of Christ,[8] however, and a person is moved by it and believes, the sign should be offered to that person in the same Spirit, but not without the Spirit.[9] In this way it is the Spirit of Christ and not a human being who leads people into the church. What the Spirit now builds will endure through the Spirit, but what a person does as a human, that will not last. Such a person's work is in vain. As David says, "Unless the Lord builds the house, they who build it labor in vain."[10]

Community of Saints

Every good and perfect gift comes from above, from the Father of lights, with whom there is no change, nor any variation from light to darkness.[11] He shares everything with us who believe in him. As Paul says, "If God is for us, who can be against us?"[12] He who did not spare his only begotten Son, but gave him up to death for us all, why should he not give us everything else? The Father wants to pour out all good things upon those who believe his Word and walk justly and faithfully before him. His promise to Abraham shows us this: "I am God

---

[1] Luke 24:36-53; Acts 1:1-8.   [2] Matt. 28:18-20; Mark 16:14-16.   [3] Jer. 31:31-34; Heb. 8:10-13.   [4] Eph. 1:9-14.   [5] John 16:12-15.   [6] Luke 24:44-51; Acts 1:20-26.
[7] Matt. 28:18-20.   [8] Matt. 10:19-20.   [9] Mark 13:9-11; 16:15-16; Luke 12:8-12.
[10] Ps. 127:1-2.   [11] James 1:17.   [12] Rom. 8:31-32.

Shaddai" (that is, one with authority and might, full to overflowing with all good things). "Walk before me and be steadfast, devout, and faithful to me, and I will make my covenant between me and you, and will multiply you exceedingly. This shall be an eternal covenant, that I will be your God and the God of your seed forever."[1]

In other words, "If you abide in me and steadfastly do my will, you shall have all good things in me; yes, I shall give you everything that is useful and lovely."[2] Since the Father is the fullness of all good things, he has given that fullness to the Son. Thus it is written, "For it pleased the Father that in him all the fullness should dwell."[3] And again, "The Word became flesh and dwelt among us, and we beheld his glory, such glory as befits the Father's only Son, full of grace and truth."[4] Further, it is stated, "In him dwells the whole fullness of the Godhead in reality, and you are full of the same."[5]

We, however, share in this grace of Christ through faith in the truth. Paul says, "And Christ dwells in your hearts through faith."[6] Such faith, however, comes from hearing the gospel proclaimed.[7] Through listening and paying careful attention to the gospel, we share in the community of Christ. We may recognize this from the words of John when he says, "That which we have seen and heard we declare to you, so that you may also have fellowship with us. Our fellowship is with God the Father and with his Son, Jesus Christ, our Lord."[8] He has given us everything he has heard and received from his Father.[9]

Community means that those who have this fellowship hold all things in common, no one having anything for oneself, but each sharing all things with the others.[10] Just so, the Father has nothing for himself, but everything he has, he has with the Son.[11] Likewise, the Son has nothing for himself, but all he has, he has with the Father and with all who have fellowship with him.[12]

All who have fellowship with him, and with each other, have likewise nothing for themselves, but they have all things with their Master and with those who have fellowship with them.[13] Hence, they are one with the Son as the Son is one with the Father.[14]

This is called the holy community because they have fellowship

---

[1] Gen. 17:1-6.   [2] Gen. 17:1-9.   [3] Col. 1:19; Eph. 3:19.   [4] John 1:14.   [5] Col. 2:9-10; Eph. 3:19.   [6] Eph. 3:17.   [7] Rom. 10:17.   [8] 1 John 1:1-3.   [9] John 15:11-15.   [10] Acts 2:42-46; 4:32-37.   [11] John 17:7.   [12] Rom. 8:10-11; 1 John 1:2-3.   [13] Eph. 4:1-16.   [14] John 16:13-15.

in holy things, yes, in such things whereby they become sanctified. That is, they have fellowship in the Father and the Son, who himself makes them holy in all he has given them.[1] Thus everything serves to help and improve one's neighbor, and to bring praise and glory to God the Father.[2]

Forgiveness of Sins

Just as Christ received from the Father the power to forgive the sins of whomever he wills, so he has committed this power to his bride, the church.[3] His words show this when he says, "Receive the Holy Spirit. Whose sins you remit here on earth, they are remitted in heaven, and whose sins you retain here on earth, they are retained in heaven."[4] With these words Christ indicates that he gives his church authority to forgive sins here on earth.

However, the power and key of forgiving is granted to the church and not simply to individual persons. This we see by Christ's words when he says, "If your brother sins against you, go and tell him his fault between you and him alone. If he hears you, you have won his soul. But if he will not listen to you, take with you one or two more, that every word may be confirmed by the evidence of two or three witnesses. If he does not listen to them, tell it to the church. If he refuses even to hear the church, then treat him as you would a tax collector and sinner."[5]

The individual is indeed permitted to forgive anything done against him personally if his brother improves his ways. But regarding the full power of the keys of Christ to exclude and to accept, Christ has not given that power to individual persons, but to the whole church.[6] That is why we say that anyone the church excludes is excluded, but anyone the church forgives is forgiven, here and in eternity. Apart from the church, there is no forgiveness, no goodness, no healing, no salvation, and no true comfort or hope.[7] Within the church and not outside the church, dwells God the Father, Son, and Holy Spirit, who vindicates everything and makes it holy.[8]

---

[1] 1 John 1:5-7.   [2] 1 Cor. 14:26-33.   [3] Matt. 9:1-8; Mark 2:1-12; Luke 5:17-26.
[4] John 20:19-23.   [5] Matt. 18:15-17.   [6] Matt. 18:15-22; Luke 17:3-4.   [7] Matt. 18:18.
[8] John 14:20-24; 2 Cor. 5:18-20.

Resurrection of the Body[1]

We testify that at the time of the last trumpet, the Lord himself shall descend from heaven with a mighty shout, with the voice of the archangel.[2] Then they who are in their graves shall rise and come forth; they who are godly will rise to resurrection of life, but sinners will rise to a resurrection of judgment.[3] With an incorruptible body[4] they shall appear before the terrible judge.[5] He will appoint to each his place and reward, according to the good or evil he has done during his lifetime.[6]

Eternal Life

"This," says Christ, "is eternal life, that they might know you, the only true God, and Jesus Christ, whom you have sent."[7] Thus in those who have true faith, eternal life begins here and now, and continues into the future, when it will be properly and fully revealed, as Paul testifies. He says, "Now we recognize truth as a dim word reflected in a mirror, but then we shall see it plainly, face-to-face; now we know in part, but then we shall know just as we are known."[8]

John agrees with this when he says, "Now we are children of God, but it has not yet been disclosed what we shall be. We do know that when he appears we shall be like him, for we shall see him as he is."[9] Now, it is really true that we shall see God face to face,[10] and know him who is eternal life and makes us live eternally; therefore, we who see and know him as he really is, shall rejoice with him forever.[11]

What is perishable cannot inherit the imperishable. Instead, the perishable must put on the imperishable form and the mortal put on [12] immortality. Therefore, whoever would rise again to immortal life must here be born anew to eternal life through faith in the truth.[13] If in this life we endure this working of God in us, then the Lord will transfigure our insignificant body. It will become like his glorified body,[14] and we shall see his resplendent brightness.[15] We shall be where he is, and all our joy shall be in him alone.[16] Suffering, sorrow, and pain will touch us no more.[17]

---

[1] The German term *Fleisch* is translated as "body" because it expresses most clearly the meaning of the original. The English term *flesh* is narrower in meaning and less adequate. [2] 1 Thess. 4:16. [3] John 5:25-29. [4] 1 Cor. 15. [5] Isa. 2:10-17. [6] Matt. 25:31-46. [7] John 17:3. [8] 1 Cor. 13:12. [9] 1 John 3:2. [10] 1 Cor. 13:12. [11] John 17:2-3. [12] 1 Cor. 15:50-54. [13] 1 Pet. 1:23. [14] Phil. 3:20-21. [15] 1 John 3:2. [16] John 12:20-23; 14:2-6; 17:24; 1 Thess. 4:17. [17] John 16:20-22; Isa. 25:6-9; Rev. 7:9-17; 21:1-6.

Having told what we confess to be the essentials of true Christian faith, we can say freely with an upright and confident heart, "To God alone be the glory!" We have now confessed in words what we believe with our hearts, so that through faith we may become righteous and blessed.[1]

---

[1] Rom. 10:10-17.

Faith, Creation, and the Fall into Sin

What Faith Is

Faith is not an empty illusion, as it would seem from those people who only speak of faith and know nothing more about it. They think that Christianity consists of words only. Therefore, they look upon all who confess Christ with their lips as Christians, no matter how they live.

True and well-founded faith, however, is not a human attribute. It is a gift from God,[1] given only to those who fear God.[2] That is why Paul says that not every person has faith.[3] Such faith is the assurance of what is not seen. It grasps the invisible, one and only, mighty God, making us close to God and at one with him,[4] and able to partake of his nature and character.[5] It dispels all wavering and doubt,[6] and makes our heart hold steadfastly and firmly to God through all distress.[7]

God, therefore, gives us assurance and confirms all his promises as definitely as, for example, a man holding an object in his hand is certain that he has it. In the same way, faith grasps the promise of God, which is invisible, and clings to it as though it were visible.[8]

Therefore, faith is truly a power of God, renewing people and making them resemble God in his nature, living in God's righteousness, ardent in God's love, and observing his commandments.

So that no one is made uneasy, we want to say why we ascribe such power to faith. Faith is God's gift and is given to people so that they might seek and find God. When God has been found, he stirs up and brings about all things in the believers themselves through faith. Nothing takes place in them except what God does in proportion to

---

[1] Eph. 2:1-10.   [2] Wisd. of Sol. 3:14-15.   [3] 2 Thess. 3:1-2.   [4] Heb. 11:1-3.
[5] 2 Pet. 1:3-4.   [6] James 1:5-7.   [7] Dan. 3:16-25; 6:19-28.   [8] Gen. 12:1-5; 13:14-18; Acts 7:1-8; Heb. 11:1-16.

their faith.[1] Paul tells us this with the words, "Not I, but the grace of God,"[2] and again, "I do not live now, but Christ lives in me."[3]

In this manner victorious strength is given to faith, as John says, "And our faith is the victory that overcomes the world."[4] This is indeed what God does in us through faith. Everything is effected by faith, and in this way the person is made pleasing to God and loved by him.

Source of Faith

According to the words of Paul, faith comes from diligently listening to the preaching of God's Word, which comes from the mouth of God and is spoken by those whom God sends.[5] Here, however, we do not speak of the literal but of the living Word that pierces soul and spirit,[6] the Word put by God in the mouth of his messengers.[7] The same Word prepares for salvation,[8] that is, it teaches us to know God.[9] From this knowledge of God, faith springs up, grows, and increases, and with faith comes knowledge,[10] so that the one who has faith lives and walks in God, and God in that person.[11] These intertwine and grow together, leading people to God and planting them in God.[12]

The more diligently we hear and receive the Word, the more knowledge grows. The more knowledge grows, or the more we understand God, the more faith and trust in God grow, and the more God reveals himself to us and allows us to know him.[13] Where such faith is absent, there is instead darkness and empty delusion, and people deceive and fool themselves.

We have now confessed our faith. We want to take this teaching, and now give a faithful account of what we believe, according to the measure of God's grace.

Doctrine

"You shall not add to the word I command you," says the Lord, "nor shall you take anything from it.[14] I will be with you when you speak and will teach you what you shall say."[15] It is clear from this that the teaching about Christ must be guided only by the Holy Spirit and

---

[1] Eph. 2:1-8. [2] 1 Cor. 15:10. [3] Gal. 2:20. [4] 1 John 5:4. [5] Rom. 10:17. [6] Heb. 4:12. [7] Jer. 1:4-10. [8] 2 Tim. 3:14-17. [9] John 17:6-8. [10] Rom. 10:17-18. [11] 1 John 4:16-21. [12] Eph. 3:17-19. [13] Eph. 3:14-21. [14] Deut. 4:2. [15] Exod. 4:10-12.

must not be mixed with human understanding and human wishes.[1] Peter says that prophecy does not arise from the will of humans but from holy people of God speaking at the urging of the Holy Spirit.[2] As it was in the days of old, so it should be today, that people do not speak from their human understanding, but from what the Holy Spirit says to them and teaches through them. Christ says, "It will not be you who are speaking, but my Father's Spirit speaking through you."[3] It must be like this today if the Word is to bear fruit.

That is why Christ did not want his disciples to go out until they had received the Holy Spirit and had been endued with strength from on high.[4] There are some who do not wait for this gift from God but go ahead by themselves without this grace, for the sake of worldly honor or for possessions. These are the ones of whom the Lord says, "I have not sent these prophets, yet they ran; I have not spoken to them, yet they prophesied."[5] For this reason their preaching is fruitless, and their teaching is not of Christ.

As we have said, if teaching is to bear fruit, it must be done in the Holy Spirit and in the right order,[6] as directed by him, so that it may strike home and hit the mark, piercing the heart like a two-edged sword.[7] If the teaching is not in the right order, it is not guided by the Spirit of Christ but by human understanding and presumption. Then it will not produce fruit or improvement, not even if the entire Scriptures were to be trumpeted before people.

Arrangement of Doctrine

Suppose one wishes to present Christ's teachings in the right way, teachings which have been given to people for their benefit, improvement, and enlightenment. First, it is necessary to present God in his unlimited power in such a way that people may recognize God's might, so that they may learn to commit themselves in trust to God. Next, they should be shown why humanity was created and made in God's likeness, and how humanity turned its back on this likeness[8] and fell into sin, which led to death.[9]

When humanity has seen the condition it is in and how deeply it

---

[1] Mark 7:6-9.   [2] 2 Pet. 1:19-21.   [3] Matt. 10:19-20; Mark 13:11; Luke 12:11-12.
[4] Luke 24:36-49; Acts 2:1-4.   [5] Jer. 23:21-22; 14:11-15; 14:11-15; Ezek. 13:1-12.
[6] Matt. 10:19-20; Mark 13:11; Luke 12:11-12; 2 Cor. 3:3-6.   [7] Heb. 4:12.
[8] Gen. 3:6-11.   [9] Rom. 5:12-14.

has plunged into death and eternal destruction through sin, then humanity must be shown once more the grace which Christ offers to all people. People must be shown how to find this grace and be grafted into Christ. When humanity has received Christ's grace, it should continually be exhorted to stand firm[1] and grow daily toward perfection.[2] In this way a person is guided onto the right path and made to depend upon God.

What We Teach About God

First, we teach that there is a God,[3] and that he shows himself to be God by the works of his hands. Even today he teaches us and shows us his glory in the same way.[4] Therefore, we point this out to people, bringing before their eyes this glory of God which is in all creatures, creatures who are the work of his hands. Then we testify with the power of God's own words that he alone is God.[5] He is a wellspring of all good things, showing kindness to those who seek him with all their heart.[6] He is found by the humble, remorseful, and brokenhearted.[7] Through his beloved Christ, he does not hesitate to do good for those who draw near to him. Since we have already spoken of these things elsewhere in this confession, we will leave it at that for the sake of brevity.

Idolatry

Because there is one God only, who is the source of all things,[8] people ought to set all their hope on him alone.[9] They should be seeking all healing and salvation in him through Christ,[10] following him only, obeying him, and trying earnestly to please him.[11] In short, a person should cling to God alone.[12] The opposite of this is idolatry.

Everything in which one seeks salvation, comfort, or help apart from God, be it in the saints or in anything else created, is idolatry, for it robs God of his honor. If a person forgets to find refuge in God and flees to anything created, that person makes an idol of it. For this reason Daniel refused to obey the counsel of the Chaldeans to turn from

---

[1] Acts 15:30-32; 16:40; 20:1-2.   [2] Eph. 4:11-15.   [3] Deut. 4:32-35; 6:4-7.   [4] Rom. 1:20.   [5] Deut. 32:39.   [6] Jer. 2:13.   [7] Isa. 66:1-2.   [8] Exod. 20:1-6; Deut. 4:35; 5:7-10; 6:4-5; 32:39-40.   [9] Ps. 20:1-6.   [10] Acts 4:8-12.   [11] Gen. 17:1-3.   [12] Deut. 19:8-10; 10:12-13.

God and to seek refuge in the king.[1]

Images have come from this glorification and love of created things. The wise teacher provides an example of this when he says, "It is as one who previously had a son whom he loved. After the son's death, the father made an image of him and began to worship it as a god, although a short time earlier he had lived as a man."[2] Thus people get caught up in error[3] by forgetting God and being led away from him.[4] That is why Solomon says, "The invention of shameful images is the beginning of all fornication and of turning one's back on God."[5] Again he says, "All makers of images are cursed along with the things they make."[6]

People practice idolatry not only in this way but whenever they love anything more than God, whether that be spouse, child, house, farm, money, goods, or even themselves, for thus they raise these things above God. In this way they turn their back on the commandments and will of God and give themselves up to sin. Their heart is turned away from God[7] and is set upon anything created.[8] This is truly forsaking God and setting up other gods.[9]

We say, too, that whoever calls upon the saints to help them or to intercede with God for their salvation, denies that Christ is the mediator and advocate with the Father. That person flees to something that can neither speak for him nor be of help. There is no other salvation and no other name given to people by which they may be saved except the name of Jesus Christ of Nazareth.[10]

Why God Created Humankind

Further, we teach that God created humanity solely for his honor.[11] He gave people reason, understanding, and sense for relating to all creatures so that they might know God's will and take pains to observe and keep it.[12] They are to cling to their Maker, seek him, love him, and honor him alone.

God is honored when what he has created remains as he created and ordained it and does not allow itself to be changed. God made people into heavenly beings with an inclination to what is divine, that

---

[1] Dan. 6:10.   [2] Wisd. of Sol. 14:15.   [3] Acts 7:40-43; Rom. 1:21-24.   [4] Ps. 53; Rom. 3:10-18.   [5] Wisd. of Sol. 14:11-14.   [6] Wisd. of Sol. 14:8; Deut. 27:15.   [7] Rom. 1:21-23.   [8] Isa. 1:2-4.   [9] Wisd. of Sol. 13–15.   [10] Acts 4:12.   [11] Gen. 1:26-28.   [12] Exod. 20:1-7, 23; Deut. 6:4-5; 10:14-19; 11:18-21.

they might seek and love heavenly and godly things[1] and abide by them. For this purpose God has also given people a heavenly body,[2] that is, his own breath and spirit,[3] which shall lead the earthly body to God. The heavenly body should honor and glorify God through the earthly body by inspiring and urging it to be true to how God made it, namely, with the ability to aspire to God. Paul admonishes us to do this, saying, "Set your affection on things above and not on things on earth."[4]

As it is to God's honor for people to remain in the condition and order established by God for them, so it is to God's dishonor to depart from and forsake the same.[5] Indeed, all of Creation except humanity has remained in its right place and waits for the bidding of its Master to be fulfilled. Humanity alone, to whom precedence and glory were given above all other creatures, has forsaken its place and left the order in which it was set.[6] Therefore, humanity should turn back in all haste.[7]

God Created Humankind in His Image

We teach that God, who is eternal truth, created and molded people in his image, saying, "Let us make humankind in our image."[8] That is a glorious likeness, truly one we should all rejoice over and wish for. But no one should be so foolish as to think that the Godhead is like flesh and blood, or that flesh and blood is a resemblance of the Godhead. Flesh and blood is of the earth and therefore earthly;[9] the likeness of God, however, is heavenly. So the whole of a person's life should be a reflection of God's likeness.

What God's Image Is

Christ says that God is a Spirit,[10] not, however, a spirit of lying, but of truth.[11] That is why we say the likeness of God is not flesh and blood but spirit. Now since people have been created after God's likeness and should make this likeness manifest,[12] it is God's will that people should be spiritually minded, not carnally minded.[13] For this reason

---

[1] Col. 3:1-7. [2] 1 Cor. 15:45-49. [3] Gen. 2:7. [4] Col. 3:2. [5] 1 Sam. 8:1-8; Isa. 2:1-4. [6] Gen. 3:6-12; 2 Esd. 3:4-8; Deut. 32:15-20. [7] Ps. 94:12-19; Heb. 3:7-13.
[8] Gen. 1:26. [9] Gen. 2:7; 1 Cor. 15:45. [10] John 4:24. [11] Heb. 6:18. [12] Gen. 1:27-28.
[13] Rom. 8:5-9.

God breathed on them with his own breath. He gave people the spirit of his truth and the image of his glory, to rule over the earthly body and to demonstrate and show God's character. In this way people bring glory to their Creator.[1]

For as God the Lord breathed upon the human race, it received a living soul. This wind or breath coming from God and given to the human race is a true picture and image of God.[2] Now since humans were given the spirit of truth, they were created in truth so that they might live and walk in it. This truth is God himself, whose image humanity should bear and reveal. As long as humanity lives in truth and obedience to God and allows the Spirit to rule and lead, it will continue to bear God's likeness.[3] But as soon as humanity turns away from this and allows the flesh to take over, it spurns God's likeness. Then, as Paul says, those who are carnally minded cannot please God.[4]

The Likeness of the Devil

Just as God is the Spirit of truth, so the devil is the spirit of lying and the father of lies. The lie, sin, injustice, or the spirit of lying are in the image of the devil. With such things, the devil clothes his children, whereas God adorns his children with truth. Thus one can be distinguished from the other.[5] John declares, "In this we recognize who are the children of God and who are the children of the devil."[6] Whoever chooses sin takes upon himself the likeness of the devil and renounces the likeness of God.[7]

How Adam Turned from the Likeness of God and Fell into Sin

Adam bore the true likeness of God. Therefore, God made him lord and ruler over all other created things, and made them all subject to Adam's will.[8] The one exception was the tree of knowledge and the recognition of good and evil.[9] Using that tree, God the Lord wished to test Adam to see if he wanted to be firm in his obedience. Through this prohibition God wished to show Adam, and to impress upon his

---

[1] Gen. 2:7. [2] Gen. 5:1-2. [3] John 14:15-26. [4] Rom. 8:8. [5] John 4:17-24; 8:39-47. [6] John 3:10. [7] Gen. 3:6-12. [8] Gen. 1:26-29. [9] Gen. 2:8-17.

inner being, that just as God made him lord over all created things,[1] so God is Lord over him. Adam was to cling to God and serve and obey God as his Lord, Father, and Creator.[2]

But Adam, deceived and beguiled by the counsel of the serpent, spurned such obedience and cast aside God's image,[3] that is, God's righteousness, purity, and holiness. Adam stained himself with sin,[4] with the image of the devil, whom he obeyed. Here some say that the serpent is the curiosity and desire of the flesh, but we do not wish to say this because at that time there was no mortality in Adam. We teach that it was the devil himself in the form of a serpent who deceived and beguiled Adam.[5] The arrogance of the flesh grew out of the serpent's counsel and raised itself up in Adam, as will be clearly seen.

When Eve heard the words of the serpent, she looked at the fruit. As soon as she saw that it made one clever and wise, curiosity was roused and grew in her, for she wanted to be more clever than she had been made. And so, through looking, a lust for the forbidden fruit awoke in her. As soon as she gave in to this and acted upon it, sin was born in her.[6] James says, "When lust has conceived, it brings forth sin; and sin, when it is fully grown, results in death."[7]

Now because Eve and her husband, who was enticed by her, disobeyed the command, sin was brought into the world, and through sin death has been passed on to everyone.[8] As soon as the transgression had taken place, their eyes were opened and they saw they were naked,[9] and that due to the serpent's counsel, they were stripped and emptied of all of God's grace. Thus, they knew evil and good; they knew how wicked it was to break the command of the Creator,[10] and how holy, good, and profitable it would have been to keep it.[11] Now because they saw that they had angered the Creator, shame and dread came upon them.[12] Because they were deceived and overcome by the devil, sin planted the devil's image in them, and this clung to them forever.[13] That is why the wrath of the Creator came upon them and all their descendants. This wrath could not be removed except through Christ, the offspring of the promise.

---

[1] Gen. 1:28.   [2] Deut. 6:5; 10:14-20; 11:1-6; 32:44-47.   [3] Gen. 3:1-6; 2 Cor. 11:3.
[4] Rom. 5:12.   [5] Wisd. of Sol. 1:12-16.   [6] Gen. 3:4-6.   [7] James 1:15.   [8] Rom. 5:12-14.
[9] Gen. 3:7.   [10] Deut. 27:15-26.   [11] Gen. 17:1-6; Deut. 28:1-11; Matt. 7:15-23.   [12] Gen. 3:8-10.   [13] 1 John 3:8.

What Sin Is

Sin is actually disobedience or refusing to obey God,[1] and from this all other wrongs grow as branches from a tree.[2] Evil has now taken the upper hand in the world[3] and still increases daily. Sinners go from one wrongdoing to another,[4] because they have yielded and committed their members to serve sin.[5]

All wrongdoing is sin,[6] as John says, but disobedience is the mother of all sin. Just as from obedience all the righteousness of God comes through Christ, so all sin and unrighteousness[7] comes from disobedience to God's command.

Original Sin

There is often vehement quarreling among people, one wanting this and the other that. Such strife results in more disruption and disunity than good. God is not a God of quarreling but of peace and love.[8] He has no pleasure in strife, nor has he anything to do with it, and therefore strife only leads to destruction.

We confess and teach that all humans,[9] with the exception of the one and only Christ, have a sinful nature, which they inherit from Adam.[10] It is just as Scripture tells us: "The inclination and desire of humanity is evil from youth."[11] David says likewise, "Behold, my mother conceived me in sin, and I was born in iniquity."[12] Paul also speaks plainly, "By one person sin entered the world and was passed on to all people."[13] To say it has been passed on to all of us clearly means that we have inherited it.

What Original Sin Is

The inheritance we all have from our father Adam is the inclination to sin. This means that by nature all of us have a tendency toward evil and toward taking pleasure in sin.[14] This inheritance shows itself in all of Adam's children, in all who are born according to Adam. In people, it devours and consumes everything which is good and godly,

---

[1] Gen. 3:6. [2] Rom. 5:12-14. [3] Rom. 3:23. [4] 2 Tim. 3:1-7. [5] John 8:39-44; Rom. 6:19. [6] 1 John 5:17. [7] Rom. 5:16-19. [8] 1 Cor. 14:33. [9] 2 Esd. 3:21-22. [10] 2 Cor. 5:21; Heb. 4:14; 5:3. [11] Gen. 8:21. [12] Ps. 51:5. [13] Rom. 5:16-19. [14] 2 Esd. 3:21-22.

so that no one may attain it again unless that person is born anew.[1]

Paul calls this inheritance the messenger of Satan, who strikes him on the head or buffets him with fists.[2] He is speaking here of the sinful inclination that stirs in him as in all people. John states, "Whoever says he has no sin deceives himself and is not speaking the truth."[3] He follows this with a discussion about the inheritance we have received from Adam, which he calls sin. In the book of Psalms, David says, "I was conceived and born in sin."[4] Therefore, through Adam we all have become sinful and must be justified once more through Christ if we want to have life with him.[5]

Harm Caused by Original Sin

In the first place, original sin is the cause of people's physical death. People were originally created for life. There was nothing corrupt in them, for God did not make death.[6] However, since we have all inherited sin, all, both young and old, must taste death. Truly, if Christ had not been sent into the world, there would be no more hope of life.

That is how it was planned from the beginning by the Father, and why Christ has come into the world and become the reconciliation[7] not only for us but for all people.[8] Therefore, we believe that God has brought it about that original sin, even though it rouses people to still more sin, now causes only physical and not eternal death. Thus the prophecy in Ezekiel is fulfilled, which says that the children shall not bear the sins of their fathers but shall die for their own sins.[9] Accordingly, we say that God accepts little children as they are, for indeed Christ is their reconciler.[10]

On the other hand, we say that original sin also causes eternal death because it leads and directs people into sin, and through it we all commit many sins. That is the sin which stirs up, rouses, and brings to pass all the other sins in us, as Paul indicates when he says, "Sin shows its true nature in that it causes death through what is good. So, through the commandment, sin's utter sinfulness is revealed."[11]

Thus, all people have died in Adam;[12] all have gone astray from God and forsaken him.[13] Paul writes, "There is none righteous, no, not

---

[1] John 3:3-5.   [2] 2 Cor. 12:7.   [3] 1 John 1:8-10.   [4] Ps. 51:5.   [5] Rom. 5:15-19.
[6] Wisd. of Sol. 1:13-15.   [7] 1 Pet. 1:3-5.   [8] 1 John 1:1-2.   [9] Ezek. 18:20; 33:10-19.
[10] 1 John 2:1-2.   [11] Rom. 7:13.   [12] 1 Cor. 15:21-22.   [13] Ps. 52:3-7; Isa. 1:1-4.

one. There is no one who understands; there is no one who asks about God. They have all turned aside and have become unfit. Not one of them does good, no, not one. Their throat is an open sepulchre; they have used their tongues for treachery. The poison of asps is on their lips, and their mouth is full of cursing and bitterness. Their feet are swift to shed blood, and destruction and misery lie along their path. The way of peace they do not know, and there is no fear of God in their minds."[1]

In this way we show people how far they have distanced themselves from God and submerged themselves in their sins. We show them also that all sin has its source and origin in embracing what is unrighteous.[2] People embrace what they ought not to embrace, and leave what they ought to accept. They love what they ought to hate, and hate what they ought to love.[3] Thus they are turned aside and led away from God by just those things which should show the way to God and teach them to know God.[4] Therefore, if anyone wants to come to God, that person must give up whatever was previously appropriated wrongly, that is, all that is temporal and transitory, and must depend on God alone. This is the true repentance which the Lord wants and expects of us.[5]

---

[1] Rom. 3:10-18. [2] Gen. 3:6. [3] Matt. 10:21-25. [4] 1 John 2:15-17. [5] Matt. 10:5-10; Luke 14:33.

How People Again May Find God and His Grace

Remorse

We write now for those who seek further advice on how to free their souls from eternal destruction and death, into which sin[1] and the snares of the devil[2] have led them, and who wish to partake of the grace of Christ. With John the preacher of repentance, and with Peter and the apostles, we teach that they must repent. Those who want to repent with all their heart must first feel genuine remorse for their sins.[3] Remorse, however, means first recognizing how wrong, evil, harmful, and destructive sins are.[4] Otherwise, repentance cannot endure, and still less can the sinner receive grace.

True remorse follows the recognition of sin[5] and is the basis on which people feel repugnance and horror of their sin.[6] Yes, they even loathe themselves for being guided and controlled by sin for so long.[7] Sin is what led them away from God, for whose sake they had been put into the world.[8]

Those who are sorry for their sin and regret their enslavement to it, must from now on guard themselves against sin all the more earnestly. They must run from it as from a serpent.[9] True remorse induces earnest care and watchfulness to prevent sin from creeping up and having power over them again.[10] How true is the saying, "A person once burnt, dreads the fire!" Once burnt, that person will not so quickly touch fire again. And still more, whoever has once recognized sin will guard against it, for it burns to eternal death.[11] However, the one who does not flee from sin and hate it with all his heart shows that he has not yet really seen sin for what it is, nor the harm it can do. Otherwise, he would take it more seriously.[12] The person who has truly come to recognize sin would rather die than willingly and with his

---

[1] Rom. 1:18-32. [2] 1 Pet. 2:19-25. [3] Matt. 3:1-12; Luke 3:1-10; Acts 2:39-40; 17:30-31. [4] Rom. 7:7-13. [5] 2 Sam. 12:13-17. [6] Ps. 51:1-13. [7] 1 Pet. 4:1-3. [8] Deut. 32:15-18. [9] Sir. 21:1-4. [10] Rom. 6:16-23. [11] Sir. 21:1-4; Rom. 5:14-17. [12] Ps. 101:1-4.

heart consent to sin in word and deed. On the contrary, all the days of his life, the one who repents would feel regret and sorrow for the sin previously committed[1] and for having angered God, his Creator.[2]

Repentance

Remorse, then, leads to true repentance, and repentance means to humble and submit oneself before God because of one's transgressions.[3] Such repentance means to humble oneself before God, to bow down, and to be ashamed because of one's wickedness. This shame brings about a genuine return, so that one hastens to God, cries aloud, and prays to him for forgiveness and grace.[4] At the same time, that person begins to conquer his flesh, brings it into subjection, bridles it, and feeds it with hyssop.[5]

The recognized sin fills a person's conscience with fear and leaves the person with no peace. Then the restless conscience searches where help and healing may be found. As David says, "I lift my eyes to the hills; where will my help come from? My help comes from the Lord, who made heaven and earth."[6] Every anxious and broken heart, every fearful and troubled heart, if it flees to him, will find peace and comfort. Scripture assures us of this with the words, "Upon whom shall I look but upon the one who is of a broken and contrite spirit."[7]

We also want to point out that the kind of shallow remorse and repentance that is customary in the world carries no weight with God. If a person says today, "I am sorry for my sin," and yet commits the same sin again tomorrow, that one will not receive grace. God wants to draw near to those who seek repentance with a sincere heart; God will start his work in them and perfect it.[8]

People Are Grafted into Christ

God draws near to the one whose heart is fearful, who is sorry for his sin, and who does not know where to turn in his distress. The world itself is too restricted for him, and he lifts up his heart to God alone.[9] God will show himself to this person, provide comfort in his sorrow, and point to his Son, who says, "Come to me, all you who are heavily burdened, and I will give you renewed strength. Put on my

---

[1] Tob. 4:1-6.　[2] Deut. 32:19-25.　[3] Gen. 3:8-10.　[4] Ps. 51:1-4.　[5] 1 Cor. 9:24-27.
[6] Ps. 121:1-2.　[7] Isa. 66:2.　[8] James 4:1-10.　[9] Isa. 58:6-10.

yoke, for it is easy, and my burden is light."[1] Such a call the Lord extends to us through his servants whom he has chosen from the world[2] to be his witnesses.[3] Those who hear his voice and come to him will never be rejected.[4]

We teach further that Christ came into the world to bring salvation to sinners.[5] As it is written, "This is the Father's will, that every one who sees the Son and believes in him shall not be lost, but shall have everlasting life."[6] We teach also that a person may be planted and grafted into Christ through faith. This is how it takes place. As soon as a person hears the gospel of Christ and believes it from the heart, he receives the seal of the Holy Spirit. As Paul says, "After you believed, you were sealed with the Spirit of the promise. That is the Holy Spirit, who is the pledge of our inheritance, the promise that we who belong to God shall be redeemed, to the praise of his glory."[7]

This Spirit of Christ, promised and given to all believers, makes them free from the law or power of sin and grafts them into Christ.[8] He makes them one with him in mind, in his very character and nature, so that they become one plant and organism with him.[9] Christ is the root or stem; we are the branches. As he himself says, "I am the true vine, and you are the branches."[10] Thus we are one substance and essence with him, truly one bread and body.[11] He is the head, and we are all members, belonging one to another.[12]

Christ is the root and the vine, and we are grafted into him through faith. Just as the sap rises from the root and makes the branches fruitful, so the Spirit of Christ rises from the root, Christ, into the branches and twigs, to make them all fruitful. The twigs are of the same nature as the root and bear its kind of fruit.[13] Christ shows this in a parable: "No one gathers figs from thistles or grapes from thorns. No good tree can yield bad fruit, nor can a bad tree bring forth good fruit, but each tree is known by its own fruit."[14] Christ is a good tree, a true vine; hence, only good can flourish and be fruitful in him.[15]

Thus each person becomes one with God and God one with that person, as a father is one with his son. Each person is gathered and brought into the church of Christ, so that each may remain in God

---

[1] Matt. 11:28.   [2] John 15:16.   [3] Acts 1:7-8.   [4] John 6:28-37.   [5] 1 Tim. 1:15.
[6] John 6:39-40.   [7] Eph. 1:10-14.   [8] Joel 2:27-29; Acts 2:14-21; Rom. 8:1-10.   [9] 1 Cor. 2:10-16; 2 Pet. 1:2-4.   [10] John 15:1-6.   [11] 1 Cor. 10:14-21.   [12] Rom. 12:1-5; 1 Cor. 12:20-27.
[13] Rom. 11:16-24.   [14] Matt. 7:16-23; 12:33-35; Luke 6:43-46.   [15] John 15:1-9; Rom. 11:16-18.

with the church and serve him in one Spirit.[1] In that way, each one may be a child and inheritor of the covenant of grace confirmed by Christ.[2]

God's Covenant

God's covenant[3] is an everlasting covenant, existing from the beginning and continuing into eternity. It shows that it is his will to be our God and Father, that we should be his people and beloved children. Through the covenant, God desires continually to pour into us through Christ every divine blessing and all good things.[4]

That such a covenant of God existed from the beginning is shown in that God created people in his own likeness.[5] All was well with them, and there was no corrupting poison in them.[6] Even when people were deceived and robbed of this likeness by the counsel of the serpent,[7] God's purpose nevertheless endured.[8] The covenant which he had previously made expresses this clearly, namely, that he should be our God and we his people.[9] Out of this comes a promise to take away the devil's power through the woman's offspring.[10] This makes it clear that it was God's intention to redeem us from the devil's power and restore us as his children.[11]

Thus, God made his covenant first with Adam,[12] and then more clearly with Abraham and his descendants.[13] Now he has made this covenant with us through Christ and has established and confirmed it through Christ's death.[14] Just as a will is not valid until the death of the one making the will, in the same way God gave his Son up to death,[15] so that we would be redeemed from death through him and be the children of his covenant forever.[16]

The Old Covenant

The old covenant, insofar as it is called old, was given to the people of Israel without the dispensing of the Spirit of grace, because

---

[1] Eph. 2:18-22.   [2] Acts 3:19-25.   [3] In these articles, the German term *Testament* is translated by "covenant" rather than "testament" because Riedemann is not referring to Old or New Testament. Instead, he is speaking of God's old relationship with the Israelites, or of the new relationship God has created with humans through Christ. Christian literature in English more often refers to the relationship of God to humans as "covenant" than as "testament."   [4] Gen. 17:3-10; Lev. 26:9-13; Ezek. 37:13-14; 2 Cor. 6:14-18.   [5] Gen. 1:26-27.   [6] Wisd. of Sol. 1:12-14.   [7] Gen. 3:1-6.   [8] Heb. 6:17-20.   [9] 2 Cor. 6:16.   [10] Gen. 3:14-15.   [11] John 1:12; Eph. 1:3-5.   [12] Gen. 3:8-15.   [13] Gen. 17:19; 28:10-15.   [14] Heb. 7:18-28.   [15] Heb. 9:11-16.   [16] Acts 3:17-26.

their stubborn hearts were not circumcised, and because sin was not taken from them.[1] Thus the apostle declares, "It is impossible to remove sins through the blood of bulls and goats."[2]

Esdras agrees with this word: "When you led the children of Israel out of Egypt, you brought them to Mount Sinai. Bending down the heavens, you shook the earth, making it quake and the depths tremble, and terrifying the people of that time. And your glory passed through the four gates of fire, earthquake, wind, and cold, to give the law to Jacob's descendants and your command to the posterity of Israel. Yet you did not take their wicked hearts from them, so your law could not become fruitful in them."[3]

Now because hearts were not changed by all this, and people remained the same old people, the old covenant was not a covenant with heirs, but one of servitude. Paul makes this clear when he speaks of the two covenants represented by two women. The covenant originating on Mount Sinai bears children born into bondage; it provides them no freedom.[4]

Although the old covenant brings bondage with it, yet it also ushers in something better and more perfect. Because something better has come, that is, the covenant of God is more perfectly and more clearly revealed, that which is dark and imperfect must come to an end.[5] Paul says, "Moses put a veil over his face so that the children of Israel could not gaze at the radiance while it was fading."[6]

The apostle testified that the old covenant does come to an end: "Since God promised a new covenant, the old one fades away. What decays and becomes old is near its end."[7] This does not mean that God's covenant is finished and done with, but rather that the imperfect revelation of it is finished. Its obscurity is ended. The result is that the covenant will be revealed in its power and clarity. This has been accomplished in Christ. Because of the surpassing clarity of its revelation,[8] the apostle speaks of the new as better.[9] More of this later.

The Law

The law is the word that bears witness to the old covenant, the covenant of bondage.[10] It is called a yoke of bondage[11] because it only

---

[1] Acts 7:51-53. See note 3 on page 98.   [2] Heb. 10:4.   [3] 2 Esd. 3:17-20.   [4] Gal. 4:21 26; Exod. 20:1-17.   [5] Heb. 7:18-19.   [6] 2 Cor. 3:11-18.   [7] Heb. 8:10-13; 2 Cor. 5:17.   [8] Heb. 7:22.   [9] Phil. 3:7-8.   [10] Gal. 4:21-24. See note 3 on page 98.   [11] Gal. 5:1-5.

requires, exhorts, and demands; yet on account of its weakness, it is not able to provide.[1] Where the Spirit is not added to the Word, it will not bring about the righteousness that stands before God.[2]

Nevertheless, it does make people conscious of sin, striking and terrifying their conscience so that they may be moved to seek and ask for something better.[3] Therefore, the law is our taskmaster until we are in Christ.[4] Through Christ, the promise of the Father is poured out on all who believe in his name.[5] This promise is the Spirit of grace. If we allow this Spirit to rule and lead us, he sets us free from the law.[6] Paul says, "If you are led by the Spirit, you are not under the law."[7] Christ is the end of the law and brings righteousness for everyone who has faith.[8]

Christ is not the end of the law, however, in the sense that he overthrows God's law or makes it nothing. Paul says, "Do we nullify the law through faith? Never! We uphold the law."[9] So the law, insofar as it is spiritual, is not abolished. In its spiritual nature, it is truly established and ordained. Through the spirit of Christ, it is fulfilled and perfected in accordance with God's will.[10] Therefore, the law alone, insofar as it is the literal word,[11] which kills, has been abolished by Christ. Christ has given us his Spirit, which joyfully and without compulsion accomplishes God's will within us.[12] Thus we are no more under the law, and yet we are not without God's law.[13]

Everything expressed literally, insofar as it is of the letter, whether written by Paul, Peter, or any other apostle, we call law and command, for so it is. That letter only kills, like the letter of the law of Moses. But insofar as it is spiritual and is spiritually received and acted upon, it is a word of grace, even though written by Moses.[14] That is why those who do not have the Spirit of Christ can only be servants of the letter of the law and not of the gospel.[15]

The Gospel

The gospel is a joyful message from God and Christ, proclaimed, put into practice, and accepted through the Holy Spirit.[16] It is a word of liberty that sets people free and makes them devout and blessed.[17]

---

[1] Rom. 8:3; Heb. 7:28.　[2] Rom. 3:19-20.　[3] Rom. 7:7-14.　[4] Gal. 3:21-24.　[5] John 14:16; Acts 1:1-8; 2:1-22, 32-33.　[6] Eph. 1:12.　[7] Gal. 5:16-18.　[8] Rom. 10:4.　[9] Rom. 3:31.　[10] Rom. 7:14-16.　[11] Eph. 2:8-16.　[12] 2 Cor. 3:6-9.　[13] 1 Cor. 9:19-21; 2 Cor. 3:7-18.　[14] Rom. 7:6-25.　[15] Rom. 8:1-9.　[16] Isa. 61:1-2; Luke 4:16-19.　[17] Rom. 8:1-2.

As Paul says, "The gospel is the power of God, providing salvation to all who believe it."[1] And again Paul says, "It is the true grace of God on which you have taken your stand and by which you will find salvation, if you hold fast to it as you have received it."[2]

This word shows us that God has restored his promised grace through Christ,[3] making us heirs of his grace and sharers in its fellowship.[4] It raises up the conscience that has been beaten down by the law and accomplishes what the law demands but cannot achieve. It makes people children of God,[5] and at one with him.[6] They become a new creation[7] with a godly character.[8]

All this, however, is not inscribed in stone or printed on paper but on the tablets of the human heart; inscribed, not with pen and ink, but with the hand of God, that is, with his Holy Spirit.[9] God has promised, "I will write my law in their mind and plant it in their inner being, so that no one need say to his brother, 'Know the Lord.' They shall all know me, from the least of them to the greatest."[10] That is the living Word, piercing soul and spirit,[11] through whom all who would inherit the promise must be born.

The New Covenant

Since the old covenant[12] comes to an end because of its obscurity and imperfection,[13] God has established a perfect covenant and revealed it to us. This covenant remains unchanged through eternity,[14] as God promised in days gone by. "The time is coming," says the Lord, "when I will make a new covenant with the house of Israel, but not like the covenant I made with their fathers when I led them by the hand out of the land of Egypt, because they did not hold to it."[15]

The new covenant is a covenant of grace, of the revelation and knowledge of God, as the words from Jeremiah declare: "They shall all know me, from the least to the greatest."[16] This knowledge comes to those who receive the Holy Spirit.[17] Thus God's covenant is confirmed by Christ and sealed and established by the Holy Spirit.[18] This was promised in Scripture: "And it will happen in the last days, says

---

[1] Rom. 1:16; 1 Cor. 1:18.   [2] 1 Cor. 15:1-2.   [3] Gen. 3:14-15; 17:1-5.   [4] 1 John 1:5-10.   [5] Rom. 8:2-4.   [6] James 1:17-18.   [7] 2 Cor. 5:14-17.   [8] 2 Pet. 1:3-4.   [9] 2 Cor. 3:3-11.   [10] Jer. 31:33-34; Heb. 8:6-11; 10:15-17.   [11] Heb. 4:12.   [12] See note 3 on page 98.   [13] 2 Cor. 3:14-18.   [14] Heb. 7:18-28.   [15] Jer. 31:31-34.   [16] Jer. 31:34; Heb. 8:6-12.   [17] John 16:12-15.   [18] Heb. 9:14-15.

the Lord, that I will pour out my Spirit upon all people; your sons and your daughters shall prophesy. Yes, even upon my servants, both men and women, I will pour out my Spirit in those days."[1]

This is the covenant of childlike freedom, and we are its children if we let ourselves be guided by its seal and submit to its influence.[2] Paul also says, "The law of the Spirit has made me free from the law of sin and death."[3] Whoever is made free by Christ is free indeed.[4] Therefore, Paul says, "Stand fast in the liberty with which Christ has made us free, and do not again become entangled with the yoke of bondage."[5] If you allow yourself to be led into the yoke of bondage, you are led from the Spirit to the letter, and Christ is of no use to you. For this reason, those who do not have the Spirit are not the children of this covenant.[6]

Infant Baptism

Infants have not been born of God in the Christian sense, that is, through the proclamation of the Word, through faith and the Holy Spirit.[7] Therefore, they cannot receive true baptism, which is acceptance into the church of Christ. Now, since all who are born of Adam share in his heritage, any who wish to be incorporated into the church of Christ must be born of Christ in the Christian way.[8] They may then be accepted in the right way, which Christ revealed to his church.[9]

As said above, the birth of Christ took place through the proclamation of the Word. Mary believed the angel and received the Holy Spirit through faith. The Spirit worked together with her faith so that she conceived Christ,[10] and he was born of her. Whoever wishes to be born in the Christian way must first, like Mary, hear the Word and believe it.[11] Thus when that person's faith is sealed with the Holy Spirit, one may in truth be accepted into the church of Christ.[12] This is how it was done by the apostles.

Nowhere do we find that the apostles baptized children; on the contrary, we find that they obeyed their Master's instructions and teaching. They said, "If you believe, you may indeed be baptized."[13] This implied, "If you do not believe, you may not be baptized."

---

[1] Joel 2:28-29; Acts 2:17-21. [2] Gal. 4:4-7. [3] Rom. 8:2. [4] John 8:36. [5] Gal. 5:1-4. [6] Rom. 8:8-9. [7] James 1:17-18; 1 Pet. 1:3-5. [8] 2 Esd. 3:10-11; 7:48-53; Rom. 5:12-15. [9] Matt. 28:18-20; Mark 16:15-16. [10] Matt. 1:18-25; Luke 2:4-7. [11] Luke 1:30-38. [12] Eph. 1:12-14. [13] Acts 8:36-38.

There are several reasons why we hold infant baptism to be useless and wrong. First, nowhere in all of Scripture do we find one little
word in which it is even considered, much less commanded. Second,
we find that the popes in their decrees have commanded that children
who can recite the Lord's Prayer and the Apostles' Creed should be
baptized. If this practice had already existed, the popes would not
have needed to command it. Therefore, this is obviously something
planted by humans, and so it must be uprooted.[1] Third, baptism is the
bond of a good conscience with God.[2] And fourth, the covenant of
grace is a covenant of the knowledge and recognition of God.[3]
Children, however, know neither good nor evil,[4] and that is reason
enough for us to reject infant baptism, even if we had no other reasons.

Alleged Reasons for Infant Baptism, with Responses

First Reason
To defend their folly, those who baptize infants first put forward
Christ's command, "Go and teach all nations, baptizing them in the
name of the Father, the Son, and the Holy Spirit, instructing them to
observe all I have commanded you."[5] Here, they say, they are commanded to baptize all peoples. Little children are also people.
Therefore, one ought to baptize infants, and if possible, also to teach
them afterward.

At the same time, they acknowledge that the apostles baptized
believers, and that this should still be done. Where Jews or Gentiles
wish to come to faith, they must first be taught; and then when they
confess their faith, they may be baptized.

Response
One should first teach the nations[6] and then, as infant baptizers
themselves say, baptize them upon confession of their faith.[7] Since little children are also people, they must accordingly first be taught, and
then baptized. Why then do infant baptizers baptize children before
teaching them and before faith has been confessed?

It is no answer to reverse the order of the words and say that we
baptize children when we can and teach them afterward. In the end,

---

[1] Matt. 15:13.   [2] 1 Pet. 3:18-21.   [3] Jer. 31:34.   [4] Deut. 1:39.   [5] Matt. 28:19-20.
[6] Matt. 28:19-20.   [7] Acts 8:36-38.

they have to admit that the apostles taught the people of their day. After the apostles taught them, they baptized them upon confession of their faith.[1] The apostles have taken this ordinance from the above-quoted words of Christ, "Teach all nations, and baptize them."[2] That order should not be changed. Thus, since children are included in the term "nations," one must either apply this command to them, or point to a different command which applies to children.

Second Reason

Now, they say, if we are not to baptize infants because they cannot believe and confess, or because we cannot teach them, then it would also follow that we should not feed them, because they do not work. For Paul says, "Whoever will not work shall not eat."[3] So we should let the children die of hunger.

Response

Here as in many other places, Scripture is drawn upon to testify against itself. Paul does not say, "If anyone does not work, neither should he eat," but "If anyone does not want to work, neither should he eat."[4] He is not speaking of little children who are not able to work but of those who are able and do not want to work. So this text does not apply. It does no more than resist the truth, as Jannes and Jambres did, striving to crush it with contrived words.[5]

Third Reason

Another argument that is brought forward is Peter's saying: "This is promised to you and your children, and to those who are still far off, whom God the Lord will call."[6] They say that here baptism is promised to children, and that therefore it is right to baptize them and wrong to deny them.

Response

The defenders of infant baptism refuse to see that it was not the act of baptism that moved the people and caused them to gather at the first Pentecost. Instead, it was the words the disciples uttered under the impulse of the Holy Spirit among them.[7] The people were amazed, wondering what this new thing might be. However, when

---

[1] Acts 2:22-41; 8:29-38; 10:44-48; 16:13-15, 27-34. [2] Matt. 28:19-20. [3] 2 Thess. 3:10. [4] 2 Thess. 3:10-12. [5] Exod. 7:9-13; 2 Tim. 3:8. [6] Acts 2:38-39. [7] Acts 2:38-41.

several persons mocked them and claimed that their words came from having drunk too much wine, Peter stood up and said, "These men are not drunk, as you suppose, since it is only the third hour of the day. No, this is what God promised in times past through the prophets:[1] 'I will pour out my Spirit upon all people, and your youths will prophesy.' "[2]

The disciples testified that this promise and gift of God had been given to them through Christ, and they now spoke out of that experience.[3] Upon hearing that, the people became very eager, wishing to receive such a gift as well, since it had been promised to all of them. They were moved to ask earnestly what they should do to acquire it.[4] Then Peter opened his mouth and said, "Everyone of you repent and be baptized in the name of Jesus Christ for the forgiveness of your sins, and you shall receive the gift of the Holy Spirit; for it is promised to you and to your children."[5]

Whoever is willing to see knows well the promise Peter is speaking of here, and why the people sought it with such eagerness. Without question, he speaks of the outpouring of the Holy Spirit promised in times past[6] but given them through Christ.[7] Moved by this, the people asked what they should do to receive this gift which was promised them. Peter replied that they should repent and, showing the fruits of repentance, be baptized in the name of Jesus Christ. Then their sins would be forgiven and the Holy Spirit would be given to them.[8] That is the right understanding of this passage, and those who interpret it differently deceive and mislead themselves.

Peter includes children when he says, "It is promised to you and your children,"[9] Thus he means that the promise is especially given to the whole house of Israel, to all the descendants of Abraham.[10] Therefore, his hearers are the children of the covenant and of the promise.[11] Likewise, Paul says, "To whom belong the rights of children: glory, covenant, law, worship services, and the promise. Their heirs are the patriarchs, from whom Christ descended."[12]

If Peter had been speaking of the promise of baptism, which can not be proved by a single word, he could easily have said to them, "Bring your children here and have them baptized." This, however,

---

[1] Acts 2:15-17.   [2] Joel 2:28-29.   [3] John 4:25-42; 16:12-15.   [4] Rom. 9:30-33.
[5] Acts 2:37-39.   [6] Joel 2:28-29.   [7] John 14:26.   [8] Luke 24:45-49.   [9] Acts 2:39.
[10] Gen. 17:1-7.   [11] Acts 3:25.   [12] Rom. 9:3-5.

he did not do. Therefore, this argument is false. Of baptism, he says only that they should repent and be baptized and give themselves to a new life. Then they will receive the Holy Spirit, who causes all this to happen in them.[1]

Fourth Reason

Next, they quote Christ's words, "Let the little children come to me, for of such is the kingdom of heaven." Then they say that to bring children to Christ must mean through baptism, and that is what Christ meant when he said, "You shall not forbid them."[2] So whoever refuses to baptize infants, sins against this word.

Response

We gladly admit that Christ rebukes the disciples for forbidding parents to bring children to him. But we do not admit that it follows that we should baptize them. Christ did otherwise; he did not baptize them, neither did he command his disciples to do so. Therefore, they should rightly remain unbaptized until they are able to understand what the covenant of the knowledge of God demands.[3] But how does Christ respond to the children? He wishes them well, takes them in his arms, and lays his hands upon them.[4] Let us leave it at that and not invent anything of our own.

They say that Christ's laying his hands upon the children is also a sacrament and sign of acceptance, so why not baptize them? We reply: If Christ had received the little children with the laying on of hands, then he would have given us an example that we should receive them into the church through this sign. Hence, let us instead simply adhere to what he has shown us with the laying on of hands, and not introduce another sign to please ourselves, such as baptism of children. If Christ had meant baptism, he would have commanded that the children who were brought to him should be baptized. This he did not do. Therefore, even if their argument were right that since Christ accepted the children through the laying on of hands, and so we too should accept and not reject them—it would still be wrong to baptize children.

Since Christ did not baptize the children, his own deeds show that he was not using the laying on of hands as a sign of acceptance

---

[1] Acts 2:38-41. [2] Matt. 19:14; Mark 10:14; Luke 18:16. [3] Jer. 31:33-34. [4] Matt. 19:13-15; Mark 10:13-16; Luke 18:15-17.

into church membership. Baptism is always the first sign by which we are commanded to accept people into the church and community of Christ, as we see in the words from Matthew: "Teach all nations, baptizing them."[1] The laying on of hands, however, is a sign of confirmation,[2] or of entrusting to someone a further task in the church.[3] If a baptized member sins and is separated from the church, that person may, after repentance, be reaccepted, and this is confirmed by the laying on of hands. So we see that infant baptism is not at all proved by Christ's laying his hands on the children.[4]

On the contrary, we have to say that here the evangelist is simply describing how Christ showed his kindness and love to the children, taking them in his arms and kissing them. Nothing more is meant.

Fifth Reason

Those who try to uphold infant baptism also bring forward the words of Christ to Nicodemus: "One cannot enter the kingdom of God without being born through water and Spirit."[5] They say that if little children are not baptized, neither can they receive salvation. At the same time, they say that water comes first, and only then the Spirit comes, meaning that one may first baptize children, and then later teach them faith.

Response

To understand Christ's meaning, one must note with whom one is dealing, and what that person's concern is. Nicodemus comes to the Lord to ask him about the way of life, and the Lord shows him the way so well that Nicodemus marvels and is amazed.[6] He has to become a new person, or be born anew,[7] and the new birth must take place through water and the Spirit.[8] In the first place, Christ mentions the water because John's baptism of water was told to Nicodemus and known by him. This same John, with his teaching and baptism, was a messenger and forerunner of Christ.[9] In the second place, baptism by water means putting to death the old person, the sinful nature,[10] so that we are conformed to the death of Christ.[11] From John's baptism, Nicodemus clearly learned this dying to the old person, since John preached repentance.[12]

---

[1] Matt. 28:18-20. [2] Acts 8:14-17; 19:4-6. [3] Acts 13:1-3; 1 Tim. 4:14. [4] Matt. 19:13-15. [5] John 3:5. [6] John 3:1-5. [7] 2 Cor. 5:17. [8] John 1:33; 1 Pet. 1:23; James 1:17-18. [9] Isa. 40:3; Mal. 3:1. [10] Rom. 6:3-6. [11] Phil. 3:8-10. [12] Matt. 3:1-11; Mark 1:2-8; Luke 3:1-18.

Christ shows him further that the death of the old person is not sufficient. One must also become alive again. This cannot take place except through baptism, or the gift of the Holy Spirit. However, nothing is restored to life without first dying,[1] and sinners are not able to receive the Spirit of God.[2] Therefore, the water baptism of repentance must first take place, so that baptism with the Spirit may follow. As John was a messenger and forerunner of Christ,[3] so is the baptism of water a forerunner of the baptism of the Spirit.[4] Just as John could not be a forerunner of Christ without teaching and preaching,[5] so water baptism cannot happen without being preceded by preaching.[6]

Sixth Reason

A passage from Mark is also quoted: "John was in the wilderness, baptizing and preaching the baptism of repentance for the forgiveness of sins."[7] Here they say, "Baptism comes before teaching and preaching; therefore, it makes no difference if we first baptize the children, provided they are afterward taught the faith."

Response

Even though the word "baptizing" does come before "teaching," it does not follow that one ought to baptize before one finishes teaching. Nor does it follow that John did so, even though his office and task was to teach and preach. Thus John himself says,[8] "I am a voice that cries out."[9] Even though the Gospel writer mentions baptism first, he does not at all mean to say that John baptized before he finished teaching. He wants to say that after baptism had been carried out, John did not cease teaching but continued to lead the people onward,[10] teaching them to prepare the way for the Lord.[11] This is the Gospel writer's true meaning.

The words of Mark in the same passage show us that this is the true interpretation, and not the interpretation from others noted above. Mark says, "John was in the wilderness, baptizing and teaching."[12] If one would consider this only according to the literal words, it would follow that he baptized and taught in the wilderness. But he did not do that, as can be seen in Luke's words: "In the wilderness,

---

[1] 1 Cor. 15:29-36.   [2] Wisd. of Sol. 1:4-5.   [3] Isa. 40:3; Mal. 3:1.   [4] Acts 2:4.
[5] Matt. 3:1-11; Mark 1:1-8; Luke 3:1-3.   [6] Matt. 28:19-20; Mark 16:15-16.
[7] Mark 1:4.   [8] Isa. 40:3-8; Mal. 3:1-3; Matt. 3:1-11.   [9] John 1:19-23.   [10] Mark 1:4-8.
[11] Matt. 3:1-3; Mark 1:1-3.   [12] Mark 1:4.

the word of God came to John, the son of Zachariah, and he went into all the country round Jordan, preaching the baptism of repentance."[1] So it is clear from this that one should not understand Mark's words in that way. John was in the wilderness, however, until the day when he appeared before the Israelites.[2]

Finally, they bring forward circumcision[3] to prove the rightness of their infant baptism. However, if one looks at the truth, about which we want to speak later, this is in reality a powerful argument *against* infant baptism. Thus, their strongest reasons have almost all been mentioned, and we do well to realize that they are baseless. Their purpose is not achieved. They only harm themselves by twisting the Word of God[4] for the sake of their pleasure and worldly gain.

The Baptism of Christ and His Church

Because baptism is a covenant of the knowledge and grace of God,[5] it is also, according to the words of Peter, the bond of a good conscience with God, the bond of those who have recognized God.[6] As has been said, the knowledge of God comes from hearing the word of the gospel. Therefore, we teach that baptism should not be for little children but only for those who have heard the Word, believed it, and have recognized God.[7]

All mortals are born with Adam's character, inherit his nature, and share in the fellowship of his sin.[8] Therefore, Christ, who was to abolish sin and destroy its power,[9] was conceived in a completely different way,[10] as discussed above. Thus, those who inherit Christ's nature[11] shall share in his fellowship, become members of his body,[12] and must also be born of him, not in the Adamic way but in the Christian way. This birth comes about through the Word, faith, and the Holy Spirit.[13] Whoever receives the Word in faith becomes God's child.[14] Thus the apostle John says, "To all who received him, who believed in his name, he gave the power to become children of God. They are not born of human descent, nor of the will of the flesh, nor of human will, but of God."[15] Paul says the same: "It is not the natural children who

---

[1] Luke 3:2-3.   [2] Luke 1:80.   [3] Gen. 17:10.   [4] 2 Cor. 2:17; 2 Pet. 3:16.   [5] Jer. 31:33-34; Heb. 8:8-13; Heb. 10:8-18.   [6] 1 Pet. 3:18-22.   [7] Luke 7:24-35; Acts 2:14-41; 11:11-17; 16:8-15.   [8] 2 Esd. 3:4-22; 7:47-56; Rom. 5:12-14.   [9] 1 John 3:1-6.   [10] Matt. 1:18-25; Luke 1:26-38; 2:1-7.   [11] 2 Pet. 1:1-4.   [12] 1 Cor. 6:15.   [13] 1 Pet. 1:3-5; James 1:17-18.   [14] John 3:1-5.   [15] John 1:12.

are children of God, but the children of the promise. They are counted as descendants."[1]

Since we are to be born of God in the spiritual way of Christ and not in the human way of Adam, we must carefully consider how the birth of Christ took place. It occurred, as already noted, in faith and through the working of the Holy Spirit.[2] Whoever wishes to have Christ's nature and character must also be born of God.[3] That person must, with Christ, be God's child.[4] This is what Peter says with the words, "You have been born anew, not of mortal but of immortal seed, and this seed is the word of truth."[5]

Here is how this birth takes place. If the Word is heard and believed, then faith is sealed with the power of God, with his Holy Spirit.[6] The Spirit immediately renews the person[7] after that person has been dead in sin,[8] restoring to life the one who stands before God in righteousness. That person has been made into a new creature,[9] a new person after God's likeness,[10] and has become renewed in this likeness.[11] Whoever is born in this way should receive baptism as a bath of rebirth.[12] This signifies being inscribed in the covenant of the grace and knowledge of God.[13]

As Abraham was commanded to circumcise in his house,[14] so Christ was to baptize in his house, as the words that he spoke to John the Baptist indicate: "Let it be so now, for it is fitting for us to fulfill all of God's righteousness."[15] Abraham could not circumcise a child in his house until the child was born to him, nor could his descendants after him. In the same way, no one can be baptized in the house of Christ unless that person is first born of Christ through the Word and faith.[16] Whoever is born in this manner is baptized upon confession of faith.[17]

History has shown us that all the apostles did the same, and we follow them.

The Manner of Baptizing, or How One Baptizes

For baptism to take place, there must be at least two persons: the one who baptizes, and the one who is baptized. The baptizer first calls a person to repentance and points out that person's sin. Then the bap-

---

[1] Rom. 9:8. [2] Luke 1:26-38. [3] 1 Pet. 1:3-5. [4] Rom. 8:14-16. [5] 1 Pet. 1:23. [6] Eph. 1:12-14. [7] Rom. 12:2. [8] Eph. 2:1-10. [9] 2 Cor. 5:17. [10] Gen. 1:27. [11] Eph. 4:20-32; Col. 3:1-11. [12] Titus 3:1-7. [13] Jer. 31:33-34. [14] Gen. 17:10-11. [15] Matt. 3:13-15. [16] 1 Pet. 1:1-5. [17] Acts 8:35-38.

tizer shows how the sinner may come to God, find grace with him,[1] and discover how baptism is a bond with God.[2] In this way the person becomes convinced of the benefit of baptism and is moved to desire it. This desire and request are a prerequisite for baptism.

After a person has made this request, the baptizer asks the baptismal candidates if they believe in God the Father, the Son, and the Holy Spirit.[3] Whoever is to be baptized must confess their faith. Further, the baptizer asks each candidate whether they reject the world, sin, and the devil, since these must be rejected.[4] Do they want to yield themselves to God with all their heart, soul, and body,[5] henceforth to live no more for self but for God and his church, and to allow God alone to rule over and to use their entire body?[6]

If this is their wish, the baptizer asks those requesting baptism whether they are certain and assured in their heart that this is the truth, and that Christ is the only way to life. If they likewise make this confession, the baptizer asks if it is their wish to bind themselves to God and be baptized.[7] After affirming that wish, the persons requesting baptism are told to humble themselves on their knees before God and the church.

The baptizer and the congregation kneel with the baptismal candidates to ask God's forgiveness for their sins. Then the baptizer takes pure water and pours it over each one ready for baptism, saying, "I baptize you in the name of the Father, the Son, and the Holy Spirit.[8] In accordance with your faith, God has forgiven your sins and drawn you into his kingdom.[9] Henceforth, sin no more, that nothing worse may happen to you."[10]

Since in baptism a person's sins are left behind and forgiven,[11] and the church has the key, baptism should take place before the church.[12] However, if it is not possible to reach the church, the baptizer may do it alone.[13]

Who May Teach and Baptize

Not everyone may take on the office of teaching and baptizing. As James declares, "Dear brothers, not many should presume to be teachers, for we all sin frequently, and we who teach will be judged

---

[1] Matt. 3:1-10; 4:17; Mark 1:1-8; Luke 3:1-9; Acts 2:36-40; 3:12-21; 8:14-38. [2] 1 Pet. 3:18-22; Acts 3:17-26. [3] Acts 8:37. [4] Matt. 10:34-39; 16:24-25; Mark 8:31-35; Luke 14:25-33. [5] Rom. 6:12-13. [6] Rom. 14:7-8. [7] 1 Pet. 3:21. [8] Matt. 28:19. [9] Luke 7:39-50; Col. 1:9-14. [10] John 5:14. [11] Acts 2:38. [12] Matt. 18:15-18. [13] Acts 8:29-38.

more strictly."[1] No one should accept such authority unless that person is chosen in an orderly and correct manner by God in the church community.[2] The apostle says to the Hebrews, "Let no one take this honor upon himself, unless chosen by God, as Aaron was. Christ also did not take on himself the glory of being made a high priest."[3] Likewise, his ministers should not put themselves to the fore but wait until God selects them.

Elections

If the church needs one or more ministers, the members must not elect to please themselves but must wait on the Lord to see whom he chooses and indicates.[4] The believers should pray earnestly, asking God to care for them, to answer their need, and to show them whom he has chosen for his ministry. After members continue earnestly in prayer, those recognized through God's counsel to be suitable are presented to the church. If there are many, we wait to see by the use of the lot whom the Lord has chosen.[5] If, however, there is only one or just as many as are needed, we need no lot, for the Lord has shown him or them to us. Therefore, we accept him or them in the fear of God, as a gift from him. Appointment to the service is later confirmed before the church through the laying on of the elders' hands.[6]

However, no one is confirmed in his service unless he has first been tested and revealed to the church. He must have the reputation of leading a good life,[7] so that he cannot become a victim of slanderers. Many people ask, "Who chose the first leader?" We answer, "God did." In the Old Testament, when Israel had turned away from him, God repeatedly showed his grace by giving them a savior out of their midst, one who again set them on the right way, that he might prove that he was Israel's God.[8]

Now he has done this anew, since people have turned away from God, have estranged themselves from God, and have departed and forsaken him. For the sake of those remaining, God has not withdrawn his mercy. Instead, when the time had come, he again wished to have compassion on us so that the slanderers would have less cause. Thus, God placed his Word in the mouth of the person who had held

---

[1] James 3:1-2. [2] Acts 13:1-3. [3] Heb. 5:4-5. [4] Acts 13:1-3. [5] Acts 1:21-26.
[6] Acts 6:1-6; 1 Tim. 4:14; 2 Tim. 1:6. [7] 1 Tim. 3:2-10. [8] Judg. 2:16-18.

the position of preacher among people who professed to be Christians, but whose lives were not in keeping with their words, in order to bring them back. God himself gave witness to the Word in the power of its effect.[1] Through this, our ears have been opened to hear the Word, and God himself has made it fruitful in us, to his praise.

Differences in the Offices

In the church, Paul says, God has first appointed apostles.[2] These are the ones who are sent out by God and his church in accordance with the command of the gospel, to go throughout the country and establish the obedience of faith for his name's sake.[3] This they do by teaching and baptizing.[4]

Second, there are bishops and shepherds,[5] who have the same office of teaching and baptizing as the apostles, except that they remain in one place and care for the church of Christ. Then there are helpers, who serve alongside the shepherds, exhorting the people to remain true to the teaching they have received.[6] There are also rulers, who direct each person, whether in the home or in the church, so that everything is done correctly and well.[7] This is done so that the church will be cared for with timely assistance. These people are simply called servants of those needs.[8]

Finally, there are elders, who serve in the church wherever and however need requires. They work with the servants to consider diligently the needs of the church community and to promote its well-being. In this way they help the servants bear the burden so that the whole church does not need to be concerned with every small matter.[9]

Concerning Abuse of the Lord's Supper

Through Christ, God has appointed a right order in everything, for people's benefit, improvement, comfort, and blessedness. The enemy has, however, twisted and contorted all things to bring harm and destruction to people.[10] The Lord's Supper[11] was given to us as a comfort and to remind us of God's grace, but the enemy has distorted it in

---

[1] Jer. 1:9; Luke 21:14-15. [2] 1 Cor. 12:28; Eph. 4:11-14. [3] Rom. 1:1-5; 16:25-27. [4] Matt. 28:16-20; Mark 16:14-16. [5] 1 Tim. 3:1-7; Titus 1:5-9. [6] 1 Cor. 12:4-8. [7] Rom. 12:4-8; 1 Cor. 12:1-11; 14:40. [8] Acts 6:2-6; 1 Tim. 3:8-10; Titus 1:5-9. [9] Acts 15:2-6. [10] Sir. 39:20-32. [11] Matt. 26:17-29; Mark 14:12-31; Luke 22:14-30; 1 Cor. 11:20-29.

such a way that it brings about death. What greater harm is there than turning away from the right observance of this meal toward idolatry, that greatest of abominations![1] That is what the children of Israel did in misusing their silver and gold for making a calf, to their own great dishonor and shame. These ornaments had been given them for their use, adornment, and honor. But they said, "These are our gods that have led us out of Egypt." In that way they stole the honor from God and gave it to a graven image made with their own hands.[2]

People today do the same with bread. They reject the usage as instituted by Christ, in which the meal becomes a comfort.[3] They make something idolatrous out of it, which is an abomination to our God. It is idolatry to honor as God that which is not God, and to look for him where he is not.[4] "God does not live in temples made by human hands." These words are a proof that he is not in the bread, because bread is always made by human hands.[5] Therefore, God is not in the bread.

To this some reply, "That is said of the Father, who does not live in temples made with human hands. But the Son, during his sojourn on earth, entered and lived in temples made with human hands,[6] and we are speaking of him."[7] However, we point out that this reference is to God, who never dwelt in houses and never will. Christ, however, during his incarnation, lived in such dwellings.[8] This fact, as well as his whole life, proved that he was human.[9] Insofar as he was a human, he was not found in more than one place at one time.[10] His whole life shows that he was not everywhere at the same time, as the apostle testifies: "He was found in form and habit as a person,"[11] except that he was without sin."[12] Humans are not present everywhere at the same time. Now, since nothing save sin was excepted, being present everywhere was not excepted.

Furthermore, they say, "That was true during his lifetime, but now that Christ is transfigured, he is present everywhere." We answer that when he held the Last Supper with his disciples, he had not been transfigured,[13] and therefore he was not everywhere.[14] Since he

---

[1] Deut. 32:15-22. [2] Exod. 32:1-6. [3] Matt. 26:19-29; Mark 14:22-25; Luke 22:14-30; 1 Cor. 11:20-26. [4] Exod. 20:4-6; Bar. 4:6-7. [5] 1 Kings 8:27; Isa. 66:1; Acts 7:48-49; 17:24-25. [6] Luke 2:42-46. [7] Acts 7:48-50. [8] Mark 2:1-2; *incarnation* means Christ fully human, in the flesh. [9] Phil. 2:5-8; Heb. 5:5-9. [10] Mark 1:35-37. [11] Phil. 2:5-8. [12] Heb. 4:15. [13] Matt. 26:26-29; Mark 14:22-25. [14] John 17:24-26.

was not everywhere before the transfiguration, he was not present in every individual piece of bread. Since he was not in the bread at that time when he himself said the words, "This is my body,"[1] why do people want to use the same words now to bewitch Christ into bread and thus invent a god?

The human form which Christ took upon himself was not present everywhere at once either before or after he was glorified; he remains in his place beside the Father. This is proved by Christ's words, "You always have the poor with you, but you will not always have me."[2] From this it is clear enough that the person Jesus Christ is not in more than one place. Although the divine nature of Christ is universal and everywhere, it does not follow that he wants to be taken and eaten in bread as if he were a god.

However, we do truly confess that God, or the Deity, reaches into all created things, into each according to its nature: into wood as wood; into bread as bread; into humans, whom he has especially made to be a dwelling for himself,[3] as humans. Then why do some seek him in bread, other than the way just mentioned, or in this bread rather than in any other bread? It is only deception, and it leads away from God.

Second, if out of the bread they have made an idol, or as they say, a Christ, they want to sacrifice him again to the Father. This is contrary to the word from Hebrews which says that Christ with one sacrifice has accomplished everything.[4] Thus, they are worse than the [Jewish leaders] who crucified him once, whereby he sacrificed himself to the Father.[5] These people, however, sacrifice him often and must sacrifice him often. In fact, they never cease to crucify him, for which they ought truly to be ashamed, since they dare to call themselves by his name.

Third, Judas sold him once,[6] but these people sell him repeatedly, and thus treat him in a worse manner than Judas did. They have turned the Lord's Supper into a moneymaking business, snatching money as a bird-catcher snatches birds. Thus they have amassed much property and gained many adherents. But now let us leave the many other abuses and consider the right observance of the Lord's Supper.

---

[1] Luke 22:19. [2] Matt. 26:11; Mark 14:6-7; John 12:7-8. [3] 1 Cor. 3:16; 6:19; 2 Cor. 6:16-18. [4] Heb. 10:8-14. [5] Heb. 9:14. [6] Matt. 26:47-50; Mark 14:43-46; Luke 22:47-48; John 13:27-30.

The Lord's Supper

The Lord Christ, the Savior of the world,[1] was sent by the Father so that those who believe in his name might have eternal life,[2] be renewed after the divine likeness,[3] and be grafted into his nature.[4] Christ has gained access for us to his Father and his Father's grace by means of his own death for us,[5] who should bear a resemblance to his death. Therefore, wishing to return to the Father from whom he had come,[6] Christ wanted to show this grace to the disciples, whom he had chosen from the world. His purpose was that, after he had gone from them, they might remember his grace and know for what purpose they had been chosen and accepted by God.[7] Then they would not need to be without hope like the rest, who know nothing of God.[8]

Therefore, he took a loaf of bread, thanked his Father, broke it, and gave it to his disciples, saying, "Take this and eat it; it is my body, which is broken for you. Whenever you eat it, do it in remembrance of me." He took the cup in the same way and said, "All of you drink from this.[9] It is the new covenant in my blood, which is shed for you for the forgiveness of sins. When you drink it, do so in remembrance of me."[10]

In taking the bread and giving it to his disciples, Christ wanted to demonstrate the fellowship of his body and to show his disciples that they had become one body, one living organism, and one nature with him.[11] Paul interprets it as follows: "We who are many, all partaking of the same bread, are one loaf and one body."[12] In saying this, however, Christ did not give them his body to eat, his flesh and blood,[13] as the deceiver has twisted the Lord's Supper and made it into idolatry. But as we have said, Christ taught his disciples that they were members of his body. As the bread is made into a loaf by bringing together many grains,[14] so we, many human beings who were scattered and divided and of differing opinions and purposes, are led by faith to be united. We have become one plant, one living organism[15] and body of Christ,[16] holding to him in one Spirit.[17]

The Lord portrayed it to them more clearly in still another para-

---

[1] Isa. 62:11; John 4:42.   [2] John 6:29-40; 20:30-31.   [3] Eph. 4:20-24; Col. 3:1-10.
[4] 2 Pet. 1:2-4.   [5] Eph. 2:17-22.   [6] John 14:1-3.   [7] John 15:1-11; to bear much fruit.
[8] 1 Thess. 4:13.   [9] Matt. 26:26-29; Mark 14:22-25; Luke 22:14-20; 1 Cor. 11:23-26.
[10] Luke 22:20.   [11] John 15:1-9.   [12] 1 Cor. 10:17.   [13] John 6:29-37.   [14] Rom. 12:4-5;
1 Cor. 12:12-13.   [15] Rom. 11:17-24.   [16] 1 Cor. 6:15-20.   [17] Rom. 12:1-3; Phil. 2:1-5.

ble, in which he said, "I am the vine, you are the branches."[1] Here he shows once more, distinctly and clearly, that his disciples are one plant, one organism, one substance, and one body with him. Therefore, it is clear enough that this alone is Christ's meaning.

In breaking the loaf for them and directing them to eat,[2] Christ shows that they must bear the likeness of his death and be ready to die like him, if they would have a share in his grace and become heirs of God. As Paul says, "We are heirs of God and joint heirs with Christ, if only we suffer with him, so that we may be raised to glory with him."[3]

This is the right interpretation and truly what Christ means, as proved by his own words in the Gospel of Luke: "This is the new covenant in my blood that is shed for you."[4] Here he does not say, "This is my blood. Drink of it." Instead, he says, "This is the new covenant." So, what is the new covenant? Is it eating the body of Christ and drinking his blood? On the contrary! Let someone show us a single word where that is promised! Oh, what great folly, not even wanting to see and know! God has indeed promised a new covenant, not of the body or of eating flesh and blood, but of the knowledge of God. The Word says, "This shall be the covenant that I will make with them. I will set my law within them and write it on their hearts, and all of them shall know me."[5] Through this knowledge, a person is led to God,[6] is grafted into him, and becomes a fellow member of his nature and essence.[7] By this knowledge also we are led into the one mind and will of Christ.[8]

He gives them wine, made from many grapes that have become one drink, with the words, "This is the new covenant in my blood."[9] It is as though he would say, "The new covenant is ratified and confirmed by my blood. I have led you into such a covenant of grace, making you partakers of it,[10] so that you now have become one loaf of bread and one body with me through faith.[11] Henceforth, led by one Spirit, you may walk in one mind and have one purpose,[12] in order to prove that you are my disciples."[13]

This meal, this sharing in the bread and wine of the Lord, is therefore a sign of the fellowship of Christ's body. All the members, in taking part, declare themselves with all the others to be of one

---

[1] John 15:1-8. [2] Matt. 26:26; Luke 22:19. [3] Rom. 8:16-17. [4] Luke 22:20. [5] Jer. 31:33; Heb. 8:10. [6] Wisd. of Sol. 7:17-28. [7] 2 Pet. 1:2-4. [8] Rom. 12:1-2; 1 Cor. 2:16. [9] Luke 22:20. [10] Heb. 9:14-15. [11] 1 Cor. 10:16-17. [12] Acts 2:42-47; 4:32. [13] John 13:35.

mind, one heart, and one spirit with Christ.[1] That is why Paul says, "Examine yourself before eating this bread and drinking from this cup, for all who eat and drink unworthily, eat and drink judgment upon themselves."[2] In effect, he says, "Examine yourselves well, and only then consider if you truly share in Christ's grace[3] and are a true member of Christ as you declare yourself to be. If you are not, in partaking of the meal, you bring judgment upon yourself."[4]

---

[1] 1 Cor. 10:16-31. [2] 1 Cor. 11:28-32. [3] John 14; 16:13-20. [4] 1 Cor. 6:12-20; 10:10-24.

The Christian Way of Life

Community of Goods

All believers have fellowship in holy things, that is, in God.[1] He has given them all things in his Son, Christ Jesus.[2] Just as Christ has nothing for himself, since all he has is for us, so too, no members of Christ's body should possess any gift for themselves or for their own sake. Instead, all should be consecrated for the whole body, for all the members.[3] This is so because Christ also did not bring his gifts for one individual or the other, but for everyone, for the whole body.

Community of goods applies to both spiritual and material gifts. All of God's gifts, not only the spiritual but also the temporal, have been given so that they not be kept but be shared with each other. Therefore, the fellowship of believers should be visible not only in spiritual but also in temporal things.[4] Paul says one person should not have an abundance while another suffers want; instead, there should be equality.[5] This he shows by pointing to the law about manna. According to that rule, the one who gathered much had nothing extra, and the one who gathered little had no lack, since each was given the amount needed.[6]

Furthermore, the Creation still testifies today that at the beginning God ordained that people should own nothing individually but should have all things in common with each other.[7] However, by taking what they should have left, and by leaving what they should have taken,[8] people have gained possession of things and have become more accustomed to accumulating things and hardened in doing so. Through such appropriating and collecting of created things, people have been led so far from God that they have forgotten the Creator.[9] They have even raised up and honored as gods the created things

---

[1] 1 John 1:1-3.   [2] Rom. 1:16-17.   [3] Phil. 2:1-8; 1 Cor. 12:12-27.   [4] Acts 2:42-47; 4:32-37.   [5] 2 Cor. 8:7-15.   [6] Exod. 16:16-18.   [7] Gen. 1:26-29.   [8] Gen. 3:2-12.   [9] Rom. 1:18-25.

which had been made subject to them.[1] That is still the case for those who depart from God's order and forsake what God has ordained.

Now as has been said, however, created things which are too high for people to grasp and collect, such as the sun, the whole course of the heavens, day, air, and so forth, show that not only they, but also all other created things, were made common for all people.[2] Because they are too great to be brought under human control, they have remained common, and humans have not possessed them. Otherwise, since people had become so evil through wrongful acquisitions, they would also have wrongfully taken possession of such things and made them their own.[3]

It is therefore true that the rest is likewise not made by God for anyone's private possession. This is shown in that people must forsake all other created things as well as the high things when they die, and carry nothing with them as their own.[4] For this reason Christ counts all temporal things as alien to people's true nature and says, "If you have not been faithful with other people's property, who will entrust you with property of your own?"[5]

Because what is temporal is not ours but is alien to our true nature, the law commands that no one should covet someone else's possessions,[6] that is, set his heart upon them or claim them as his own.[7] Therefore, whoever will adhere unwaveringly to Christ and follow him must give up acquiring things and holding property.[8] Christ himself says, "None of you can become my disciple if you do not give up all your possessions."[9] Whoever is to be renewed into the likeness of God must abandon what leads away from God, that is, grasping and collecting material possessions. Otherwise, God's likeness cannot be attained.[10] That is why Christ says, "Whoever does not receive the kingdom of God as a little child shall not enter it."[11] Christ also says, "Unless you overcome yourselves and become as little children, you shall not enter the kingdom of heaven."[12]

Whoever has become free from created things can then grasp what is true and divine. When the true and the divine become one's treasure, the heart turns toward that treasure, emptying itself from everything else[13] and regarding nothing any longer as its own but as be-

---

[1] Wisd. of Sol. 13:1-3; 15:14-19.   [2] Gen. 1:25-31.   [3] Gen. 3:2-6; 2 Esd. 3:4-7; 7:12-15; Rom. 5:12-14.   [4] 1 Tim. 6:6-9.   [5] Luke 16:9-13.   [6] Exod. 20:17; Deut. 5:21.   [7] Luke 16:11-12.   [8] Matt. 10:37-39; Mark 8:34-38; Luke 9:23-26.   [9] Luke 14:33.   [10] Eph. 4:20-32; Col. 3:1-11.   [11] Mark 10:15; Luke 18:17.   [12] Matt. 18:1-4.   [13] Luke 12:33-40.

longing to all God's children.[1] Therefore, we say that as all believers share spiritual gifts,[2] still more should they express this in material things and not covet or claim them for themselves, for they are not their own.[3] They will honor God, show that they partake in the fellowship of Christ,[4] and be renewed into God's likeness.[5] The more a person is attached to property and claims ownership of things, the further away he is from the fellowship of Christ and from being in the image of God.[6]

For this reason, when the church came into being, the Holy Spirit reestablished such community in a wonderful way. "No one said any of the things they possessed were their own, but they had all things in common."[7] This admonition by the Spirit is true for us even today. In the words of Paul, "Let each one look not to your own interests but to the interests of others." In other words, "Let each one look not to what benefits yourself, but to what benefits many."[8] Where this is not the case, it is a blemish upon the church that should truly be corrected. Someone may say that this only applies to what took place in Jerusalem and therefore does not apply today. In reply, we say that even if it did only happen in Jerusalem,[9] it does not follow that it should not happen now. The apostles and the churches were not at fault, but the opportunity, the right means, and the right time were lacking.

This, therefore, should never be a reason for us to hesitate. Instead, it should move us to greater and better effort, for the Lord now gives us both the time and the occasion. It was not the fault of either the apostles or the churches, as is shown by the ardent efforts of both. The apostles directed people to the church with great diligence and spared no pains to teach them true surrender, as all their epistles still prove today.[10]

The people, especially those from Macedonia, obeyed with all their hearts, as Paul bears witness, saying, "I want to tell you of the grace given to the churches in Macedonia. Their joy was most abundant since they had been confirmed through much suffering, and their poverty, though it was great indeed, overflowed as riches in simplicity. I can testify that they voluntarily gave according to their means and beyond their means. They begged us earnestly and insistently to allow them to share in the support of other believers. In this

---

[1] Acts 2:44-45; 4:32-37. [2] 1 John 1:3. [3] Luke 16:11-13. [4] 1 Cor. 10:16. [5] Eph. 4:22-24; Col. 3:1-10. [6] Gen. 1:25-27. [7] Acts 2:44-45; 4:32-37. [8] Phil. 2:2-4. [9] Acts 2:38-45; 4:32-37. [10] Phil. 2:1-11; Rom. 14:7-8.

they exceeded our hopes, giving themselves first to the Lord and then also to us, by the will of God."[1]

On the basis of this, we can recognize that the churches favorably inclined their hearts to practice community and were willing and ready to do so, not only in spiritual but also in material things. They wished to follow Christ their Master, become like him, and be of one mind with him.[2] He went before us in this way and commanded us to follow him.[3]

Separation from the World

Through Christ, God has chosen for himself a people to be his own.[4] He has bestowed his Spirit on them that they might be of his nature and character, no longer carnal but spiritual.[5] It is as Paul says, "You are no longer in the flesh; you are in the Spirit, if the Spirit of God dwells in you. Anyone who does not have the Spirit of Christ does not belong to him."[6] Therefore, the church of Christ is not of the flesh but of the spirit, and there is no church of Christ except the gathering of those whom the Holy Spirit brings together, directs, and teaches. Those who surrender themselves to be ruled by the Spirit yield themselves to the church of Christ,[7] in which the Holy Spirit works.[8] But those who give in to serving sin and being ruled by it cut themselves off from the church of Christ and become estranged from it. Once they have left the church, they sink further and further into ruin.[9]

For this reason we on no account admit that we have cut ourselves off from the true church of Christ. On the contrary, we have drawn near to the church and yielded ourselves to it, so that Christ, who works in the church, may also work in us, and we through this may be assured of being God's children.[10] We belong to the community of the church of Christ, the fellowship of the children of God, where there are no longer slaves,[11] but all are children through faith in Jesus Christ.[12]

We have to say that it is not we but all baptizers of infants who have forsaken the church and the community of Christ and have cut

---

[1] 2 Cor. 8:1-5. [2] Phil. 2:5-8. [3] Matt. 10:22-25; Luke 14:33. [4] 1 Pet. 2:9-10.
[5] Acts 2:1-12. [6] Rom. 8:9. [7] Rom. 6:8-18. [8] Joel 2:27-29. [9] Isa. 1:1-9; Ps. 1:4-6.
[10] Rom. 8:10-17. [11] Gal. 4:1-7. [12] Gal. 3:21-26.

themselves off from it. They have fallen away and have become so corrupt that they do not recognize what the true church of Christ is, and how the church proves itself to be the church of Christ. If on points that out to them, they answer, "The saints, who had the Holy Spirit, did that, but we are unable to do so."[1] They do not know that the church of Christ is a house of the Holy Spirit, and that no one belongs to it who does not have this Spirit.[2] As Paul says, "Whoever does not have the Spirit of Christ, does not belong to Christ."[3]

God has chosen this church for himself and has separated the members from all peoples, so that they might serve him[4] with one mind and heart[5] and through the one childlike Spirit. Therefore, as has been said, no slaves are to be found in the church, but only children.[6] Thus, the church has not separated itself; instead, God has separated it from all other peoples.[7] That is also the reason why, as a sign of the covenant, he has given the church baptism, with which all who surrender themselves to God are received into the church.[8]

However, because of our many sins, God allowed us all to drift away. We all turned from good to evil,[9] and twisted the order of the church into evil, and abused it, so that we all walked in darkness. This continued until God, who does not want the death of the sinner,[10] had mercy on us. Once more he let the true light of his grace shine and brought his truth to light. The wise teacher teaches us, "My child, do not neglect to turn back to the Lord, and do not put it off from one day to the next."[11] Accordingly, we have hastened to turn back to the Lord, to keep the ordinances which we had forsaken, and to thank God, who has accepted us.

We have turned toward the church of Christ, not away from it. We have left the gatherings of profane and impure people, and we wish that everyone would do the same.[12] That is why we call everyone to repentance[13] and tell whoever is willing to hear, not to harden their hearts[14] and thus bring the wrath of God upon themselves.[15] If some will not repent and will not keep the true ordinances of God, but remain in sin, we must let them go their way and leave them to God.

---

[1] Acts 6:2-8; 7:55-60.   [2] 1 Cor. 6:13-20; 2 Cor. 6:14-18.   [3] Rom. 8:1-9.   [4] John 4:21-24.   [5] Acts 2:42-47.   [6] Gal. 4:1-7.   [7] John 15:19.   [8] Matt. 28:19-20; Mark 16:15-16.   [9] Rom. 3:9-12.   [10] Ezek. 18:32; 33:11.   [11] Sir. 5:7.   [12] 2 Cor. 5:16-17.   [13] Acts 17:29-31.   [14] Heb. 3:10-15; 4:6-7.   [15] Ps. 2:1-6.

About Temples and Why We Do Not Attend Them

God the Lord has built a temple for himself. This temple is his church, in which he wants to be honored. He does not wish to plant the memory of his name in any other place, because the outer ceremonies have been brought to an end. In Christ Jesus the real and true service of God has begun. It takes place through the one and only Spirit.[1] Therefore, everything else that takes place through human choice is no service of God, however much it may give that impression. There is no divine service except in the true church of Christ, the church without spot or blemish,[2] the church sanctified by Christ himself. The gathering in temples, however, is a rabble and a gathering of prostitutes, adulterers, and all unclean spirits, which God hates. In such temples there is no divine service[3] but, on the contrary, blasphemy and contempt of the Almighty.[4] This has persuaded us to flee from their gathering and avoid it.[5]

The buildings of stone and wood originated, as the history of several of them shows, at a time when this country was forced by the sword to make a verbal confession of the Christian faith. Temples which had been dedicated to their gods were then transformed into churches (as they were wrongly named) for the Christians. Thus, the buildings originated through the instigation of the devil and were built up through sacrifice to devils. Paul says, "What the heathen sacrifice, they offer to demons and not to God, and I do not want you to be in fellowship with demons."[6] That is not God's will either, for Christ has nothing in common with Belial.[7] In the Old Testament too, God commanded that such places should be utterly destroyed so that Israel might not share in pagan fellowship. He does not command that these places be changed and used properly, but that they be broken down completely.[8]

At that time the people failed to do this and left the root in the ground.[9] Thus not only failed to convert heathen practices to right ones, but they also deserted the right usage and began to indulge in all kinds of idolatry. Today things are changed so much that what the heathen of old called "gods" are now called "saints." Because the root was left in the ground, they have gone farther and built one house

---

[1] 1 Cor. 6:12-20; 2 Cor. 6:14-18; John 4:19-24. [2] Eph. 5:25-30. [3] Rom. 1:24-32.
[4] Ps. 36:1-5. [5] Prov. 1:10-16. [6] 1 Cor. 10:20. [7] 2 Cor. 6:15. [8] Exod. 34:8-16; Num. 33:50-52; Deut. 7:25-26; 12:1-3. [9] Judg. 2:1-3.

after another for their gods, or "saints," as they call them, and filled them with their idols.[1] With this they show that they are their fathers' children and have not left their company.[2]

We know that God hated such places since their beginning,[3] and still hates them. No true service of God is found there. On the contrary, God is continually dishonored and despised.[4] Therefore, we also avoid them and flee from them so we will not share their fellowship and again fall away from the truth we have recognized. Otherwise, God would turn from us as he turned from Israel.[5] At the same time, if our path leads us through such a church building, we are not defiled before God by passing through. But to take part in such fellowship, or to listen, or to learn anything there—that is what Paul means: "I do not want you to be in fellowship with demons."[6]

Why We Do Not Associate with Priests

Priests have taken upon themselves the office of proclaiming the gospel, yet they teach only the literal word and the law. They do not have God's strength, namely, the Holy Spirit, which makes a person worthy of such an office.[7] Therefore, we cannot listen to their voice, for it is the voice of strangers and not of those sent by God,[8] who himself says, "My sheep do not hear the voice of strangers."[9] All mere words are now alien, because the gospel has come. Paul says, "The Lord is the Spirit, and where the Spirit of the Lord is, there is freedom. Now the glory of the Lord is reflected in all of us from our uncovered faces, and we are being transformed into his likeness with ever-increasing glory. All this comes from the Lord, who is the Spirit."[10]

That priests do not have the Spirit of the Lord is shown by their drunkenness, greed, vanity, pride, swearing, and all kinds of unchastity.[11] In the book of Wisdom, we read, "The Holy Spirit dislikes those who have only the outer appearance of wisdom and righteousness. He withdraws from those whose thoughts are without understanding, or when evil takes the upper hand."[12] Because these things are found in them, priests cannot preach the word of the gospel.

---

[1] Deut. 32:15-17.   [2] Matt. 23:29-33.   [3] Num. 33:50-52.   [4] Ps. 36:1-5.   [5] Jer. 7:1-12; Amos 5:1-9; Acts 7:7.   [6] 1 Cor. 10:20.   [7] 2 Cor. 1:8-12.   [8] Jer. 23:21-32.   [9] John 10:4-5.   [10] 2 Cor. 3:17-18.   [11] Gal. 5:16-21.   [12] Wisd. of Sol. 1:5.

The gospel is proclaimed in the strength of the Spirit,[1] as Scripture tells us: "The Spirit of the Lord is upon me, because he has anointed me and sent me to preach the gospel."[2]

How priests act also shows that they do not preach the word of the gospel, but only the literal word. They put people under pressure to hear their teaching by means of stocks, imprisonment in dungeons, torture, banishment, and death. If they were servants of the Spirit, they would have the strength and working of the Spirit within themselves,[3] which would tell them that such action would make them slaves, not children. Therefore, they establish only a servile congregation, and slavery has nothing to do with Christ.

"You are no longer slaves, but all are children," says Paul.[4] The free Spirit produces childlikeness through his own work and inspiration in people[5] and not through the bullying by the priests and by those who follow them. Because the priests do not have the nature and order of the Spirit, which belong to the teaching of Christ, they show that they are not servants of the Spirit but of the letter.

The service of the new covenant is not one of the letter but of the Spirit, performed in the strength of the Spirit of Christ. Speaking of this service, Paul says, "Our ability and competence is from God, who has sent us and made us capable of being servants of the new covenant; not of the letter, but of the Spirit. The letter kills, but the Spirit gives life."[6] All who dare to preach the gospel in any way except in the strength of Christ's Spirit, and who come and run before Christ, are thieves and murderers. Thus Christ said, "All who come before me only to slay, to steal, and to destroy are thieves and murderers. Therefore, command Christ's flock not to listen to them."[7]

Since the teaching of Christ is not of the letter but of the Spirit,[8] it cannot be taught by those who are carnally minded. That is why John says, "Do not receive into your home or welcome anyone who comes to you and does not bring these teachings of Christ. If you welcome such persons, you participate in their sins."[9] This is why we do not receive priests into our homes nor associate with them. We buy nothing from them and sell nothing to them when they demand it, not even food or drink. Nor do we work in any business connection with them, so that we do not participate in their sins.[10]

---

[1] 2 Cor. 3:3-6. [2] Isa. 61:1-2; Luke 4:14-19. [3] Luke 9:49-56. [4] Gal. 4:7. [5] Rom. 8:14-17. [6] 2 Cor. 3:4-6. [7] John 10:8. [8] 2 Cor. 3:4-6. [9] 2 John 1:6-11. [10] 1 Tim. 5:22.

Marriage

Marriage is a union of two in which each one undertakes to care for the other, and the second agrees to obey the first. Through their agreement, two become one; they are no longer two but one. If this is to be a godly union, the two must come together in accordance with God's will and order, not through their own action and choice. That means that neither shall forsake the other, but together they shall endure good and bad times as long as they live.[1]

Marriage consists of three stages or levels. First is the union of God with the soul or spirit,[2] then that of the spirit with the body,[3] and third that of one person with another, that is, a man with a woman. [4] This is not the first but the last and lowest level. It is recognizable and understandable by all and therefore serves as a picture to teach and to demonstrate the invisible or higher levels.[5] As the man is head of the woman,[6] so the spirit is head of the body, and God is head of the spirit.

Through this we see how marriage instructs us and leads us to God, for if we regard it rightly, it teaches us to know God and to cling to him. However, where marriage is not seen in the right way, it leads people away from God and brings about death. Since there are few who perceive it correctly and many who perceive and observe it incorrectly, Paul says it is good for a man not to touch a woman, in case he is swept away in his ignorance to his own ruin.[7] So we will speak of marriage insofar as God enables us.

Since woman was taken from man and not man from woman,[8] man has the lordship and woman has weakness, humility, and submission.[9] Therefore, she should be under the yoke of her husband and obedient to him.[10] This was commanded by God, who said to her, "Your husband shall be your lord."[11] Therefore, a woman should look up to her husband, seek his counsel, and do nothing without it. When she fails to do this, she rejects her God-given place in the order of Creation and encroaches upon the lordship of her husband. She also turns her back on the commands of the Creator and on the promise of submission she gave her husband when they were united in marriage, which is to honor her husband as a wife should.[12]

The man, on the other hand, as one in whom something of God's glory is seen, should have compassion on the woman as the weaker in-

---

[1] Gen. 2:21; Matt. 19:3-8; Mark 10:2-9; 1 Cor. 6:16; 7:10; Eph. 5:28-32. [2] 1 Cor. 6:17. [3] Gen. 2:7. [4] Mal. 2:10-16. [5] Eph. 5:23-30. [6] 1 Cor. 11:3. [7] 1 Cor. 7:1-8. [8] Gen. 2:22; 1 Cor. 11:3-8. [9] 1 Pet. 3:1-6. [10] Rom. 7:2-3. [11] Gen. 3:16. [12] 1 Cor. 11:7-9.

strument.[1] He should go before her in love and kindness and care for her not only in temporal but still more in spiritual things. He should faithfully share with her all he has been given by God. He should go before her in honesty, courage, and all Christian virtues, so that in him she may have a mirror of righteousness, an invitation to piety, and a guide who will lead her to God.[2] Where the husband does not do this, or does it carelessly and superficially, he turns his back on the glory that was given him by God and on God's order.[3]

To both, the man and the woman, is ordained what belongs to each one, because it is God's will to lead us into deeper knowledge and understanding. Even as the man should accept and love the woman, should care for her, and rule over her, so the spirit desires to provide and rule over the body, and God over the spirit.[4] Again, as the woman should obey the man,[5] so also what is earthly should obey what is heavenly, namely, the spirit. A person's actions should not be determined by what is earthly and of the flesh, but rather by the counsel of what is heavenly, and be ruled by that.[6] The heavenly body, namely, the human spirit, however, should look to the One from whom it has come[7] and allow itself to be governed and led by God alone.[8] When this takes place, the marriage is observed rightly in all three levels and remains close to God.

Marriage must not come about through the will of the flesh, or for the sake of beauty, youth, money, possessions, or any other earthly thing. That is not of God but comes from the devil. The angel says to Tobias, "Hear what I say, and I shall tell you who they are who are ruled by the devil, namely, those who marry with no heed for God in their heart but only to satisfy the lust of the body, like a mule or horse that knows no better. Over such people the devil prevails indeed."[9] Thus we see that a marriage contracted out of physical desire will end in ruin.

It is clear, then, that such a thing should not take place. One should not choose according to the flesh but wait for this gift to come from God.[10] One should pray earnestly to God to send, in accordance with his divine will, the partner he has provided, for such a one will be a help toward life and salvation.[11] After praying, one should ask one's parents and not one's own flesh, that through them God might reveal

---

[1] Eph. 5:22-23; 1 Pet. 3:1-7. [2] 1 Tim. 3:1-4. [3] Gen. 3:17-19. [4] Rom. 8:3-9. [5] 1 Cor. 11:3; 1 Pet. 3:1-4. [6] Col. 3:18-23. [7] Gen. 2:7. [8] Rom. 6:12-13. [9] Tob. 6:16-17, from the Froschauer Bible. [10] 1 Cor. 7:7. [11] Gen. 24:7.

whom he has appointed. This choice should be accepted with real gratitude as a gift from God, whether young or old, rich or poor—whoever is shown by God through the counsel of the parents. What God has thus joined together, humans should not separate.[1] Such a couple should be married openly in the presence of the church by an ordained Servant of the Word.[2]

The man should also be the husband of only one wife,[3] as Christ is the head of one church.[4] Since marriage is a picture of Christ and his church, it must truly resemble what it represents. That is why a man must have only one wife.

Adultery

As we have seen, marriage is a union of two, in which each one undertakes to care for the other, and the second agrees to obey the first. The marriage is confirmed through the agreement of both. Conversely, where this agreement is violated by one or the other party, the marriage is broken.[5] If the husband does not preserve his honor, which represents the glory of God, and does not guide his wife and lead her to godliness, he has already broken the marriage with her.[6]

If the husband breaks the union with his wife in this way, he soon sins on the second level, that is, against his spirit, for he lets himself be ruled by the flesh instead of the spirit. So he becomes superficial and forsakes his lordship.[7] Again, when his spirit is overcome and weakened by his flesh, he falls to the third level and breaks his union with the Creator, by whom he is led.[8]

Likewise, if the woman gives up being obedient to the husband who faithfully guides her, she breaks the union and commitment made with him.[9] If she sins in this way against her husband, she too goes on to sin on all three levels, as just described. If a husband has been careless or superficial, and so has been first to break the marriage, and then wants to drag his wife after him, she should let the broken marriage go. She must hold to what is unbroken, that is, to obedience to the Spirit and to God. Otherwise, she will fall prey to death along with her husband.[10]

---

[1] Matt. 19:3-6; Mark 10:2-9.   [2] Sir. 26:3-4.   [3] 1 Tim. 3:2.   [4] Eph. 5:22-31.   [5] Mal. 2:13-16.   [6] 1 Cor. 11:3, 7.   [7] Rom. 8:5-9.   [8] Gen. 3:6-11.   [9] 1 Pet. 3:1-6.   [10] Gen. 3:6-11.

However, when the husband does his part but his wife acts without his counsel, she acts against her marriage vow in small things as well as great, and deprives her husband of his honor and lordship.[1] If the man permits her to do this, he participates in her sin, as Adam did with Eve[2] in consenting to eat the forbidden fruit. Both then became the prey of death, for they had broken the marriage with their Creator and transgressed his order.[3]

The Lord Christ says of adultery, "Whoever looks on a woman lustfully has already committed adultery with her in his heart."[4] The third level, adultery of the flesh, occurs when the husband goes to another woman or the wife to another man. If one partner commits adultery in this way, the other should put the offender away, and they should have nothing in common until the erring partner shows real fruits of repentance. If one partner has intercourse with an unfaithful partner before that one has repented, they commit adultery with each other, even though they were husband and wife before. It is no longer a marriage because it is broken until it is healed through repentance. Therefore, both should be rebuked by separation.[5]

Government

The government is appointed by God as a rod of his anger, to discipline and punish evil and wicked people.[6] Paul calls the government a servant of God's vengeance,[7] by means of which God will avenge their sins and bring the evil they have done upon their own heads. Then their wickedness will not spread, and the whole earth will not be blemished and unclean because of it.[8] One should therefore be obedient to rulers as to those who are appointed by God to protect us,[9] as long as they do not attack the conscience or demand what is against God.

Peter exhorts us, saying, "Submit yourselves to every human authority for the Lord's sake, whether to the king as supreme, or to governors who are sent by him."[10] Paul says, "Remind the people to be subject to the government, to obey magistrates, and to be ready to do every good work."[11]

The more diligent one is in being obedient and subject to the author

---

[1] Eph. 5:23-28; 1 Pet. 3:1-6.   [2] Gen. 3:6-8.   [3] 2 Esd. 4:4-7; 7:20-24; Rom. 5:12-14.   [4] Matt. 5:27-28.   [5] 1 Cor. 5:1-5.   [6] Isa. 10:5-15.   [7] Rom. 13:4.   [8] Gen. 9:1-6.   [9] Rom. 13:1-7.   [10] 1 Pet. 2:13-17.   [11] Titus 3:1.

ities, the more pleasing one is to God. Whoever resists that, resists what God has instituted.[1] However, if rulers command and act against God, one should not comply with their demands but obey God rather than people.[2] The conscience has been set free and is reserved for

God alone. God, and no human being, may be its overlord and teach and direct it wherever and however he pleases. Wherever the government presumes to encroach upon the conscience and control people's faith, it is robbing God of what is his, and obedience to it would be wrong.

Since the office of government is appointed and instituted by God, it therefore is right and good. Even when it is misused, however, the institution still remains as it was ordained and thus is to be honored. Even if positions in the government are held by godless men, governmental authority is not thereby annulled.[3] God allows such men to hold office for the greater punishment of the people.[4] But just as a wicked government is given to the nation by God as a punishment, so is a disobedient nation given to the wicked government. The two will tear each other apart, and both will finally be destroyed.[5]

Why Government Has Been Established

God has established government because people turned away from him and lived according to their own desires. God said, "My Spirit shall not always be in conflict with people, for they are flesh."[6] That is why after the Flood he established the government to be a rod of his anger,[7] to shed the blood of those who have shed blood.[8]

Later, Israel had again turned away from the Lord, who was their King. They had forsaken him and wanted an earthly king. God said to Samuel, "They have not rejected you, but me; they do not want me to reign over them. They do to you as they have always done. Since the day I led them up out of Egypt, they have forsaken me and served other gods. Therefore, listen to their voice, and give them a king."[9]

From these words we see how the authority of the government grew and where it came from, namely, from the wrath of God. We read in Scripture, "You said, 'Give us a king.' So in my anger I gave you a king, and in my wrath I took him away."[10] These words show us that

---

[1] Rom. 13:1-2   [2] Acts 5:29.   [3] Rom. 13:1-7.   [4] Isa. 3:4-12.   [5] Gal. 5:14-15.
[6] Gen. 6:3.   [7] Isa. 10:5.   [8] Gen. 9:5-6.   [9] 1 Sam. 8:7-9.   [10] Hos. 13:10-11.

governmental authority was not given from grace but from disfavor and anger, because the people had turned away from God. Since they forsook God and followed the flesh, the flesh had to rule over them.

The government is a picture for us, a sign and reminder of people's estrangement from God.[1] It ought to encourage all people to reflect upon their predicament and to hurry back to God in order to be restored to the grace they have lost. There are few, however, who think this way. Most people remain in their sins.

Above all, the government, as long as it exists, continues to be a sign that God's wrath toward sinners has not yet come to an end.[2]

Whether Rulers Can Be Christians

The Jewish government, which was present until Christ came, is a symbol of the old kingdom that comes to an end when the new kingdom begins. The Scriptures tell us, "The scepter shall not depart from Judah until Christ, the hero, comes."[3] The old has come to an end in Christ, who now sits on the throne of his father, David,[4] and has become King of all true Israelites. He has established a new regime that is not like the old and is not supported by the temporal sword.[5]

The regime of the Jews, who until then were God's people, came to an end in Christ, and the Jews had their regime taken from them. This signifies that in Christ the old regime shall be no more, but Christ alone will rule over Christians with his spiritual sword.[6] The power of the worldly sword has been taken from the Jews and given to the Gentiles. This change shows that God's people are not to use the worldly sword or rule with it. Instead, they should be led and ruled by the spirit of Christ alone.[7] This is addressed to heathen, thus indicating that the heathen and unbelievers are not submitting themselves to the spirit of Christ and therefore will be punished and disciplined with the sword. So we see that governmental authority has its place outside Christ, not in Christ.[8]

God is King and Commander of his people in Christ alone, as it is written, "God has set a government over every people, but over Israel he alone is Lord."[9] Just as he is a spiritual King, so he has spir-

---

[1] 1 Sam. 8:7-22.   [2] Rom. 13:3-4; 1 Pet. 2:13-17.   [3] Gen. 49:10.   [4] Ps. 2:1-7.
[5] Matt. 28:18; Phil. 2:9-11.   [6] John 16:13-15; Rom. 8:1-17; Rev. 1:16.   [7] Heb. 4:12-13.
[8] Rom. 13; Titus 3:1-7; 1 Pet. 2:6-18.   [9] Sir. 17:17.

itual servants, and with all of them he wields a spiritual sword that pierces soul and spirit.[1]

The Son was appointed by the Father,[2] as Scripture tells us: "I have set my king upon my holy hill of Zion."[3] He was not given in anger, like the earthly king, but in blessing,[4] and he has become a source of blessing to us all. It had, indeed, been promised that in him all peoples should be blessed.[5] Therefore, just as the old order was established to demand blood for blood,[6] this ruler has been appointed to protect and to save people's souls.[7] As the old order was to punish evil,[8] so the new is to recompense it with good. As the old way was to hate the enemy, so the new way commands us to love him.[9] Christ is King of all kings, and at the same time the complete opposite of all the rulers of this world. Therefore he says, "My kingdom is not from this world. If my kingdom were from this world, my servants would be ready to fight for me."[10]

Christ calls into being a completely different kingdom and regime.[11] He wishes his servants to submit themselves to it and become like him.[12] That is why he says to them, "The princes of the world are called gracious lords, and the powerful exercise rulership over the people, but you should not be like that. Let the one who is the greatest among you be your servant."[13] Thus the glory of Christ and of his servants consists in relinquishing all worldly glory. The more completely a person gives it up, the more glorious that person becomes in Christ's kingdom. This is shown in the words, "Whoever desires to be exalted shall be abased, and whoever is humble, shall be exalted."[14]

The full blessing of God is in Christ our King,[15] and he himself is the blessing.[16] Therefore, all that was given in wrath must come to an end in Christ. It has no place in Christ. Governmental authority was given in wrath,[17] so it cannot find a place in Christ or be part of him. No Christian is a ruler, and no ruler is a Christian, for the child of blessing cannot be the servant of wrath.[18] In Christ, temporal weapons are not used. Instead, spiritual weapons are used in such a way that people neither deserve nor need the methods of punishment or discipline used by the world.[19]

---

[1] Heb. 4:12. [2] Matt. 28:18; Phil. 2:9-11. [3] Ps. 2:6. [4] Hos. 13:10-11. [5] Gen. 12:1-3; Gal. 3:8. [6] Gen. 9:6. [7] John 12:47. [8] Exod. 21:12-17. [9] Matt. 5:21-24.
[10] John 18:36. [11] Phil. 2:5-11. [12] Matt. 10:37-39; Luke 14:26-27. [13] Matt. 20:25-28; Luke 22:25-27. [14] Mark 9:33-35; 1 Pet. 5:5-6. [15] Col. 1:19-23. [16] Gal. 3:8-9. [17] Hos. 13:11. [18] Luke 9:51-56. [19] Rom. 13:7-10.

Someone may say, "It is necessary to use force because of wicked people." We have already answered this by saying that the power of the sword has passed to the heathen for the punishment of their evildoers. That is not our concern. Paul says, "What have I to do with judging outsiders?"[1] No Christian can be a ruler in worldly society.

In reply, someone might say, "According to this view, the way to life is closed to those who hold government office." We deny this, for Christ says, "Come to me, all you who are weary and heavy laden, and I will refresh you and give rest to your souls."[2] This shows it is open for all, for rulers as well as subjects. Whoever comes to him will not be rejected in any way.[3]

If rulers were to put aside their glory as Christ did, and humble themselves with him,[4] allowing only Christ to work through them, then the way to life would be as open to them as to others.[5] When Christ begins to work in people, he causes them to do nothing but what he himself did during his life on earth, and we know that he fled from those who wanted to make him a king.[6]

However, if their spirits remain unbroken and they will not give up their greatness, Christ himself says, "Those who do not give up all that they have, yes, even their own life, cannot be my disciples."[7] From this it is clear that not only governmental authorities but all who still cling to created things and do not give them up for Christ's sake- such people are not Christians.[8]

Warfare

Christ, the Prince of Peace, has prepared a kingdom for himself, namely, the church, and has won this kingdom by shedding his own blood. Therefore, all worldly warfare in this kingdom has come to an end. This is what was promised through the prophets: "The law will go out from Zion, the word of the Lord from Jerusalem. He will judge between the nations and will settle disputes for many peoples. They will beat their swords into plowshares and their spears into grape knives, pruning hooks, and scythes. From that time on, nation will not take up sword against nation, nor will they train for war any more."[9]

Therefore, Christians should not take part in war, nor should they

---

[1] 1 Cor. 5:12. [2] Matt. 11:28. [3] John 6:37. [4] Phil. 2:5-8. [5] Gal. 2:20. [6] John 6:15. [7] Matt. 10:37-39; Luke 14:33. [8] Matt. 19:27-30. [9] Isa. 2:1-4; Mic. 4:1-4.

use force for purposes of vengeance. Paul exhorts us not to avenge ourselves but to leave retribution to the Lord, who says, "Vengeance is mine; I will repay."[1] Since vengeance now belongs to God and not to us, it ought to be left to him and not be practiced by us. Since we are Christ's disciples, our lives should be examples of his nature. Jesus could have repaid evil with evil, but he did not.[2] He could, indeed, have protected himself against his enemies by striking down with a single word all who wanted to seize him.[3] But he did not, nor would he permit others to do so. He said to Peter, "Put your sword in its place."[4] This shows how our King, with a powerful army, sets out against his enemies, how he defeats them, and how he exercises vengeance! He restores Malchus's ear that had been struck off.[5] Jesus also says, "Whoever wants to be my disciple, let him take up his cross and follow me."[6]

Christ wants us to act as he did. Therefore, he commands us in these words: "It was said to the people of old, 'An eye for an eye, and a tooth for a tooth.' But I say that you should not resist evil. If someone strikes you on your right cheek, turn and offer him the other one.'"[7] That makes it clear that you ought neither to avenge yourself nor go to war. Instead, as the prophet says, offer your back to those who strike and your cheeks to those who tear at the beard.[8] That means we should suffer with patience and wait upon God, who is just. He will requite the evil.[9]

Some may wish to say that David, who was loved by God, went to war, and so did other saints;[10] thus when war is justified, we may do the same. But we say no to that. David and the other saints went to war, but we ought not to, because of the words quoted above: "It was said to the people of old, 'An eye for an eye, and a tooth for a tooth.' But I tell you, do not resist evil."[11] Here Christ makes the distinction. There is no need for many words, for it is clear that Christians cannot take part in war or avenge themselves.[12] Whoever does so forsakes and denies Christ and is untrue to Christ's nature.

---

[1] Deut. 32:35; Rom. 12:14-21; Heb. 10:30. [2] 1 Pet. 2:19-23. [3] John 18. [4] Matt. 26:51-54; John 18:10-11. [5] Luke 22:47-53. [6] Matt. 16:24-25; Mark 8:34-35. [7] Matt. 5:38-48. [8] Isa. 50:6. [9] Deut. 32:35-36; Joel 3:1-2. [10] Gen. 14:14-16; Num. 31:1-8; Josh. 6:1-16; 8:1-29; 9:1-2; Judg. 4; 1 Sam. 17:20-52. [11] Matt. 5:38-39. [12] Luke 9:51-56; Rom. 12:19.

Taxes

Since the government and its authority have been ordained and commanded by God, the payment of taxes to the government is also ordained and commanded. As Paul says, "You must also pay tribute."[1] For this reason we willingly pay interest, taxes, tribute, or whatever it may be called, and do not oppose such payments in any way, for we have learned this from our Master, Christ. He not only paid it himself,[2] but he also commanded others to do so, saying, "Give to Caesar what is Caesar's, and to God what is God's."[3] Therefore, we, as his disciples, do our best to keep this command, and we do not oppose the government in this mattter.

However, for taxes that are demanded for the specific purpose of war, executions, and bloodshed, we give nothing, not out of disrespect or obstinacy but in the fear of God. We thus do not partake in other people's sins.[4] One might say, "You ought to pay tribute where tribute is due, and you do wrong to refuse it."[5] We reply, "In no way do we refuse to pay tribute where and how it is due." God, as said above, has decreed that the government should receive taxes, which they have to collect yearly,[6] and we do not refuse to pay these.

Yet it does not follow from Paul's words that one should submit to every whim of rulers. In the same passage Paul says, "Give to all what is due them; tribute to whom tribute is due." He does not say, "Give whatever and however much they want," but he says, "Give them their dues,"[7] that is, yearly taxes decreed by God.[8] Yet those taxes which God has *not* decreed, namely, those taxes which are not annual, are given, not as a duty and as the ruler's due, but unwillingly, because of pressure and coercion by the authorities.

Therefore, paying such taxes does not follow from the above-quoted words of Paul, nor from the words of Christ when he commands to give to Caesar what is Caesar's.[9] Christ was speaking of the yearly taxation that was first introduced when Augustus was emperor, and was then continued.[10] At that time there was neither war nor rumors of war; therefore, money was not collected or contributed for warfare. It was rather as if the count were to put a tax on the wood on his land in such a way that whoever takes wood away in a cart should

---

[1] Rom. 13:1-7; 1 Pet. 2:13-17; Sir. 17:17; 1 Sam. 8:10-22.   [2] Matt. 17:24-27.
[3] Matt. 22:15-21; Mark 12:13-17; Luke 20:20-25.   [4] 1 Tim. 5:22.   [5] Rom. 13:7.
[6] 1 Sam. 8:7-18.   [7] Rom. 13:6-7.   [8] 1 Sam. 8:11-17.   [9] Matt. 22:15-21; Mark 12:13-17; Luke 20:20-25.   [10] Luke 2:1-5.

pay one gulden a year, whoever takes it in a barrow half a gulden, and whoever carries it home himself a quarter gulden. The Lord spoke of such taxes, and not of war taxes, when he said that one should not refuse to pay what is Caesar's. These taxes we pay willingly. In those cases where our consciences would be violated, it is our duty and our wish to obey God rather than people.[1]

Making Swords

Since Christians should either beat their swords into plowshares or put them aside,[2] they should also not make them, for they are used solely to kill or wound people. Christ has not come to destroy people,[3] and therefore his disciples should refuse to do so, too. Thus Christ says, "Do you not know to what Spirit you belong?"[4] This is as though he would say, "Does the Spirit of grace teach you to destroy other people? Or do you wish to live according to the flesh and turn away from the Spirit, whose children you have become? Do you not know that I have not come to destroy people? If you want to be my disciples, you must let my Spirit rule over you and not live according to the flesh.[5] For whoever obeys the flesh cannot please God."[6]

Now, since Christians should not practice vengeance,[7] neither should they make the weapons by which others carry out vengeance and destruction, in order not to take part in other people's sins.[8] Therefore, we do not make swords, spears, muskets, or any such weapons. However, what is made for people's benefit and daily use, such as bread knives, axes, hoes, and the like, we can and do make. Someone might say, "But these could be used to harm and kill others." Yet even so, they are not made for that purpose, so there is nothing to prevent our making them. If such a tool should ever be used to harm someone, we do not share the guilt. The one who misuses it will have to accept the judgment.[9]

Making Clothes

It is our duty and our wish to serve our neighbor by working hard at making all kinds of things that may be needed. In this way

---

[1] Acts 5:29. [2] Isa. 2:1-4; Mic. 4:1-3. [3] John 12:47. [4] Luke 9:55. [5] Gal. 3:2-14. [6] Rom. 8:6-8. [7] Matt. 5:21-24; Rom. 12:14. [8] 1 Tim. 5:22. [9] Ezek. 33:18-20; Gal. 5:16-21.

God will be praised and our industry and conscientiousness recognized in work that is honestly done.[1] For no one, however, do we make clothing that serves pride, ostentation, or vanity, such as an exaggerated cut, elaborate braiding, floral decoration, or embroidery work. We wish to keep our conscience clean before God.[2]

We have been chosen by God not only to refrain from making and using such things, but also to testify against them and make people aware of those sins.[3] Now since we must testify that we oppose this, we cannot partake in making or producing it. James says, "Pure and undefiled service of God is to keep oneself unspotted from the world."[4] With God's help, that is what we want to do as well as we are able, always striving for this as long as we live.

Whether a Christian Can Go to Court or Sit in Judgment

As we have explained, temporal things do not belong to us. Therefore, a Christian cannot quarrel or go to court because of them. On the contrary, if a person's heart is turned from the world and set upon that which is of God, that person should prefer to suffer injustice. Paul says, "You fail completely because you have lawsuits with one another. Why not rather let wrong be done to you? Why not rather let yourselves be harmed and defrauded?"[5] If Christians should not sue one another, then going to court and sitting in judgment are completely eradicated among Christians.[6]

Hence, it also follows that no Christian may take part in the proceedings of a worldly court of law, for Christians do not judge in this way. Paul says, "What have I to do with judging those who are outside?"[7] Judging and bringing lawsuits have ceased in the church of Christ. The reason Christians must not judge those who are outside their assembly is that the latter have not placed themselves under the Spirit of God, so they should not be judged in the light of that Spirit. The Lord has said, "My Spirit will not strive with people forever, for they are flesh."[8] The church of God is not concerned for temporal matters about which those outside the church are in the habit of quarreling. Therefore, God has not given his Spirit to judge in such matters.

A young man wanted Jesus to speak to his brother about sharing his inheritance with him. Jesus answered him, "Who made me a judge

---

[1] Eph. 4:15-24; 2 Thess. 3:3-12.   [2] Isa. 3:16-24.   [3] John 16:7-11.   [4] James 1:27.
[5] 1 Cor. 6:7.   [6] Matt. 5:39-42.   [7] 1 Cor. 5:12.   [8] Gen. 6:3.

between you?"[1] In effect, he said, "What is your quarrel to me, the quarrel between yourselves over what is temporal? I have not been sent by God to judge such matters. I have come to implant what is of God,[2] so that whoever wishes may find it in me and receive it.[3] You, however, do not search for what is divine but for what is earthly and worldly. Therefore, go, and let those in authority decide for you."[4] Whoever seeks the things of this world does not seek what is in Christ and therefore cannot have such matters decided by Christ. As with Christ, so with his followers; they have not been appointed to judge over that which is temporal.

Christ shows that Christians may not go to court when he says, "If any one will sue you and take away your coat, let him have your cloak also."[5] In effect, Jesus is saying, "It is better to let people take everything than to quarrel with them and find yourself in a strange court." Christ wants us to show that we seek what is heavenly and belongs to us,[6] and not what is temporal or alien to us.[7] Thus, it is evident that a Christian can neither go to court nor be a judge.

Swearing

Just as the law was an introduction to the wider grace and knowledge of God, so also are the commandments. In the Old Testament, God the Lord had no other purpose for the practice of swearing than to direct people to his name,[8] so that they would learn to know him, cling to him,[9] and give him alone the honor.[10] By commanding his people Israel to swear by his name,[11] God, who is the truth, meant to teach them to speak the truth and to abide by it. He also forbade them to use his name lightly or in vain.[12] Thus he wished to say that they should be careful in all their speech, so that they might be found to be servants of God, that is, of the truth. For this reason, God threatened not to consider guiltless anyone who speaks his name lightly or in vain, that is, being careless about the truth.

It is true that in the Old Testament, God gave the command to swear. Yet in the New Testament, since God's will has been fully revealed, God commanded people "to speak the truth and to walk in it," or "to know God truly and to cling to him."[13] David expresses the

---

[1] Luke 12:13-14.   [2] Isa. 61:1-2; Luke 4:16-19.   [3] John 7:38.   [4] Sir. 17:17.   [5] Matt. 5:40-41.   [6] Col. 3:1-2.   [7] Luke 16:19-25.   [8] Gal. 3:21-24; Heb. 7:18-28.   [9] Deut. 10:20-22.   [10] Deut. 32:39-40.   [11] Deut. 10:20.   [12] Exod. 20:7; Deut. 5:11.   [13] John 1:1-18.

same thought when he says, "Whoever swears by God is praised, but the mouth of those who speak lies must be closed."[1] Who can deny that here swearing means speaking the truth and clinging to it?

Although in the Old Testament we are given the command to swear, in the New Testament this command means to know God and to cling to him. These words show the same teaching: "Before me every knee shall bow; by me every tongue shall swear. They will say of me, 'Truly, righteousness and strength are in the Lord.' "[2] Paul explains the prophet's words thus: "Every knee shall bow to God, and every tongue shall confess him."[3] Here he shows that what is called swearing in the Old Testament, in the New Testament means acknowledging God and clinging to him alone.[4] The law has become a guide to a better knowledge and hope; through it we draw near to God.[5]

Since the light of divine grace has appeared and become more brightly revealed in Christ, the ministers of the new covenant no longer present to us the shadow.[6] Instead, they display the glow of the light of truth in its clarity. Paul, as one who has no veil before his face, can say plainly, "Let each reject lying, and speak truth with his neighbor, for we are all members of one body."[7]

Someone might say, "But surely Israel was also commanded to speak the truth and hate lies,[8] so that cannot be the meaning." We respond by agreeing that Israel was indeed commanded to speak the truth. At that time, however, the status of being an heir had not been distinguished from that of bondage. Even though the spirit of bondage was not able to grasp the real truth,[9] God nevertheless wanted to show them, by means of swearing by his name, that there is no other truth.[10] Whoever would walk in the truth, must come to it and become firmly grounded in it through the name of God.[11] This is what God wanted to teach us about swearing in the Old Testament.

At that time being an heir was not distinguished from the state of bondage. Therefore, those who had the spirit of being an heir were still bound by the outward ceremony of the law.[12] Paul explains it this way: "As long as the heir is a child, the heir is in no way different from a servant, though lord of all. The heir is under tutors and governors until the time appointed by the father. In the same way we, being still children, were in bondage to outward regulations until the

---

[1] Ps. 63:11.　[2] Isa. 45:23-24.　[3] Rom. 14:11.　[4] Jer. 31:31-34.　[5] Heb. 7:18-19.　[6] 2 Cor. 3:11-18.　[7] Eph. 4:25.　[8] Ps. 15:1-3.　[9] Rom. 8:1-15.　[10] 2 John 1:4-6.　[11] John 8:12-47.　[12] Gal. 3:21-26.

time was fulfilled when God sent his Son. He redeemed us from the law, so that we might become children of God."[1]

Now the shadow has departed, and the light has dawned.[2] Being an heir is separated from being in bondage;[3] the covenant of being an heir is ratified. Henceforth, there are no more servants, but all are children[4] who have received the childlike spirit and have been brought by it into the covenant of the knowledge of God. God himself now testifies and accomplishes everything in his people which previously had been accomplished by swearing an oath.[5] Swearing by God's name[6] was meant simply to show that among his people, God is the one who confirms, empowers, and fulfills all things. So now, since the truth is revealed,[7] the shadow or outward sign must come to an end, and the Spirit of truth must be allowed to testify in us with power.

That is why Christ says, "It was said to our forebears, you shall not swear falsely. But I say to you, do not swear at all, neither by heaven, for it is God's throne, or by the earth, for it is his footstool, nor by Jerusalem, for it is the city of the great King. Nor shall you swear by your head, because you cannot make one hair white or black. Let your yes be yes, and your no be no; for whatever is more than these is from the evil one."[8] And the evil one is the devil, who does everything in people that causes God to be reviled.[9]

It is clear to everyone and no one can deny that what God desires of us Christians is true worship performed in spirit and in truth. Such worship is more perfect than the service of the old covenant.[10] That is why we are not only to abstain from swearing falsely but are not to swear at all.[11] In this way, Christ teaches us to give honor to God alone and to humble ourselves before him as those who of themselves cannot do anything.[12] Since we cannot do anything, we cannot even promise to do something of ourselves, let alone swear to do it.[13] Therefore, it is clear that on account of our weakness and unworthiness, we ought not to swear, so that we do not rob God of his honor.

They say further, "We ought not to swear by created things, but we may indeed swear to the truth by the Creator. Since he has sworn by himself,[14] we thus are here not forbidden to swear by him, but we are forbidden to swear by created things." We reply that God has sworn by himself,[15] but we ought not to do so, for what God promis-

---

[1] Gal. 4:1-7. [2] Col. 2:13-17. [3] Gal. 4:4-8. [4] Heb. 9:11-15. [5] Rom. 8:10-17; Jer. 31:33-34; Heb. 8:7-10; 10:8-17. [6] Deut. 10:20; Ps. 63:11. [7] John 1:1-18. [8] Matt. 5:33-37. [9] Matt. 13:39. [10] Luke 1:5-17. [11] Matt. 5:34-37. [12] John 15:4-7. [13] James 5:12. [14] Gen. 22:15-18; Ezek. 33:11. [15] Ps. 110:4.

es, he both can and will do.[1] He thus has the right to swear. We, however, do not have that right, for by ourselves we cannot do anything. Moreover, Christ forbids us to swear not only by the Creation but also by the Creator, as shown in these words: "Do not swear at all."[2]

If one is not to swear by the creation, which is indeed less than God, then one must certainly not swear by God, who is much higher and greater. Who shall presume to use the greatest of names when the use of the lesser is forbidden? One should not swear by the higher, which is even worse than swearing by what is lower.

Thus we see Christ's words: "Woe to you, blind leaders, who say, 'If anyone swears by the temple, it means nothing; but whoever swears by the gold of the temple, is bound by the oath.' You blind fools! Which is greater, the gold or the temple that makes the gold sacred? You also say, 'To swear by the altar is nothing, but to swear by the sacrifice upon the altar, binds one to the oath.' You blind fools! Which is greater, the sacrifice or the altar that makes it sacred? Whoever swears by the altar includes in his oath everything upon the altar, and whoever swears by the temple, swears by it and by the one who dwells in it. Whoever swears by heaven, swears by the throne of God and by him who sits upon the throne."[3]

Here it is evident that Christ desires oaths to be sworn even less by the things which are greatest than by those which are smallest. In the same way, he rebukes the [Pharisees] because they find fault with small offenses and ignore the greatest ones. He indicates to them that the temple is more than the gold within it, and the altar more than the gift upon it. Therefore, to swear by the temple and altar is a greater sin than to swear by the gold in the temple and the gift on the altar, since one swears not only by the temple but also by him who dwells within, that is, he swears by God. Likewise, whoever swears by heaven swears by God's throne and by him who sits upon the throne. That is why Christ calls those people blind leaders, who filter out gnats and swallow camels.[4] They focus on the smallest details of the law and ignore the greatest.

Thus it is clear that one ought not to swear at all, as James says: "Above all, dear brothers, do not swear, not by heaven, nor by earth, nor by anything else. Let your yes be yes, and your no be no."[5] Do this, as has been said, so that we do not encroach upon God's honor

---

[1] Deut. 32:40. [2] Matt. 5:34. [3] Matt. 23:16-22. [4] Matt. 23:16-24; Luke 11:42.
[5] James 5:12.

and glory. Since we can do nothing without God,[1] and since he has to do everything in us, let us give him the honor. James teaches us that if it is the Lord's will, I will do it,[2] and furthermore, that whoever knows what is good and fails to do it, commits a sin.[3]

Greeting

Greeting is well wishing,[4] and therefore we ought to wish what is good to all who desire good. So when members of the church community meet each other, they should greet one another with this good wish, offering the blessed gift of the peace of Christ, which the Lord has given us.[5] Christ teaches his disciples to do this: "Whatever house you enter, say, 'Peace be with you.' If there is one within who is of the same mind, your peace will rest upon that person; but if not, your peace will return to you."[6]

From these words we learn that both the person who greets and the one who is greeted must be children of peace, if God's blessing is to take effect. The peace of Christ cannot rest upon one who is not in harmony with the gospel or does not wholeheartedly desire it. However, the Lord's greeting should not be spoken superficially, or with the lips only, but from the whole heart, in firm faith, and with the confidence that God will certainly grant this good wish. It should be as though God himself were expressing the wish through that person.[7] Whoever receives such a greeting should accept it with the same confidence and wholehearted longing.

God the Lord will bless the greeting and grant the wish expressed, that the Lord be with those to whom it is offered,[8] and always remain with them.[9] Like Mary's greeting to Elizabeth,[10] it will be a source of joy. But if a greeting is given thoughtlessly or frivolously, it is sin, for God's name is used in vain.[11] God detests that; whoever does it will not be considered innocent or remain unpunished. Just as the one sins who extends the greeting frivolously, so does the person who accepts it carelessly and without reverence before God. Also, whoever offers the greeting to those who do not want it, such as gamblers, drunkards, and the like, is misusing God's name. So let those who fear God beware of this and protect their soul from evil.

---

[1] John 15:5. [2] James 4:13-15. [3] James 4:17. [4] Matt. 10:11-13; Luke 1:28, 39-45; 10:5-9. [5] John 14:27. [6] Matt. 10:13; Luke 10:1-12. [7] Mark 13:11; Luke 12:11-12; 21:9-15. [8] Judg. 6:12, 23. [9] Matt. 28:19-20. [10] Luke 1:41. [11] Exod. 20:7; Deut. 5:11.

Shaking Hands and Embracing

To shake hands and embrace are signs of peace, love, and unity in God, signs by which those who are in the church community show that they are of one mind, one heart, and one soul.[1] This we learn from Paul's words: "When Peter, James, and John saw the grace of God that was given to me, how the gospel was entrusted to me as it was to them, they gave to me and Barnabas the right hand and were united with us."[2] Here we see a sign of unity, peace, and love.

When hands are clasped within each other, people show that their hearts are likewise knit together. The same is true of embracing. Just as people put their arms around one another, so each enfolds the other in their heart.[3] Because these two signs are signs of peace, they should be observed strictly and firmly in the church in the fear of God, and in a way that expresses their inner meaning. One member of the church should receive another with this reverence.[4]

However, if one person acts in this way toward another without having one's heart turned in that direction, that person is a hypocrite and the truth is not within him.[5] In the world, where shaking hands is a sign of friendliness, a Christian may use the handshake as such with people of the world. When a handshake, however, is a sign of swearing an oath, it should not be used.[6]

However, since both shaking hands and embracing mean the same thing, therefore, in order not to offend, and also to avoid a situation in which the flesh might be tempted to sin,[7] a brother should only embrace his brothers, and a sister embrace her sisters. In this way they express what is in their heart. Between brothers and sisters, this love should only be expressed by shaking hands and not by embracing, because nothing should be allowed to bring the teaching of Christ into disrepute or dishonor.

Prayer

Prayer ought to come from a true heart. It should take place in spirit and in truth:[8] Only that way is it pleasing to God. The heart of the person who prays in this manner must first[9] put aside all that is wrong, since God does not hear sinners.[10] That person must strive, as

---

[1] Acts 2:42-46; 4:32. [2] Gal. 2:9. [3] Phil. 2:29. [4] Rom. 12:1-10; 1 Pet. 1:22. [5] John 3:16-18. [6] Prov. 17:18. [7] Matt. 18:6-10. [8] John 4:23. [9] Sir. 18:23-24. [10] John 9:31.

far as it is possible, to be at peace with all people, and above all with believers.[1] Christ says, "If you come before the altar to lay your sacrifice upon it, and remember at the same moment that your brother has something against you, then go and first be reconciled to him, and then come and sacrifice your gift."[2] Therefore, all who would offer the fruit of their lips to God, namely, thanksgiving and prayer, must first be reconciled to all, so that none of the believers has anything against them.

Furthermore, if you have something in your heart against anyone, forgive that person, as Christ teaches when he says, "When you stand praying, forgive, if you have anything against anyone, so that your Father in heaven will also forgive you your trespasses."[3] When your heart is thus purified, it must be adorned with true faith and real trust.[4] Yes, you must have such trust in God that you firmly and securely believe that God, as a father who always seeks the best for his children, will hear you and grant your request.[5] The words of Christ point to this: "If you who are evil can still give your children good gifts, how much more will your Father in heaven give the Holy Spirit to those who ask him?"[6]

Whoever prays in faith will receive. Those who pray in faith will not cease to make their request to God; they will not allow any concern to hinder them. If there is a delay, and it seems as though God does not respond, they will wait with all patience, firmly confident that God will not withdraw but rather will grant their request.

If those who have prayed turn their heart to something else and thus draw away from their request and cease to pray, they can receive nothing, since they have not persevered in faith.[7] About this, James says, "If any of you would ask anything of God, ask in faith, never wavering. Whoever doubts or ceases to make requests is a fickle person. Such a person need not expect to receive anything from God."[8]

However, we are children of Christ's Spirit. If we, because of our weakness, do not know how to come before God so that our requests and prayers are acceptable to him, then, says Paul, "The Spirit helps us in our weakness. We do not know what to pray for, as we ought, but the Spirit intercedes for us mightily, with sighs too deep for words. He who searches our hearts knows the Spirit's intention, because the Spirit intercedes for believers in accordance with God's will."[9]

---

[1] Rom. 12:4-5. [2] Matt. 5:21-24. [3] Mark 11:25-26. [4] James 1:5-8. [5] 1 John 5:13-15. [6] Matt. 7:7-11. [7] Jer. 29:10-13; Matt. 7:7-11; 21:21-22; Mark 11:22-24; Luke 22:39-46; John 14:10-14; 15:7; 16:23-27. [8] James 1:5-8. [9] Rom. 8:26-27.

God desires to be honored and worshiped in this one Spirit,[1] and therefore we ought to await his prompting and learn of him. Then what the Spirit puts into our understanding will be heard by God and will be pleasing to him, and since he hears us, we shall receive what we have asked of him.[2]

Singing

Paul says, "Sing and make melody in your heart to the Lord with psalms, hymns, and spiritual songs."[3] For this reason we say that to sing spiritual songs is good and pleasing to God as long as they are sung in the right way, that is, genuinely, in the fear of God, and as prompted by the Spirit of Christ.

Such songs are called spiritual because they are inspired and composed at the urging of the Spirit[4] and because they rouse people to live in devotion to God. Since they are composed at the inspiration of the Spirit of Christ, they should be sung in the same Spirit, if they are to be sung rightly, so that people can benefit by singing them.

Where this does not happen, and one sings songs only for sensual joy, for sweet sound, or for some similar reason, one misuses them, changing them into what is carnal and worldly. In such cases one is not singing songs of the Spirit but of the letter. Whoever enjoys listening for the music's sake does not hear the song in the Spirit. The singing will not bear fruit for that person. A person who does not sing or listen to spiritual songs correctly, sins greatly against God. Sin arises because such a person uses God's Word for sensual enjoyment and sin, rather than for salvation and as encouragement toward a more godly life.[5] In this way a song can cause harm, for though it is in itself spiritual, yet to that person it is no longer spiritual but worldly, for it is not sung in the Spirit.

Those who sing songs in the Spirit hear every word with deep thoughtfulness, consider its true meaning, why it has been used, and how it may be of inner help to them.[6] Those who sing this way offer praises to the Lord, to improve themselves and others, and to be encouraged to live in devotion to God. To sing thus is to sing well; any other way is in vain. We must add that we do not permit the singing of any but spiritual songs in our life together.

---

[1] John 4:21-24. [2] 1 John 5:14-15. [3] Eph. 5:19; Col. 3:16. [4] 2 Pet. 1:19-21.
[5] Ps. 50:14-23. [6] 2 Tim. 3:14-17.

Fasting

Fasting is a way of chastening and subduing the body in order to humble and more easily control it. Fasting has arisen among those who love God, as a help to crucify their flesh and conquer its lusts. They can then adhere to God all the more freely and joyfully.

Ungodly people have abused and spoiled the meaning of fasting.[1] They fasted for the sake of gain, thinking they could get something from God. Such fasting is worthless, as the words of Isaiah show: "They say to God, 'Why do we fast since you do not see it? We afflict our soul, and you take no notice!' " To this question the Lord answers, "Because you do not fast properly. For though you fast, your desires remain, and you press your debtors no less than before. Your fasting leads to quarreling and striking with your fist the one you are exhorting. Such fasting prevents your voice from being heard in heaven. Do you think I find pleasure in the fast in which you torture yourself for a day, twist your neck about like a hook, and lie on the ground in a hair shirt? Is that called fasting? Is that a day pleasing to the Lord?"[2]

From these words it is clear how the ungodly have twisted and misused fasting. Although they, as well as the papists, have not stopped sinning, they think by such means to wipe out their sins and to reconcile themselves to God. As Isaiah says, "Though you fast, your passions remain." It is as if he wishes to say, "What is the good of your fasting, since you chastise yourselves by denying only the needs of the body, while allowing free rein to all other human passions? Is that a fast or a day that pleases God?[3] Far from it! Your forefathers who drew near to me did not fast in that way."

We see that fasting is good and pleasing to God when it is properly observed, as the following words prove: "You no longer fast as you fasted earlier, so that your voice might be heard in heaven."[4] This refers to the true fasting as carried out by the saints of old. They denied themselves the craving of the flesh and broke away from it entirely. They refused to do wrong and concerned themselves with God alone. They clung to him and served him in true faith, and through this fasting, their voices rose up to heaven.

The Lord shows us that he is pleased with such fasting when he says, "Loose the yoke of him that is in bondage to you, that is, wipe out his debt; let the oppressed go free, and break all his bonds; give bread

---

[1] Titus 1:10-15. [2] Isa. 58:3-5. [3] Isa. 58:3-4. [4] Isa. 58:3-8.

to the hungry; bring the orphan to your house and feed him; clothe the naked, and do not turn your face away from the needy. Is not this the fast that is pleasing to me? Then will your light break forth as the morning, and your health shall flourish; your righteousness shall go before you, and the glory of the Lord shall surround you."[1] That is a fast pleasing to the Lord, and all the saints practiced it diligently. They were therefore called friends of God. Even today, whoever would please God with fasting should follow their example.

Celebrating

Festivals are not to be kept for the sake of their outward appearance, which is no more than a shadow or picture of what is to come. The true reality of a holy day is Christ himself.[2] In him, the shadow must give way; the outer festivities must recede before the essential or true celebration, in which the Lord delights. Celebrating in this manner means earnestly seeking to obey God, to do his will and please him,[3] to meditate upon his Word day and night,[4] to do good and desist from evil and the enjoyment of evil. In summary, this means living and walking in the Spirit.[5] Such is the true celebration that God demands, as Scripture tells us: "Blessed is the person who does this, and the son of man who keeps to it, who observes the Sabbath without desecrating it, and holds back from doing anything evil."[6]

That is how God commanded us to keep his holy day,[7] and we should now observe it to the best of our ability. But celebrating as it is done in the world is an abomination to God.[8] The evil and shameful things that people are unable to do during the week because of their work, they do on the holy day, using it in this way for unholy pursuits. They would have been better off without such a day of celebration.

Yet we also have a day of rest on which we read and hear the Lord's Word.[9] By means of this, we allow our hearts to revive and continue in the grace of God. Because it is usual for all people to observe Sunday, we keep the same day in order to avoid any offense, since which day is observed is a matter of indifference. We do this not because of the Law, which is annulled in Christ,[10] but as we have said, to concern ourselves with the Word of God.

---

[1] Matt. 25:31-46; Isa. 58:6-8. [2] Col. 2:16-17. [3] Isa. 56:1-7. [4] Ps. 1:1-3. [5] Gal. 5:16-18. [6] Isa. 56:1-2. [7] Exod. 20:8-11; Deut. 5:12-15. [8] Isa. 1:10-15. [9] Exod. 23:10-12; 35:1-3. [10] Col. 2:13-16.

Buying and Selling

We allow none of our members to be traders or merchants, since this is a sinful business. The wise teacher says, "It is almost impossible for a merchant or tradesman to keep free from sin."[1] "As a nail is driven firmly into a fissure between stones, so is sin wedged between buying and selling."[2] Therefore, we allow no one to buy in order to resell, as merchants and tradesmen do. But when we buy what is necessary for the needs of our house or craft, and then use the materials and sell what is made-that is in order and is no sin.

What is wrong, however, is to buy an article and sell it for a profit in the same condition as one bought it.[3] This makes the article more expensive for the poor; it is stealing bread from their mouths and forcing them to become nothing but slaves to the rich. Paul says, "Let the thief give up stealing."[4] Some may argue that the poor can also benefit if one takes commodities from one country to the other. Such people use poverty as a pretext while seeking their own profit first, and think only of the poor as those who have an occasional penny in their purse. Therefore, we do not permit our people to trade but say with Paul that they should labor, working with their hands at honest work, that they may have something to give to the one who is in need.[5]

Innkeepers

Neither do we allow any of our members to be public innkeepers, serving wine or beer, since this is associated with much that is depraved and godless. Drunken and idle young fellows gather at the inn and give vent to their high spirits in disorderly behavior. Innkeepers are forced to allow this and to listen to their blasphemy. For this reason we do not believe that anyone who fears God may follow this occupation. Merely for the sake of money, none should have to permit such profanity, nor to listen to it, and thereby participate in the same sins.[6] That is why the wise teacher says that it is nearly impossible for an innkeeper to be free from sin.[7]

We do, however, receive someone who is stranded, who has nowhere to go, and who calls at the home of one of our members. We will serve the one in need, and freely and without charge provide

---

[1] Sir. 26:29. [2] Sir. 27:1-2. [3] Sir. 26:29; 27:2. [4] Eph. 4:28. [5] Eph. 4:28.
[6] 1 Tim. 5:22. [7] Sir. 26:29; Wisd. of Sol. 19:13-17.

help and hospitality. This we regard as right, for it was practiced by the believers of old who were quite hospitable.[1]

Drinking Toasts

Drinking toasts is a cause of evil and of disobeying God's commandments. We do not allow it among us because it gives rise to drunkenness, which squanders and destroys both soul and body.[2] You may say that a small drink taken in friendship, since it is enjoyable and desirable, is not wrong. That may be. But we answer that drinking toasts lures a person on to drink when that person would otherwise not do so. Therefore, drinking toasts is unnatural, sinful, and wrong.

When persons are not prompted by thirst but are persuaded to drink in order to please others, they transgress God's order[3] and forget about the Creator as well as about their identity. Such drinkers want to be cock of the roost in showing how much they can drink, downing one drink after another. But they forget what is written: "Woe to those who are great drinkers of wine, and who encourage others to become drunk."[4] "They do not see what the Lord does, nor consider the work of his hands. Thus they land in prison because of their ignorance, and the jaws of hell are opened exceedingly wide over all of them, to swallow their arrogance and foolhardiness as well as everyone who takes pleasure in such things."[5]

Consequently, drinking toasts is fundamentally wrong, no matter how it is done. It is an invention of the devil to catch people, to draw them into his net, and to make them his servants. He then misleads them into all sin and causes them to forsake God. Therefore, flee from drinking toasts even more than from a serpent.[6]

Meetings

When we gather for a meeting, we wish to have our hearts encouraged and awakened in the grace of God, so that we may walk in the sight of the Lord with greater earnestness and diligence.[7] First, the people are encouraged to consider seriously the reason for gathering and prepare their hearts for prayer, so that they may be worthy

---

[1] Heb. 13:2; 1 Pet. 4:9; Gen. 18:1-8; 19:1-3. [2] 1 Cor. 6:9-10; Eph. 5:3-5. [3] 1 Tim. 4:1-5. [4] Isa. 5:22. [5] Isa. 5:12-14. [6] Sir. 21:2-4. [7] 1 Cor. 14:26.

before the Lord to intercede[1] for the concerns of the church and all its members.[2]

After that, we give thanks to God for all the good things he has given us through Christ.[3] We thank him for accepting us into his grace[4] and revealing to us his truth. This is followed by an earnest prayer to God to keep us faithful and devout to the end, and to supply all our needs. We ask him to open our hearts so that we may profit from his Word by accepting it and keeping it.[5]

When prayer is ended, the Servant of the Word proclaims the Lord's Word faithfully, according to the grace God gives him, encouraging us to fear the Lord and to remain true to him. After this has transpired, the servant commits the congregation to the Lord and dismisses them, each one going to his own place.[6]

When we gather to celebrate the meal of remembrance, or the Lord's Supper, the people are encouraged and taught for two or three days beforehand. They are told clearly the meaning of the Lord's Supper, how it is observed, and how they should prepare themselves to be worthy to receive it.[7] Each day should include prayer and thanksgiving. When this has taken place and the Lord's Supper has been observed, all sing a hymn of praise to the Lord. Then the people are exhorted to live in accordance with what they have just expressed. They are commended to the Lord and allowed to depart.

Education of Children

"You parents," says Paul, "do not provoke your children to anger. Instead, bring them up in the nurture and instruction of the Lord."[8] For this reason, our education of children is such that we do not allow them to carry out their headstrong will and carnal habits. In such countries as Moravia, where we have many households, we have schools in which we bring up our children in godly discipline and teach them from early childhood to know God.[9] We do not permit them to go to other schools, since they teach only the wisdom, art, and practices of the world and are silent about divine things.

Our practice is as follows. After the child is weaned, the mother takes the child to school. Women, recognized as competent and con-

---

[1] Sir. 18:23. [2] 1 Tim. 2:1-4. [3] Rom. 8:26-34. [4] Eph. 2:1-13. [5] Col. 1:1-14.
[6] Prov. 1:7; 9:1-10; Sir. 3:17-22; Num. 6:22-26. [7] 1 Cor. 10:14-22; Matt. 26:26-28; Mark 14:22-24. [8] Eph. 6:4. [9] Tob. 1:1-12.

scientious in this task, have been appointed by the church to care for the children. As soon as the little ones can speak, they are taught about God's Word and learn to speak God's Word.[1] They are also taught about prayer, and such things as children can understand. The children remain with these women until their fifth or sixth year, that is, until they are able to learn to read and write.

When they are ready for this, they are entrusted to the schoolmaster, who continues to instruct them in the knowledge of God, so that they may learn to know God's will and strive to keep it. The teacher observes the following order with them: When they assemble for school each morning, they thank the Lord together and pray to him. Then for half an hour the teacher preaches a children's sermon. He tells them how they ought to honor and obey their parents, teachers, and those in authority over them.[2] The teacher uses stories from the Old and New Testaments to illustrate God's promise to good children, and on the other hand, God's punishment to disobedient and headstrong children.[3]

Through obedience to parents, the schoolmaster teaches them obedience to God and how to do God's will.[4] He teaches them to have reverence for God as their almighty Father, to love, honor, serve, and worship God above all things, and to be faithful to him alone, from whom they have all good gifts.[5] Thus we teach our children from infancy not to seek what is temporal, but what is eternal.[6]

The children stay with the schoolmaster until they reach the stage when they can be taught to work. Then each is set to the work for which each child is recognized as gifted and capable. When they have thus been educated, and when they have learned to know and believe in God,[7] they are baptized upon their confession of faith.[8]

Church Discipline

Paul says, "Put away the evil that is among you."[9] Therefore, in the fear of God we watch over one another, since we should protect and keep each other from all wrongdoing and from such evils as deserve exclusion. That is why we admonish one another, warning and rebuk-

---

[1] Deut. 6:20-25; 11:18-21. [2] Exod. 20:12; Deut. 5:16; Sir. 3:1-8; Eph. 6:1-3; Col. 3:20.
[3] 1 Sam. 2:30-34; 3:11-14; 4:17-22; Sir. 3:8-15. [4] Gen. 18:17-19. [5] Tob. 4:14; 14:9-11;
Deut. 6:10-25; 11:1-9; Matt. 22:36-40; Mark 12:28-31; Luke 10:25-28; James 1:17.
[6] Col. 3:1-3. [7] Jer. 31:33-34; Heb. 8:8-10. [8] Acts 8:29-38. [9] 1 Cor. 5:13.

ing each other persistently. Should anyone disregard or not accept the rebuke, the matter is brought before the church. If someone will not listen to the church, that person is then excluded and banned.[1]

A different method is used for major sins. Paul says, "If anyone who is called a brother is sexually immoral or covetous, or if he is an idolater, a slanderer, a drunkard, or a swindler, you must not even eat with him."[2] Such a person is separated from the church without admonition, since the judgment of Paul is already spoken.

When a person is banned, we have no fellowship with him and nothing to do with him, so that he may become ashamed.[3] Yet the excluded person is called to repentance, in the hope that the sinner will be moved to return all the more quickly to God.[4] If that does not happen, the church remains pure and is innocent of his sin. It has no guilt and has earned no rebuke from God.[5]

In all cases, however, a distinction is made. Whoever sins willfully should be rebuked according to the weight of that sin, and the more willful the sin, the sharper the discipline. If, however, one does not sin willfully or maliciously but through weakness of the flesh, that person is disciplined without being completely separated from the church or excluded from all fellowship. Such a member is not, however, permitted to give or accept the Lord's greeting[6] of peace.[7] In this way the erring member will humble oneself before God for the sin, and afterward guard all the more carefully against it.

Reacceptance

When a person is excluded, we have no fellowship with that person until there is true repentance. He may beg and plead, but he will not be accepted until he has received from the church the good report of a truly repentant life. The church must perceive that the Lord has again drawn near to him, been gracious to him, and accepted him. When that is recognized, the church offers the hand of fellowship, as God has commanded us. The church reaccepts the excluded person, who is once more considered a member of the church.[8]

Just as a person is first received into the church by a sign, the sign

---

[1] Matt. 18:15-17.   [2] 1 Cor. 5:11.   [3] 2 Thess. 3:14-15.   [4] 2 Cor. 7:8-11.   [5] Josh. 7:1-5.   [6] Luke 24:36; John 20:19.   [7] Matt. 10:13.   [8] Luke 17:3-4; 2 Cor. 2:5-11.

of baptism,[1] so that person is received back into the church after separation due to sin by a sign, the sign of the laying on of hands. That must be done by a Servant of the Gospel. It indicates that the repentant sinner once more has a share in God's grace and is rooted in it.[2] When this has happened, that person is received back with complete love;[3] all suspicion, complaint, and reluctance are removed. We should trust the reaccepted person as fully as we trust all other members of the church. Thus Satan cannot get the better of us. That is why reacceptance is postponed for such a long time, until, as has been said, the grace of God is again noticeably at work in the person, and the church is again able to have confidence in him.

The Whole Life, Conduct, and Adornment of Christians

First, we say with Peter that the adornment of Christians does not consist in outward show, such as jewelry, fine clothing, or similar trappings. Instead, the person's heart should be adorned with a gentle and quiet spirit. Such adornment is incorruptible, glorious, and greatly prized in the eyes of God. That is how all the saints, who had hope in God, adorned themselves.[4]

Christians, therefore, should not strive to please the world by means of outward adornment, as is done in the world.[5] There the attraction of one to another is by outward show. They take so much pleasure in outward adornment that they forget about God, and so turn their back on heavenly treasure, running after vanity until Satan has them firmly and utterly in his power.[6]

For this reason Paul says, "Do not be conformed to this world, but be transformed through the renewing of your mind, so that you may discern the will of God and that which is perfect and pleasing to him."[7] These words tell us that in order to know what is right in the eyes of God, we must lay aside all that draws us to conform to the world. We must reject anything that is obviously worldly and carnal and give ourselves wholly to the glory of God.[8]

Eagerness to adorn oneself as the world does is not only not fitting for Christians, but on the contrary, it is a sign of the non-Christian.

---

[1] Matt. 28:19-20; Mark 16:16.   [2] Rom. 11:26-27.   [3] 2 Cor. 2:5-11.   [4] 1 Pet. 3:3-5.   [5] Rom. 12:2.   [6] Isa. 3:18-24.   [7] Rom. 12:2.   [8] Rom. 8:5-8.

Godly hearts do well to reject and avoid worldly adornment and concern themselves solely with the true adornment of Christians. As is
said above, that kind of adornment belongs to the inner person.[1] Since
their citizenship is in heaven,[2] Christians ought to put on heavenly
adornment. The only thing they should learn from the children of the
world is diligence. In order to please each other, worldly people are
diligent to dress and to adorn themselves to the very utmost in accordance with the fashion of the land in which they live. How much
more should Christians pay serious attention to the ways of the land
into which they have been led by Christ, that is, a land of heavenly
reality.[3] Christians should adorn themselves in every possible way so
as to please God, who dwells in heaven.[4]

Thus, all the desire and effort of those who would follow Christ,
all their daily cares, endeavors, and prayers,[5] should be directed to
receive from God this heavenly adornment. They should seek it with
enthusiasm and persistence and forget all other adornment. They
should have in mind only the adornment of the faithful, which is true
blessedness. This blessedness will be given them in abundance.

Such diligence comes only from love to him for whose pleasure
we adorn ourselves. The greater our love to the one who dwells in
heaven, the more we will strive for the adornment in which he
delights. We want to wear it only because it pleases God.[6] Whoever
does not search for this adornment shows no great reverence for God.

Whoever longs for this adornment wholeheartedly will be clothed
by the Lord himself with holy raiment. That person will be clothed with
all kinds of Christian virtues,[7] which may be put on and worn as a gar-
ment. These garments will adorn a Christian better than a necklace of
gold.[8] Whoever recognizes this will then forget pearls, necklaces of silk
and gold, and other similar ornamentation. Instead, we will grasp and
express our faith through the one adornment of blessedness which lasts
forever and upon which we have set our heart.[9]

However, we also speak concerning anyone who made clothing
earlier, while in the world, before coming to the true recognition of the
truth. Such a person does not sin by continuing to use that clothing
until it is worn out, as long as the person does not misuse it by allowing such outward adornment to be a hindrance to oneself in striving

---

[1] 1 Pet. 3:3-5. [2] Eph. 2:19-22. [3] Col. 3:1-4. [4] Isa. 60:1-5; Matt. 5:3-12; 23:23-33.
[5] Ps. 1:1-3. [6] John 14:15. [7] 2 Pet. 1:5-11. [8] Prov. 3:1-15. [9] 1 Pet. 1:6-9.

for divine adornment. If it should be a hindrance, it would be better to throw such clothing into the fire than wear it. But after the recognition of truth, we permit no one among us to make or order such clothing. Otherwise, Satan could use the occasion to mislead that person again.

Through the grace of God, we have now given an account of our faith, teaching, and whole way of life. To the almighty God be all praise and honor! Except for those who fight willfully against the truth, everyone will be able to sense and recognize that we have written nothing except the truth. Nor have we chosen anything to suit ourselves, but we have resolved to hold faithfully to what God himself has ordained and commanded.

May the Lord our God, to his praise, bring to fulfillment the work he has begun in us all. May he establish us in his truth and keep us faithful and devout in his Son until the end, so that we may become worthy to receive the promise with all the saints. May he enlighten those who still walk in darkness, so that they may see and know the light of life. Amen.

Yes, amen.
Sit laus Deo
(praise be to God).

"Fight for the truth to the death,
and the Lord will fight for you."[1]

---

[1] Sir. 4:28.

PART 2

The God of Grace and His Separated People

How God Desires to Have a People Whom He Has Separated from the World and Chosen to Be His Bride

God the Almighty made people in his own image so that he might be known and praised by them, and his holy name be honored.[1] Since God is truth, it is clear that his only desire for people was that they reveal this image of truth and live and walk in it.[2] Thus God desired that people would appear in their true nature, in the image and glory of God.[3] No corrupting poison would be found in them.[4] But Adam and Eve were deceived by the counsel of the serpent and turned away from God's glory. They fell into sin,[5] namely, into the likeness of the devil to whom they had surrendered. Because they gave themselves to the service of unrighteousness, the wrath of their Creator came upon them, and they fell into disfavor.[6] For that reason they were driven out of the garden of Eden.[7]

That is how transgression came into the world.[8] It continued to increase more and more in succeeding generations, and God's indignation increased against them also. He wanted to forsake them, saying, "My Spirit shall not always be a judge among people, since they are flesh; I shall take it from them."[9] That is what happened to Saul[10] and many others who rejected the word of God, as the book of Wisdom testifies: "The Holy Spirit teaches rightly, that one should flee from idolaters and depart from the wicked."[11]

From this we see that in the beginning God separated the faithful from the unfaithful. Concerning the unfaithful, he says that the Holy Spirit will not dwell in those who have given themselves over to sin.[12] However, God promises the faithful that he will be their God[13] and be

---

[1] Gen. 1:26-31. [2] John 14:1-17. [3] 1 Cor. 11:7. [4] Wisd. of Sol. 1:13-14.
[5] Gen. 3:1-7. [6] Eph. 2:1-12; 5:1-6. [7] Gen. 3:23-24. [8] Rom. 5:12-14; 1 Tim. 2:14.
[9] Gen. 6:3. [10] 1 Sam. 16:14-15. [11] Wisd. of Sol. 1:4-5. [12] Wisd. of Sol. 1:4.
[13] Gen. 17:7; Jer. 31:31-37; 32:36-44.

with them at all times.[1] God instructs them to keep his commandments, teachings, and ways.[2] We see this especially in the case of Abraham,[3] who was called the father of all believers.[4] The Lord appeared to him and said, "I am God, Shaddai, the one with full authority and over-flowing with all that is good. Walk before me, be steadfast and faithful to me, and I will establish a covenant between me and you."[5]

Moses gives the same message to Israel: "If you pay attention to these laws and are careful to follow them, then the Lord your God will keep the covenant of mercy as he swore to your fathers. He will love you and bless you."[6] Now, God has always made a distinction between the faithful and the unfaithful, loving the faithful and hating the unfaithful[7] (as he still does and always will do). So he wanted this separation and distinction to be visible not only to himself but also to humans.[8] It began in Christ,[9] in whom also the restoration of salvation had been promised from the beginning.

When God the Almighty in his grace wished to show that he had pleasure in the faithful but not in the unfaithful,[10] he separated for himself one people from all other peoples, one people[11] in whom he was pleased.[12] He established his covenant with them[13] and gave them circumcision as a token. They were to circumcise the flesh of the fore-skin of every male born to them or bought by them. That was to be a distinction between the chosen people and the heathen.[14]

God also promised to be their God and to have them as his own people.[15] He said to Abraham, "I will be your God and the God of your descendants."[16] Moreover, he made yet another distinction with the words: "As for Ishmael, I have heard you; but I will establish my covenant with Isaac."[17] In effect, he was saying, "I will not establish my covenant with the bondwoman's son, born according to the flesh, but with the free son, the son born of the promise. In him I will keep the promise I made to you, and in him I will give the blessing, for his descendants are the ones who will be called your seed."

Paul interprets that word by saying, "The children of the flesh are not the children of God. Instead, the children of the promise are counted as Abraham's offspring."[18] Hence, it is evident that at the be-

---

[1] Matt. 28:20. [2] Deut. 28:1-14. [3] Gen. 12:7; 15:5-6. [4] Rom. 4:7-25. [5] Gen. 17:1-5. [6] Deut. 7:12-15. [7] Exod. 20:4-6; Deut. 5:8-10; 7:7-10. [8] Matt. 25:10-12; 2 Thess. 1:6-10. [9] John 15:9-21. [10] Exod. 20:4-6, 20. [11] Gen. 12:1-3. [12] Deut. 4:20-24. [13] Gen. 17:7-10; 26:2-5; 28:1-4. [14] Gen. 17:10-14. [15] Lev. 26:9-13; Deut. 29:7-15. [16] Gen. 17:1-8. [17] Gen. 17:19-21. [18] Rom. 9:6-8.

ginning God did not choose all of Abraham's children, as Paul declares clearly. He says, "Not all are Israelites who are born of Israel, nor are all who are descended from Abraham called Abraham's children."[1]

Scripture says, "Drive out the bondwoman and her son, for the bondwoman's son shall not share the inheritance with the son of the freedwoman."[2] If this is true, then this story implies that being an heir is separated from being a slave. The slave cannot remain in the house, whereas the children always have their home there.[3] The promise is meant for them alone, namely, that God will be their God, and they shall be his people.[4] Yes, he will be their Father, and they shall be his children.[5] Because of that he blesses them richly with all kinds of good things.[6] Thus it is written, "The Lord will send a blessing on your storehouses and on everything to which you set your hand; he will bless you in the land he will give you."[7]

However, with this outward blessing, the Lord wished to show the unfathomable riches of his grace, which will be given us in Christ.[8] From him we have received grace upon grace.[9] Moses says further, "The Lord shall make you a holy people for himself, as he has sworn to you, if you keep his commandments and walk in his ways. The whole world shall see that you are called by the name of the Lord."[10] Now Esau was also by birth coheir to the promise, since he was fathered by Isaac,[11] through whom the promise was to be fulfilled.[12] He made himself unworthy of the promise by selling his birthright to Jacob for a paltry meal,[13] and he was unable to repent of it even though he sought repentance with tears. Therefore, Esau was not counted as a son but was assigned to bondage[14] and separated from Jacob.[15]

In Jacob, who is also called Israel,[16] the promise came to pass,[17] for the tribe increased through his many children.[18] God cared for them as his people,[19] not because of their devoutness but because of his faithful promise.[20] He did not forget but held firmly to the covenant[21] he had made with the fathers.[22]

When God punished Egypt for Israel's sake, the Israelites were untouched by Egypt's plagues.[23] Thus people could know how the Lord separated Egypt and Israel from one another.[24] Israel set out[25]

---

[1] Rom. 9:6-7. [2] Gen. 21:9-12; Gal. 4:28-31. [3] John 8:31-35. [4] Gen. 17:7; Deut. 29:9-15. [5] 2 Cor. 6:18. [6] Gen. 12:1-3; 13:2. [7] Deut. 28:1-12. [8] Rom. 8:18-21. [9] John 1:14-16. [10] Deut. 28:9-10. [11] Gen. 25:19-34. [12] Gen. 17:18-20. [13] Gen. 25:31-34. [14] Gen. 27:38; Heb. 12:15-17. [15] Gen. 36:6. [16] Gen. 32:28. [17] Gen. 17:4-8. [18] Gen. 48:17-20. [19] Exod. 3:6-10. [20] Deut. 9:6. [21] Deut. 4:5-10. [22] Gen. 17:1-5; 26:1-5; 28:12-15. [23] Exod. 7:19-25. [24] Exod. 9:1-7. [25] Exod. 13:17-22.

with joy and delight in the hope of receiving the Promised Land.[1] Soon, however, the people lost that hope[2] and became so disobedient to God's Spirit[3] that the Lord considered destroying them in the wilderness.[4] But for the sake of his name and because of the prayer of his servant Moses, he did not do it.[5]

Thus the Israelites were spared, not because they were devout,[6] but because of the grace and mercy of the Almighty.[7] The covenant God made with the fathers[8] was to stand, and the promised grace[9] of the coming Christ was to be given in his time,[10] for he was to be born of them.[11] Therefore, God gave them his law,[12] statutes, and ordinances[13] so that they would observe them, walk in them, and keep them diligently.[14] They were to teach their children faithfully so that those children[15] in turn could teach their own children. In that way they would learn to fear the Lord as long as they lived[16] and would not turn from his commands to the right or to the left.[17] Then the curse that was foretold would not come upon them.[18]

These are some of the commands God the Lord gave Israel through Moses: "Beware of making a treaty with the inhabitants of the land you are entering, or they will become a stumbling block to you. Do not make friends with them. Do not give your daughters to their sons, or take their daughters for your sons, for they might turn your sons away from me and make them serve strange gods.[19] This is how you should act toward them. Smash their altars, break their pillars, cut down their groves, and burn their idols in the fire.[20] But do not act in this way toward the Lord your God.[21] Instead, go to the place he will choose[22] and bring your sacrifices and tithes.[23] There you shall serve him."[24]

Here it is clear that God does not want his people to associate with the heathen in their disorderly conduct,[25] nor to take part in their ceremonies, nor to go to the places where they practice idolatry. What the heathen seek is different from what the faithful seek.[26]

That is why God says through the prophets, "Can two walk together unless they have agreed beforehand?"[27] Believers and unbe-

---

[1] Ps. 105:37-45. [2] Ps. 106:8-23. [3] Num. 14:1-23. [4] Deut. 1:19-28. [5] Exod. 32:9-14. [6] Deut. 9:1-6. [7] Exod. 33:12-19; Rom. 9:10-26. [8] Gen. 17:4-8; 28:12-15. [9] Deut. 9:1-5. [10] Gen. 49:8-12. [11] Gen. 12:1-3. [12] Exod. 20:1-20. [13] Deut. 5:1-33. [14] Deut. 6:1-7; 11:1; 28:11-13. [15] Deut. 6:1-7. [16] Ps. 78:1-6; Deut. 10:12-17. [17] Josh. 1:7-9. [18] Deut. 27:11-26. [19] Exod. 34:12-16. [20] Num. 33:50-53; Deut. 12:1-3. [21] Deut. 12:4. [22] 1 Kings 9:1-3. [23] Exod. 23:23-25; 34:14-26; Deut. 26. [24] Deut. 10:20. [25] 1 Pet. 4:1-5. [26] Deut. 12:1-7. [27] Amos 3:3.

lievers are not agreed;[1] the Lord has chosen one and rejected the other.[2] He has said, "I have accepted you alone out of all the peoples on the earth."[3] When Esdras speaks to the Most High, he says of Israel, "Of every tree of the earth, you have chosen the vine; of all birds, the dove; of all cattle, the sheep; and of all nations, one people, your people Israel, to be the people of your inheritance."[4]

God the Lord, who is God over all gods, is separate from all idols.[5] He himself has expressed this when he says, "To whom then will you liken me, or to what image will you compare me? For I declare beforehand things that have not yet come to pass."[6] Of Christ, Paul says, "Can Christ and Belial agree?"[7] Because the believer has nothing in common with the unbeliever, God wishes to separate his people from the ungodly.[8] God himself says, "If you turn to me, I will be with you, and if you teach the devout to cut themselves off from evildoers, you shall be as my mouth. Before you fall to them, they will have to fall to you, for I have made you into a fortified wall of bronze. Though they fight against you, they shall not prevail, for I am with you to help and save you."[9]

God says further, "Depart, depart, leave that place! Touch nothing unclean! Come away and purify yourselves, you who bear the vessels of the Lord."[10] Furthermore the Lord says, "My people, come away and leave them, and cut yourselves off. Touch nothing unclean, and I will receive you and be a father to you, and you will be my children."[11] Again he says, "Come out of her, my people, so that you do not take part in her sins or become stricken by any of her plagues."[12]

As mentioned above, even as God is holy[13] and separate from all abominations, so he wishes for his people to be separated from the assembly of the wicked.[14] His people are to be a holy people,[15] according to his command: "You shall be holy, for I the Lord your God am holy."[16]

All who have eyes to see can understand why God commands his people to cut themselves off from such ceremonies. The reason is so that they would not pollute and defile themselves. Much less should they think that they are serving God when they take part and do the same as the heathen do, with their abominations, idols, and devils.[17]

---

[1] Amos 3:1-2; 2 Cor. 6:14-18.   [2] Deut. 9:1-6.   [3] Amos 3:1-2.   [4] 2 Esd. 5:20-27.
[5] Deut. 32:39.   [6] Isa. 40:18-26; 46:3-10.   [7] 2 Cor. 6:15.   [8] 2 Cor. 6:14-16.   [9] Jer. 15:19-21.   [10] Isa. 52:11.   [11] 2 Cor. 6:17-18.   [12] Rev. 18:4.   [13] Lev. 11:44-45.   [14] Jer. 15:19.
[15] Lev. 20:1-8.   [16] Lev. 19:1-4.   [17] 1 Cor. 10:20-28.

For this reason Moses said to Pharaoh, "It would not be good to sacrifice within the country, for we might sacrifice to the abominations of the Egyptians and not to our God."[1] Note that here Moses not only refuses to go to the place where they perform their abominable rites, but he will not even sacrifice in the same country.

Some may say it took place for another reason; yet the word remains clearly and distinctly expressed. No one can deny that God did not want the Israelites to serve him in Egypt any longer. The command to go had been given.[2] After the command had been carried out, the Lord told them the same again. They were to eradicate and completely demolish the places where the heathen had served their gods.[3] That was why Moses sought an opportunity to lead the people out with haste,[4] as the Lord had commanded.[5] Not only that, but the Lord even forced the haughty king to let the people go.[6] Later, when Pharaoh was hurrying after the Israelites, the Lord drowned Pharaoh in the sea.[7]

In the same way, God commanded the Israelites that, on arriving in the land to which he was leading them, they were to destroy the inhabitants of the land. God did not want them to be enticed and seduced to surrender themselves to idols by the daily sight of idolatrous ceremonies. They were also to destroy completely all places where the heathen served their gods.[8] They were not to change those places, or to convert them to right use, but to destroy them utterly.[9] Besides all that, God warned them earnestly, showing them the harm that would come upon them if they did not obey his command: "But if you will not drive out the inhabitants of the land before you, then those whom you allow to remain will become barbs in your eyes and thorns in your sides and harass you in the land in which you live. In addition, I will treat you as I meant to treat them."[10]

As long as the Israelites firmly kept these commands, the Lord cared for them as for his children. He protected them and allowed no one to harm them.[11] But as soon as they forgot and were no longer faithful to these and other commands, the Lord delivered them into the hands of those who hated them.[12] He had clearly forewarned them of this through his servant Moses,[13] especially in Moses' song of witness.[14] Joshua, too, when he was old and soon to fall asleep, warned

---

[1] Exod. 8:25-27.　[2] Exod. 4.　[3] Num. 33:51-52; Deut. 12:1-3.　[4] Exod. 5:1-9.
[5] Exod. 3:7-22.　[6] Exod. 12:12-13.　[7] Exod. 14:26-31; Ps. 106:6-12.　[8] Num. 33:50-53.
[9] Deut. 12:1-3.　[10] Num. 33:55-56.　[11] Ps. 10:13-18.　[12] Judg. 2:10-15.　[13] Deut. 4:15-24.　[14] Deut. 32:15-29.

them with these words: "You have seen the great things that the Lord your God has done[1] to your enemies and how he himself fought for you.[2] Therefore, be steadfast in keeping all the commands of God which Moses gave to you.[3] Do not turn from them either to the right or to the left.[4]

"Then the Lord your God will be with you[5] and will so fight for you[6] that one of you shall chase a thousand.[7] But if you turn back and intermingle with the remnant of these nations and make friends with them, they will become snares and traps to you. They will be thorns in your sides and barbs in your eyes[8] until the Lord drives you out of the good land and destroys you."[9] Furthermore, Joshua says, "Of all the good things the Lord has promised you,[10] not one thing is lacking. All have come about. Just as all the good things have come about, so will the Lord bring all the evil upon you that he has promised; not one evil thing will be lacking if you transgress his commandments."[11]

The land of the Israelites, their glory, rule, and later the kingdom —these all prefigure and point to Christ the King and his future kingdom. All this had been promised beforehand[12] and was later established.[13] Since that is so, the driving out means separating believers from unbelievers,[14] for unbelievers have no place in the church of God.[15] God desires to have a holy bride without wrinkle, spot, or blemish,[16] holy as he is holy.[17] The Lord, the almighty God, was not pleased when Israel allowed the heathen to dwell in the land instead of driving them out. His angel spoke to them: "I have led you out of Egypt, as I swore to your fathers, and I will never break my covenant with you.[18] You are to make no alliance with the inhabitants of this land; you are to throw down their altars. You have not obeyed me. Why did you do this? That is why I also said I will not drive out the inhabitants before you. They will become a pitfall for you, and their gods will ensnare you."[19]

God would be even more displeased today if one were to set up a church together with the world, or take the world into the church of the saints. David says the sinner has no place in the congregation of the righteous.[20] Some may say, "We do not set up a church with unbe-

---

[1] Josh. 23:3-14. [2] Josh. 6:15-20; 8:18; 10:10-14; 11:6-12. [3] Deut. 4:1-7. [4] Josh. 1:7-8. [5] Gen. 26:17-24. [6] 2 Chron. 13:1-16. [7] Lev. 26:3-8. [8] Josh. 23:12-13. [9] Deut. 28:15-32. [10] Deut. 28:1-14. [11] Deut. 27-28. [12] Gen. 49:10. [13] Acts 2:1-21. [14] Acts 5:1-16. [15] Ps. 1:4-6. [16] Eph. 5:1-7. [17] 1 Pet. 1:13-16. [18] Gen. 15:13-18. [19] Judg. 2:1-3. [20] Ps. 1:4-6.

lievers but with those who confess Christ. Even though they may have fallen into many sins or even fallen away completely, if they want to improve themselves, it is fitting for us to help them and not to turn our backs on them. In the Old Testament, the prophets did not cut themselves off from Israel even though the people had indeed done evil. They remained with the people and with earnest admonitions led them all back to God.[1] It is therefore fitting for us to do the same."

To that we reply that the prophets acted rightly and not foolishly in not cutting themselves off from Israel, in spite of the evil the people had done. This is true because at that time to be an heir and to be a servant were not distinguished from one another.[2] Although the prophets were truly heirs and the others were slaves, yet they were kept under outward rules until Christ came.[3] Now that the time appointed by the Father has come, however, heirs and slaves are separated, so that the heirs can receive their inheritance and their freedom.[4] Now, through faith in Christ, there are no more slaves but heirs.[5]

Some may say, "Those others also believe in Christ except that they have fallen into certain errors. We must help to raise up everyone who has fallen." To that we say that it is not wrong to help raise those who are fallen, if they are willing to let themselves be raised. But no one is raised up by a dead faith,[6] nor is anyone who continues to sin helped any more than Pharaoh was.[7] God raised up Pharaoh in order to display his power through him.[8]

The only real help takes place through regular preaching, followed by faith sealed with the Holy Spirit.[9] Paul says, "All who are moved by the Spirit of God are children of God."[10] This activity of God produces sons and daughters and leads them here and now into their freedom through Christ.[11] God alone is the One who has made the distinction between slaves and heirs;[12] therefore the distinction will endure. No one will be accepted into the covenant of an heir and be considered part of the community of the faithful who is not urged by the Spirit of God.[13]

Therefore, we also say that we desire to encourage everyone to improvement and to be drawn to love and God's blessedness. But this cannot be accomplished in the manner described above, for through

---

[1] 1 Kings 18:7-19; 2 Chron. 18:13-22; 24:17-21; 34:16-28.   [2] Gal. 4:1-3.   [3] Gal. 4:3-7.   [4] Gen. 21:9-12; Gal. 4:4-7.   [5] Gal. 4:7.   [6] James 2:14-17.   [7] Exod. 9:27-35.   [8] Rom. 9:17.   [9] Eph. 1:13.   [10] Rom. 8:14.   [11] Gal. 4:4-7.   [12] John 8:31-36.   [13] Rom. 8:14.

God's grace we recognize that this is not pleasing to him. The purpose cannot be attained or accomplished because this work is not directed by God. According to our Master's instructions[1] and the inspiration of his Holy Spirit,[2] the right way is first to call everyone to repentance through the Lord's Word.[3] All who respond-who give themselves up to God completely[4] and allow the Holy Spirit to work in them and lead them into a new life-all these we will joyfully accept into the church of God's children as those who have received Christ.[5] But, as Christ and the apostles did, we allow those who continue in their sins[6] to be banished and go their own ways.

If people ever say of their backsliding,[7] as you do, that they have been seduced by papistry, we answer, yes, they have been mislead, seduced, and blinded, and know nothing of God or of Christ.[8] They have God only on their lips and deny him in their lives.[9] They have tried to find salvation in created things and served the creature more than the Creator.[10] Eternal wisdom speaks of that: "These people honor me with their lips, but their hearts are far from me. They therefore worship me in vain, and I will not hear their prayers."[11]

If people have been so completely deceived, mislead, and corrupted by papistry that they have honored created things more than the Creator,[12] then they certainly are guilty of serious sin and deep faithlessness.[13] No one can deny that they have left the fellowship of the saints and surrendered to the abominations of the heathen.[14] Those who wish to be reconciled with God and return to him must separate themselves from such ungodly company.[15] They must turn completely to the Word of truth[16] and allow it to renew them.[17] Then God will once more be gracious to them[18] and accept them.[19]

That truth is symbolized in the story of the foreign wives whom the Jews had to put away in order to be reconciled with God.[20] Similarly, to be accepted by God, anyone who has become entangled in such alien commitments must break with them and join Christ.[21] Otherwise, God will drive them away as Nehemiah drove certain persons away. Anyone who leaves the church or is excluded will not be accepted back until true repentance has been done.[22] During separation from the church, the excluded member is without God and with-

---

[1] Matt. 28:19-20; Mark 16:15-16. [2] 2 Pet. 1:19-21. [3] Matt. 4:17; Acts 2:36-38.
[4] Rom. 12:1. [5] John 1:9-12. [6] Matt. 19:16-26. [7] 2 Thess. 2:3-12. [8] 1 John 3:6-11.
[9] Isa. 29:13-16. [10] Rom. 1:21-25. [11] Isa. 29:13-14; Mark 7:1-9. [12] Rom. 1:21-25.
[13] Jer. 2. [14] Ezek. 16:1-23. [15] Acts 2:36-40. [16] Ps. 119:9-16. [17] Eph. 5:25-27; Titus 3:3-7.
[18] Acts 2:38-39. [19] 2 Cor. 6:16-18. [20] Ezra 10:10-12. [21] Neh. 13:23-29. [22] 2 Cor. 2:5-11.

out Christ. John says, "Whoever transgresses and does not abide by the teachings of Christ, has no God."[1] As long as they remain separated and have no God, their preaching, baptizing, and everything they do is impure. To those who are impure, everything is impure[2] and therefore an abomination before God and counts as nothing.

Since they have departed from the Word, which is God,[3] they have no word. God therefore says to them, "Hear the word of the Lord! The Lord has reason to rebuke the inhabitants of the land, for there is no faithfulness, no belief, no love, and no knowledge of God in them. On the contrary, blasphemy, lying, killing, stealing, and committing adultery have taken the upper hand. Murder follows murder."[4]

Such people have neither the Word nor true baptism. On what basis then are people baptized today? If I must say so, they were preached to by those who were not sent, and baptized [as infants] although God had not commanded it.[5] Since they had received no command from God, their baptism is also worthless. Christ says, "Every plant which my heavenly Father has not planted shall be uprooted."[6]

That is why I say of these deluded people that they do not know Christ.[7] They have not known, received,[8] or accepted him.[9] They have heard only a verbal confession from their forefathers, from generation to generation, and have learned to repeat it.[10] The education of their own children shows us this. They teach blessedness so well that as soon as a child begins to speak, the child learns to curse. Then the parents praise him and say, "What a fine boy he will be!" That attitude is most common among the nobility, who certainly ought to oppose it.

The spirit of the parents is recognizable in their children.[11] Verbal confession, therefore, means nothing to me. The devil can also use God's name and confess him in spoken words.[12] I know what an abomination that is to God![13] I can only say I think such people have conquered and accepted Christianity in the same way the Philistines took the ark of God from Israel.[14] They slew all the Israelites and took the ark with them into their own country. There they kept it to their own harm, and to the harm of their god[15] until, growing wiser by misfortune, they had to send it home again.[16]

These so-called Christians can be compared with the heathen who were led into the land of Israel by the Assyrian king and were

---

[1] 2 John 1:9.   [2] Titus 1:15.   [3] John 1:1.   [4] Hos. 4:1-2.   [5] Jer. 23:21.   [6] Matt. 15:13.   [7] John 3:1-5.   [8] John 14:6-7.   [9] John 1:5-11.   [10] Isa. 29:13-16; Mark 7:1-9.   [11] Sir. 11:28.   [12] James 2:19; Luke 8:27-29.   [13] Isa. 1:10-15; 29:13-14; Mark 7:6-7.   [14] 1 Sam. 4:6-11.   [15] 1 Sam. 5:1, 5.   [16] 1 Sam. 6:10-16.

settled in the cities. The Lord sent lions among them to kill them, until a priest from Israel came and taught them the manner and practice of the law. Those heathen learned to serve the God of heaven. But because they continued in their abominable practices, God was not pleased with their service, and their children followed in their footsteps.[1]

That is just what can be seen in the so-called Christians of today, especially the Lutherans. They continually profess to love and serve God and yet will not give up evil, sinful practices and the whole service of the devil. They continue that way from generation to generation; as their fathers did, so do they, and even worse. John clearly states in what way they walk in the truth![2]

Something took place later, however, when God the Lord had mercy on Israel, according to his promise.[3] Through Cyrus the king, the Lord led Israel back into their land to rebuild the temple Nebuchadnezzar had broken down.[4] Cyrus said, "The Lord God in heaven has given me all the kingdoms of the earth, and he has commanded me to build a house for him at Jerusalem in Judah. Whoever among you belongs to his people (may his God be with him), let him go up to Jerusalem in Judah and build the house of the Lord God of Israel. He is the God in Jerusalem. The people of any place where a survivor may now be living should freely and without compulsion provide him with silver and gold, goods and livestock, for the house of God at Jerusalem."[5] Thus the Lord their God touched the hearts of some Israelites, and they went up to build his house.

Now, as they were building and the work was progressing, the heathen, or the leaders among those who had been living in the country, came to them and said, "Let us build with you, for we seek your God as you do, and we have been sacrificing to him[6] since Esarhaddon, king of Assyria, brought us up here."[7] Then Zerubbabel and Joshua and the heads of families in Israel answered them, "It is not fitting for you to build a house for our God with us; we will build it ourselves for the Lord God of Israel,[8] as the king has commanded us."[9] The heathen hindered the Israelites and frightened them away from their work. They tried through letters to get Artaxerxes the king to order the work to be stopped, and in that they were successful[10] until

---

[1] 2 Kings 17:18-34. [2] 1 John 2:4; 4:20. [3] Deut. 4:14-22. [4] 2 Chron. 36:19-23.
[5] Ezra 1:1-4. [6] Ezra 4:1-2. [7] 2 Kings 19:36-37. [8] Ezra 4:3. [9] Ezra 1:1-4. [10] Ezra 4:24.

the time of Haggai and Zechariah. Those prophets urged the people to continue the work of the Lord.[1]

That is a picture of how we fare with so-called Christians today. They, too, want to build with us and undertake the Lord's work. Then they hear the answer of devout Zerubbabel, Joshua, and all the chiefs of Israel: "It is not fitting for heathen to build the house of God with them."[2] So they try to obstruct the work. Their cunning and tyranny is more cruel than that of Pharaoh,[3] Antiochus,[4] or Nero in attempting to scare us from building the Lord's house. We set our hope on our God, that he will not let those so-called Christians succeed any more than he did the enemies of Judah. Through the persistence of the prophets, their work succeeded gloriously, and consequently the enemies of Israel were not allowed to build with them.

Thus we hope, in spite of what the so-called Christians do, that their fury and persecution will not scare us away from the work that the Lord our God has begun in us through Christ. Instead, we hope that God will complete it to his praise and give us richly of his manifold divine grace. For we try earnestly and with all our power to devote ourselves to do what agrees with his will and to preserve it. He has promised us,[5] "I will turn to you and let you grow; I will increase your numbers and keep my covenant with you. You shall eat last year's harvest, clearing out the old to make room for the new.[6] I will walk and dwell among you, and my soul shall not spurn you; I will walk among you and be your God, and you shall be my people."[7]

Thus we wish with all our heart that all people would be built into a holy house with us.[8] But as that is not the case, we ask God day and night to protect all whose heart he has touched, moved, and pierced. May they come and build such a house, and not be frightened away by cunning, threats, or anything else.[9] We also pray that God will move those who are not yet so moved to come to the building of the Lord's house.[10] Thus may it go forward as it began in Christ, to the praise of God the Father, through Jesus Christ eternally. Amen.

---

[1] Ezra 5:1-5; Hag. 1-2; Zech. 4:9; 6:15. [2] Ezra 4:3. [3] Exod. 5:6-14. [4] 1 Macc. 1:21-34. [5] Deut. 28:1-14. [6] Lev. 26:9-12. [7] 2 Cor. 6:16-18. [8] 1 Pet. 2:5. [9] Acts 16:14-40. [10] 1 Pet. 2:1-5.

How the House of the Lord Is Built Up in Christ, and How It Has Been Decided That in This House Separation Shall Be Perfected

Meanwhile, much has been said about the construction of the former temple at Jerusalem. It became a picture pointing to the church of God.[1] To discover the truth, it is necessary to examine this matter which concerns and affects us. We thus find, if we look at the truth and hold the matter up to the light, that in the beginning, when God created humans in his own image,[2] he created them as his dwelling place. As the sage tells us, there was no deadly poison in them, but all was well with them.[3]

Since there was no corruption in humans, it follows that all good, which is God himself, was to dwell in them. The likeness of God in which humans were created shows that very thing. But because this temple was desecrated and despoiled through the counsel of the serpent,[4] it has instead become a dwelling place of idols and all unclean spirits. In the parable about Satan, Christ shows how that happens. When the evil spirit finds no rest, he says to himself, "I will return to my house, which I have left."[5] Accordingly, says Paul, Satan carries on his work in the children of unbelief,[6] bringing about all kinds of unrighteousness so that the Spirit of the Lord will leave them.[7]

Since all this has happened, it has justifiably aroused the wrath of the Almighty[8] and brought it on the human race. In spite of all this, God is a wellspring of mercy whose streams never run dry.[9] Remembering his holy name, he did not want to give up his plan to have people be his temple.[10] He thought to restore and to repair their fall and the harm that had been done. This he had promised soon after the transgression had taken place, when he said to the serpent, "The

---

[1] Matt. 21:12-13; John 2:13-16; 1 Cor. 3:16-17; Heb. 3:5-6. [2] Gen. 1:26-27.
[3] Wisd. of Sol. 1:13-14. [4] Gen. 3:1-8. [5] Matt. 12:43-44. [6] Eph. 2:1-2. [7] Wisd. of Sol. 1:5. [8] Eph. 5:5-6. [9] Jer. 2:13. [10] 1 Cor. 3:16; 6:19; Heb. 3:6.

woman's offspring shall crush your head."[1] Since the promise, God has shown this in many ways to those who were pleasing to him, especially to those who were devoted to him from the beginning.

God remained with these devoted ones and showed himself to them[2] until the time of grace[3] came again, and the promise became strengthened in Christ. Then once more God built and established a temple for himself,[4] a temple separate from all abominations.[5] Christ is the first stone[6] and foundation,[7] and we must all be built on him.[8] He was delivered up for us[9] and was raised from the dead on the third day,[10] in order that we too might walk in a new life.[11]

Therefore Paul says, "Christ has given himself up for us that he might consecrate for himself a church, cleansing her by washing with water through the word, so that he might present her to himself as a radiant church, holy and blameless,[12] without stain or wrinkle or any other blemish."[13]

This building is not earthly and human, but heavenly and of God.[14] Therefore, it is the duty of the builders to learn their skill in heaven from the Father of all grace,[15] from whom flow all good gifts,[16] and not from humans, even if they are called doctors or masters. Christ himself says, "They must all be taught by the Lord. Everyone who hears and learns from my Father comes to me."[17] Therefore, we must first of all go to this school, and with Moses we must climb up the mount[18] to see the tabernacle, in order to take note of its form and all its decorations. We should also observe the command given by the Lord to Moses. "Take care and observe," he says, "that you create it according to the design I showed you on the mountain."[19]

Woe indeed to the foolish workers who have never been to the mountain[20] and still less have seen the example of the tabernacle![21] What kind of work can they do, since they have remained in the valley and in the encampment? They have never gone outside the camp to Christ[22] and know nothing of the size and design of the tabernacle. How can they work when they do not know how to go about it, or what is needed for the task?[23] If they bring thornbushes instead of firs,

---

[1] Gen. 3:15.   [2] Gen. 12:1-3; 15:1-5; 17:1-8; 18:16-22; 26:1-5; 28:10-15; 32:24-30.
[3] 2 Cor. 6:1-2.   [4] Amos 9:11-15; Acts 15:16-17.   [5] Isa. 52:1.   [6] 1 Pet. 2:1-5.   [7] 1 Cor. 3:11.   [8] Eph. 2:19-22.   [9] Matt. 26:47-56; Mark 14:43-50; Luke 22:47-53; 1 Cor. 11:23-26. [10] John 2:18-22; 20:11-18; Matt. 28:1-10; Mark 16:1-7; Luke 24:1-15.   [11] Rom. 6:4. [12] 1 Pet. 1:13-23.   [13] Eph. 5:2, 25-27.   [14] 1 Cor. 3:9.   [15] Exod. 31:1-6.   [16] James 1:17. [17] Isa. 54:13; John 6:45.   [18] Exod. 24:12-18.   [19] Exod. 25:40; Acts 7:44; Heb. 8:1-5. [20] Ps. 2:4-6; 15:1-5; 24:3-6.   [21] Eph. 2:19-22.   [22] Heb. 13:10-13.   [23] 1 Cor. 2:11-16.

dross instead of silver and gold, what kind of house will that be? Who will enjoy living in it?[1]

That tabernacle will certainly suffer the same fate as the tabernacle of Shiloh,[2] which the Lord abandoned along with its priests,[3] who were slain, just as the Lord had told Eli.[4] Oh, take heed and become wise! Even Moses, a servant of the Lord who had spoken with God face to face,[5] knew nothing of the tabernacle.[6] He had to receive its design from the Lord on the mountain,[7] even though it was only an image of holy things.[8] Now what will those do who are to build the holy tabernacle? Where will those who have never been up the mountain obtain the design,[9] and despite that still presume to do this work?[10] Surely they must be those of whom the Lord, the Almighty God, has said, "I did not send these prophets, yet they ran; I did not speak to them, yet they prophesied. If they had stood in my council and had heard my words, they would have turned my people from their evil deeds and evil ways."[11]

The Lord tells such prophets, "You have not cared for my flock, but have scattered them and driven them away. So I will punish you for the evil you have done. I myself will gather the remnant of my flock out of all the countries to which I have driven them, and will bring them back to their home pastures. They shall be fruitful and increase, and I will appoint shepherds over them who will tend them."[12]

Therefore, before the foundation of the world, Christ the caretaker of the holy tabernacle[13] was assigned by the Father to reveal to us the Father's eternal will[14] and to raise and rebuild again their fallen structure.[15] He does not come from Mount Sinai, as did Moses,[16] but from heaven itself.[17] However, he climbs the mount at the Father's bidding, as God had appointed him to do, and as David says: "I have set my king upon my holy hill of Zion, that he may proclaim my law; for this purpose I have instructed him and sent him."[18]

Isaiah also testifies of him with the words, "The Spirit of the Lord is upon me because he has sent me to preach good tidings to the poor."[19] Jesus Christ calls out to us and, as our prince, calls us to come

---

[1] Jer. 8:4-12; Ezek. 13:1-12. [2] Ps. 78:56-60. [3] 1 Sam. 4:17-22; 5:9-10. [4] 1 Sam. 2:31-36. [5] Num. 12:1-8; Exod. 33:11. [6] Heb. 3:1-6. [7] Exod. 24:12-18; 25:40. [8] Col. 2:16-23; Heb. 8:1-5; 10:1. [9] Eph. 2:19-22. [10] Ps. 2:1-6; 15:1-5; 24:3-6; Isa. 33:10-17. [11] Jer. 23:21-32. [12] Jer. 23:1-4. [13] Heb. 8:1-5. [14] 1 Pet. 1:18-20; John 16:13-15. [15] Amos 9:11; Acts 15:15-18. [16] Exod. 32:15-16. [17] John 3:3-8; 6:28-40. [18] Ps. 2:6. [19] Isa. 61:1-2; Luke 4:17-19.

to him:[1] "Come to me, all you who labor and are heavy laden, and I will refresh you. Take my yoke upon you and learn from me, for I am gentle and lowly in heart."[2] Since no one can come to Christ unless the Father draws him,[3] it is evident that only those can go up to build the Lord's house[4] whose hearts have been moved, whose spirits have been awakened, and who hear and obey Christ's voice calling them. They come to Christ so that they may come to the Father,[5] since no one can come to the Father except through Christ.[6] The Father shows them the design of the tabernacle or house, and all the adornment with which to make it according to his will.[7]

What does the Lord say? "No human shall see me and live!"[8] Therefore, when God starts to speak in us,[9] something must begin to die. We must hear,[10] see,[11] taste,[12] and feel the Lord God in the countenance of Jesus Christ.[13] All of this must happen before such construction can begin, as is clear from the words of Peter: "If you have come to him, the living stone, and have tasted that the Lord is gracious, let yourselves be built as living stones into a spiritual house!"[14]

If God is to draw near to a person and begin to work, that person must listen to what the Lord speaks within him. He must note, pay attention, and observe what the Lord inspires, moves, and operates in him, and allow himself to be ruled and guided by it. What he then does is no work of flesh and blood,[15] nor is it anything undertaken from personal choice.[16] As said above, it may not be undertaken by humans.

When Christ's herald comes, he cries with a loud voice, "Repent and change your lives, for the kingdom of heaven is at hand."[17] He furthermore says, "The axe is already laid to the root of the trees. Every tree that does not bring forth good fruit will be cut down and thrown into the fire."[18] Paul says, "Put to death, therefore, what belongs to your earthly nature, so that sin may no longer rule over you."[19] In another epistle he says, "Do not let sin hold sway in your mortal body, so that you have to obey its lusts; and do not allow your members to be used as instruments of wickedness."[20]

If such dying has not taken place in a person, that one cannot

---

[1] Heb. 2:10.   [2] Matt. 11:28-30.   [3] John 6:44.   [4] 1 Esd. 1:5.   [5] Matt. 11:25-27; John 10:27-29.   [6] John 14:6.   [7] Eph. 5:23-32.   [8] Exod. 33:20.   [9] Rom. 6:3-6.   [10] Heb. 1:1-4.   [11] 1 Cor. 13:12.   [12] 1 Pet. 2:3.   [13] 2 Cor. 13:5.   [14] 1 Pet. 2:2-5.   [15] Rom. 7:7-16; 8:1-9.   [16] Col. 2:16-23.   [17] Matt. 3:1-12; Mark 1:1-8.   [18] Matt. 3:10; Luke 3:7-9. [19] Col. 3:5.   [20] Rom. 6:11-14.

come to the mountain[1] and draw near to the Lord.[2] Neither can that person hear,[3] see,[4] or feel,[5] much less learn, the construction of the tabernacle from the Lord.[6] From this I conclude that all who still remain on the plain and have not climbed up the hill of the Lord have not been sent by him at all[7] and cannot speak his Word. Paul says, "How shall they preach, since they are not sent?"[8] Christ also tells us, "He whom God has sent speaks the words of God."[9] How can anyone be sent by him before he hears his voice?[10] Who can hear it and remain alive?[11] Therefore, the old self must first die[12] and be done away with,[13] as Paul teaches when he says, "Put off now your old self with the practices that belonged to your former way of life, which was corrupted through the lust of sin."[14]

Whoever has died to self and become broken through hearing the divine answer in the heart, that one comes to Christ. Christ says, "Whoever has heard and learned from the Father comes to me."[15] That is also why Moses says, "All your saints are in your hand. They shall sit at your feet and learn from your words."[16] Whoever learns thus from the Father will be awakened to a new life through faith in Jesus Christ,[17] who bears witness to this with these words: "The hour is coming and is now here, when the dead shall hear the voice of the Son of God, and they that hear shall live."[18] We should not continue in the sins to which we have died, but rather, since we are raised as he was raised, we should walk in newness of life.[19]

Those who have been on the mountain with Christ and have seen the tabernacle with all its adornments and furnishings, they and only they are able to know how to do the work to please him[20] whose dwelling it shall be.[21] This temple must be most exquisitely adorned with many precious stones and beautiful jewels, as Scripture tells us: "Behold, I will set your stones as a decoration, your foundations with sapphires, your windows of crystal, your gates of rubies, and all your boundaries of choice stones. All your children shall be taught by the Lord, and great shall be their peace. In righteousness you will be established."[22]

So Peter, as a wise master builder who will not build with hay and straw on the foundation that has been laid, since no other foundation

---

[1] Ps. 15:1-3; 24:3-6; Isa. 23:17-18. [2] Heb. 12:22-24. [3] Heb. 1:1. [4] 1 Cor. 13:12.
[5] 2 Cor. 13:5. [6] Eph. 5:23-32. [7] Jer. 23:21. [8] Rom. 10:15. [9] John 3:34. [10] Jer.
23:16-22. [11] Deut. 5:23-33. [12] Rom. 6:1-8. [13] Col. 3:5-9. [14] Eph. 4:17-32; Col. 3:5-9.
[15] John 6:45. [16] Deut. 33:3. [17] John 3:5-15; 2 Cor. 5:17. [18] John 5:25. [19] Rom. 6:1-4.
[20] Ps. 15:1-3; Matt. 5:1-12. [21] John 14:15-27; 2 Cor. 6:16. [22] Isa. 54:11-14.

can be laid,[1] tells everyone first of all to repent. He obeys the word and command of his Master,[2] who himself first called the people to repentance[3] and commanded his disciples to do the same.[4] When they have repented and laid aside sin,[5] Peter goes on to encourage them to let themselves be built into the house of the Lord. Thus he says, "If you have now laid aside all malice, you should long, as newborn babes, for the pure, sensible milk, the word of truth, that you may thrive by it, if indeed you have tasted that the Lord is gracious. You have come to him as to a living stone, rejected by the builders, but precious and chosen by God. Therefore, let yourselves be built into a spiritual temple with a holy priesthood."[6]

Similarly, Paul boasts in having laid the foundation as a wise master builder. However, anyone who wants to build on it should take heed how one builds, for fire will test every person's work.[7] Whoever wants to work on this building and set one stone upon another, must first have learned from the true master builder, Christ,[8] how the other fellow workers, such as Peter, Paul, and the rest, have built. Otherwise, he might use stones for lime and lime for stones, and the building might remain unfinished, like the tower of Babel.[9] God the Almighty has sent his Christ into the world[10] to lead the human race back to God.[11] We have received adoption as God's children,[12] and God has granted and given adoption to all who receive Christ.[13] Physical birth does not lead to that. There needs to be a birth from God, which takes place through the Word.[14]

Thus it becomes clear who they are who have accepted Christ: those who believe in his name or in his Word. To these he also says, "Whoever loves me, I and the Father will come to him and will make our home with him."[15] Note here by what means the tabernacle or dwelling of God is built. That is the way every faithful builder should go about constructing his building. That is the true pattern of all stones belonging to this house. Now Christ wants to dwell[16] in those who have allowed all the roughness or sin to be cut away,[17] who are measured by the plumb line and level of Christ, and who have brought their hearts to him, to love him.[18] Whoever builds in any other way builds with nothing but hay and straw.[19]

---

[1] 1 Cor. 3:10-12.   [2] Matt. 28:19-20; Mark 16:15; Acts 2:38.   [3] Matt. 4:17.   [4] Matt. 10:1-10; 28:19-20.   [5] Acts 2:38-41.   [6] 1 Pet. 2:1-5.   [7] 1 Cor. 3:10-15.   [8] John 2:19-22; 16:13-14; Matt 16:18.   [9] Gen. 11:1-4.   [10] John 5:33-37.   [11] 1 Pet. 3:18.   [12] Gal. 4:1-5.   [13] John 1:12-13.   [14] 1 Pet. 1:23.   [15] John 14:23.   [16] John 14:23.   [17] 1 Cor. 6:9-11.   [18] Deut. 6:4-5; Matt. 22:37; Mark 12:29-30; Luke 10:27.   [19] 1 Cor. 3:10-13.

This building will be beautifully built to please him who should dwell in it.[1] Nothing but pure love will be within, and he himself is this love.[2] Thus all God's commandments will be fulfilled,[3] for Christ himself says, "Whoever loves me, keeps my commandments."[4] But the power to love, God himself, who is love,[5] gives to us. Hence, it is clear that those who transgress his command and continue to sin, do not belong to his temple.

John says, "Whoever sins and does not abide in the teaching of Christ has no God, but he who is true to Christ's teaching has both the Father and the Son."[6] In another passage he says, "Whoever says he loves God and does not keep his commandments, is a liar and the truth is not in him."[7] It is thus undeniable that people who continue to sin do not belong to the house of God. Thus David says, "The wicked will not stand firm when judgment comes, nor can sinners stand in the congregation of the righteous."[8] This is especially true because no one can serve two masters: God and the devil.[9]

Therefore, the sage says that the Holy Spirit abhors those whose wisdom consists of deceit, and the Spirit will rise and flee from foolish thoughts. Where sin takes the upper hand, the Spirit departs.[10] If the Holy Spirit leaves such people, how can they be his dwelling, since he has withdrawn from them and does not wish to be with them?[11] Paul says bluntly, "Whoever does not have the Spirit of Christ, does not belong to him."[12]

The stones in this building vary: some contribute to it, and some do not. Anyone who goes against this will be judged accordingly.[13] Since this tabernacle is to be built as a dwelling place for God,[14] with Christ as its foundation,[15] each must take care what he brings, and with what he builds. Although the first temple was only an image,[16] God gave exact instructions concerning what materials were to be used in building it. These were gold, silver, and brass; yellow, purple, and scarlet silk; goats' hair, rams' skins dyed red, and badgers' skins; acacia wood, oil for the lamps, spices for anointing oil, and sweet incense; onyx stones and other mounted gems.[17]

Just as God instructed the Israelites on how to build, so Christ has instructed us on what we should bring to his house and how it should

---

[1] 1 Cor. 6:19; Lev. 26:11.   [2] 1 John 4:16.   [3] Rom. 13:8.   [4] John 14:15; 15:10.
[5] 1 John 4:16.   [6] 2 John 1:9.   [7] 1 John 2:4; 1 John 4:20-21.   [8] Ps. 1:4-6.   [9] Matt. 6:24.
[10] Wisd. of Sol. 1:4-5.   [11] 2 Chron. 15:1-3.   [12] Rom. 8:9.   [13] Acts 17:16-31.   [14] 1 Cor. 6:19; Eph. 2:19-22.   [15] 1 Cor. 3:11-13.   [16] Heb. 8:5; 10:1.   [17] Exod. 25:1-18.

be brought. The builders who would build on this foundation[1] need first to be planted and deeply rooted in Christ,[2] and to have grasped his full nature,[3] mind, and character.[4] This, however, they cannot achieve unless the Father moves them.[5] It does not depend on human will or effort but on God's initiative.[6] Although a person may try of his own ability and shout until the veins swell in his throat, yet his word will not yield fruit. This is true because the word is only a dead letter, giving no life and having no power.

The person who is sent by God, however, and has God's Word in his mouth,[7] speaks the Word that pierces soul and spirit.[8] This Word shall not pass away void. Just as rain cannot fall from heaven and return without bearing fruit, even less will God's Word fail to bear fruit.[9] Therefore, whoever will build this house must receive the tools from the Lord in heaven, tools for preparing the stones and wood. As the Scripture says, "They will sit at your feet and learn from your words."[10] These tools will cut where they are wielded to the praise of God, for God himself will be the tool[11] that prepares everything.[12]

Even though a person speaks with the tongue of angels,[13] if God does not speak through him, he does not speak God's Word,[14] because God is the Word.[15] But when God speaks through a person and wishes to build his temple in that one, God first cuts away what is coarse and wild and is not fitting for his house. He does this through the preaching of repentance.[16] When any receive the Word and repent, God places them on the foundation of Christ,[17] provided they die to sin and become like him in death. They will then be revived through faith and restored to a new life,[18] which comes about not through human power,[19] but by God's grace and work.[20]

Since this is done not by human effort but by God's action,[21] Paul exhorts us as follows: "Yield your members to be instruments of God and his righteousness, so that they may be holy."[22] If God is to do anything good in a person, that person must surrender himself to God.[23] Otherwise, the good cannot be done in him. Just as a person cannot do anything good of himself, so God does not want to do anything in him, unless he gives himself with all his heart to be God's instrument.

---

[1] 1 Cor. 3:10-11. [2] John 15:1-5; Eph. 3:17; Col. 2:7. [3] 1 Pet. 1:3-5. [4] 1 Cor. 2:11-16. [5] John 6:44. [6] Rom. 9:16. [7] Jer. 1:1-10. [8] Heb. 4:12. [9] Isa. 55:8-11. [10] Deut. 33:3. [11] John 1:1-3. [12] Heb. 3:1-4. [13] 1 Cor. 13:1. [14] Jer. 23:21. [15] John 1:1. [16] Matt. 3:1-12; Mark 1:1-8; Luke 3:1-14. [17] 1 Cor. 3:11. [18] Rom. 6:1-4. [19] Deut. 8:1-3; Zech. 4:6. [20] Eph. 2:1-10. [21] 1 Cor. 15:20-28. [22] Rom. 6:19. [23] Prov. 1:22-31.

Then that person's surrendered will interweaves itself with the divine will in such a way that the divine will and the human will become one. From now on, God desires, chooses, and works everything in that person. The person allows himself to become God's instrument[1] and thus may say with the beloved apostle Paul, "Now I live no more, but Christ lives in me."[2] This is the way God works in people.

On the other hand, if a person keeps back anything, chooses for himself, or wants or undertakes something on his own and not with God, God's work is hindered and can make no progress. Such a person remains unprepared for this building and will not be suitable for it. God works in the person who surrenders himself, and God gives proof of his power[3] in the person's renewal.[4] Through this work God enables the person to partake of his Son's[5] nature and character,[6] and even, in part, of his unlimited power. This we read in the words, "All things are possible to the one who believes."[7]

However, when people of the world say that they cannot obey what God has commanded, it is clear that they are not believing but unbelieving, and do not wish to bear patiently the Lord's work. They do not want to submit to his taking away what displeases him, nor allow the Lord to plant in them what he wishes,[8] in order to make them into fitting, precious, and living stones in this building.[9]

It is most unfitting to erect this building with unbelievers. The reason we do not set up a church with the world is that to the believers, all things are possible, yes, all things are light and easy.[10] We recognize that the world has no faith, but instead has an empty delusion,[11] which is dead before God.[12] Faith produces righteousness through the hand of God,[13] but unbelief produces sin through the hand of the devil.[14] What accord is there between Christ and Belial,[15] that their children should work together to build a dwelling for the Lord? Then John says, "Whoever does right belongs to God, but the one who sins is of the devil."[16]

Paul therefore says, " 'Depart and leave them; be separate from them, and I will receive you; I will be your Father, and you shall be my sons and daughters,' says the Lord Almighty."[17] Christ, who brings to the Father one people out of all peoples,[18] commands the new cove-

---

[1] John 15:4-5. [2] Gal. 2:20. [3] Deut. 8:1-4. [4] Titus 3:1-7. [5] 1 Cor. 2:9-10.
[6] 2 Pet. 1:3-8. [7] Mark 9:23. [8] John 15:1-2. [9] 1 Pet. 2:5. [10] Mark 9:23. [11] Matt. 11:30. [12] James 2:17. [13] Gen. 22:1-18; James 2:18-26. [14] Eph. 2:1-12. [15] 2 Cor. 6:15.
[16] 1 John 3:7-10. [17] 2 Cor. 6:17-18. [18] John 10:16; 15:12-20; Eph. 2:13-22.

nant as a greater security, so that there may be a distinction between his people and all other peoples.[1]

Circumcision separated the Jews from the heathen.[2] God did not wish to have heathens in his worship services,[3] nor did he wish his people to learn the ceremonies of the heathen.[4] In fact, he threatened that if they did that, he would do to them as he had intended to do to the heathen.[5] For the same reason, at the time of the apostles, unbelievers were not permitted to join the believers.[6] Paul, too, separates the faithful from the unbelievers.[7] Accordingly, we also wish in this matter and in all things, to be worthy to receive with him the promise of the inheritance. This is possible, insofar as it is in us to follow Christ as our Master. With his help we will keep his command and covenant, not turning aside from it to the right or to the left.[8] May he give us and all others who wholeheartedly want it, his grace to do this,

through Jesus Christ our Lord.

Amen.

---

[1] Matt. 28:19-20; Mark 16:15-16; Luke 22:20; 1 Cor. 11:25.   [2] Gen. 17:7-10.
[3] Exod. 12:43; Ezra 4:1-3.   [4] Deut. 12:1-3.   [5] Num. 33:55-56.   [6] Acts 5:3-13.
[7] Acts 19:9; 2 Cor. 6:14-7:1.   [8] Josh. 1:7; 23:6; Deut. 5:32-33; 12:32; Prov. 4:27.

Concerning the Covenant of Grace
Given to God's People in Christ

In accordance with his own merciful and compassionate nature[1] and out of pity, God the Almighty wanted to save the corrupted human race from ruin.[2] He also desired to fulfill his promise of the coming Christ, and so he sent the Word of grace,[3] by whom all things were made[4] and still continue to exist.[5] In Mary, the virgin previously chosen, the Word became incarnate through the working of the Holy Spirit,[6] so that he might be like us in everything, except in sin alone.[7] Scripture says, "Children of a family are of one flesh and blood. In the same way, Christ shares our flesh and blood so that through death he might break the power of the one who had power over death[8] and deliver those[9] subject to lifelong bondage through fear of death."[10]

Christ came[11] as he was sent by the Father.[12] Through himself he revealed and proclaimed the eternal will of the Father,[13] the word of grace,[14] and the name of the Father.[15] Thus he said, "I will declare your name to my brothers; in the presence of the congregation, I will sing praise to you."[16] Again he said, "I have revealed your name to those whom you have given me out of the world. They were yours, you have given them to me, and they have kept your word. Now they know that all you have given me comes from you. I have taught them the words you have given me, and they have received them, and know in truth that I came from you, and that you have sent me."[17]

From those words we can see what Christ did during his earthly life. He gathered those who already belonged to the Father and led them into the liberty of an heir.[18] He did this so they would become

---

[1] Exod. 20:1-6.   [2] Gen. 3:14-15; Rom. 5:12.   [3] Gen. 49:10; Deut. 18:15.   [4] John 1:1-3.   [5] Col. 1:15-17.   [6] Matt. 1:18-21; Luke 2:1-7; *incarnate* means embodied, fully human.   [7] Heb. 4:15-16.   [8] Heb. 2:14-18.   [9] Gal. 3:25-29.   [10] John 5:24-29.   [11] Heb. 10:5-7.   [12] John 6:29-40.   [13] Eph. 1:3-12.   [14] Isa. 61:1-6; Luke 4:16-19.   [15] John 17:1-7.   [16] Heb. 2:12; Ps. 22:22.   [17] John 17:6-8.   [18] Gal. 4:4-7.

like Christ, conform to his image[1] in complete obedience to the Father,[2] and come into one sheepfold, the sheepfold of his divine promise.[3] He revealed this in the words, "I have still other sheep that are not of this fold; I must bring them in too, so that there will be one flock and one fold."[4] Therefore, Jesus began to search earnestly for his sheep, first in Israel,[5] and then, when the fold had been established and the covenant of God's grace had been confirmed by Christ's death,[6] in the whole world. That fulfilled the words of the prophet: "I have appointed you for a light to the Gentiles, to be my salvation to the ends of the earth."[7]

That covenant, which has been confirmed in Christ,[8] leads to an imperishable,[9] not a perishable hope. The new birth that leads to that imperishable hope must also never end but remain forever. Christ appeared in order to bring it about, proclaiming the gospel of God,[10] the Word of the Father.[11] Those who believe the Word,[12] write it in their hearts,[13] and keep it;[14] they are born as God's children.[15] Peter agrees with that when he says, "Those who are born again by the word of truth, are not of perishable, but of imperishable seed."[16]

All who are begotten through that seed are made eternal in their nature and are led into the kingdom of Christ, which abides forever.[17] Peter says that those who do the will of God remain in eternity.[18] The bride thus becomes like the bridegroom. Because this all takes place through the Word, it needs to be proclaimed diligently,[19] in keeping with Christ's Word and command.[20] Christ will make the Word living and active,[21] and cause it to increase, but that means cutting away a person's old customs and habits, in fact, the whole of his old life[22] with all its works.[23] Birth according to the flesh counts for nothing and has nothing to do with the matter.[24] Paul explains it like this: "They who are the children of the flesh are not the children of God; it is the children of the promise who are then reckoned as heirs."[25] Only to those who are born of God does Christ give the power to become God's children, not to those who are born of human will, or of flesh and blood.[26]

---

[1] Rom. 8:29. [2] John 14. [3] Eph. 2:17-22; Col. 1:12-22. [4] John 10:16. [5] Matt. 10:5-6. [6] Matt. 28:19-20; Mark 16:15. [7] Isa. 49:6; Acts 13:1-3. [8] Heb. 9:11-12. [9] 1 Pet. 1:3-5. [10] Luke 4:16-19; Rom. 15:16. [11] John 17:8-14. [12] John 6:60-69. [13] Jer. 31:33. [14] Matt. 13:23. [15] John 1:12-13. [16] 1 Pet. 1:23. [17] Rev. 22:1-5. [18] 1 Pet. 1:22-23. [19] 2 Tim. 4:1-5. [20] Matt. 28:19-20; Mark 16:15. [21] 1 Cor. 3:7. [22] 1 Cor. 5:1-5. [23] Eph. 4:21-32; Col. 3:1-10. [24] John 1:10-13. [25] Rom. 9:1-8. [26] John 1:12-13.

What need is there of many words, although the devil loves to quarrel?[1] The covenant of being an heir, which was promised earlier by the mouth of the prophets,[2] is now established in Christ.[3] In that covenant the freedom of the children is revealed;[4] they are set free from bondage[5] and led into their holiness and inheritance.[6] As children, they may now use the good things their Father[7] has given them in Christ.[8] Therefore, let us allow truth to be truth, as it will remain in all eternity.[9] It will go badly with anyone who strives against it;[10] it will be hard to kick against the goad,[11] since the Lord has commanded that nothing be added to the truth and nothing taken from it.[12]

In this covenant of being adopted as an heir,[13] in which God in Christ[14] has separated heirs from slaves,[15] the heirs will not serve God in outward ceremonies,[16] but in a childlike spirit and in truth.[17] Paul says, "So now there are no more slaves, but all are heirs through faith in Christ."[18] Through the mouth of the prophet, God says, "Surely they are my people, children who will not be false. Therefore I am their savior."[19] Now since the distinction is made in Christ, it remains eternally. It takes place only through the Holy Spirit,[20] who distinguishes those who are moved by the Spirit of God and are God's children from those who do not have God's Spirit and are none of his.[21] Though it should displease the whole world, yet the Lord's counsel alone, and not ours, must stand. We wish to abide by it with his help, not allowing ourselves to turn from it in all eternity.

Because the world knows nothing of God,[22] we may be asked quite pointedly whether we are certain that all who are received in our meetings have the Holy Spirit. We answer that as far as it is given us to know, we are certain everyone who believes is sealed with the Holy Spirit.[23] But God has reserved for himself the knowledge of whether a person does not believe as he has confessed. We leave that to God's power until the time he shows it to us. Then such a person would be excluded, in accordance with God's command to put away evil.[24] That is why, if we want to be found faithful as messengers of the One who has sent us and faithful ministers of our task, our duty here is to be watchful. But we should not turn to human arrogance and opin-

---

[1] James 3:14-18. [2] Jer. 31:31-34. [3] Heb. 9:11-12. [4] Rom. 8:9-17; Gal. 4:4-7.
[5] John 8:28-32. [6] Gal. 4:4-7. [7] Matt. 5:38-48. [8] Rom. 8:17. [9] 1 Esd. 4:33-40.
[10] Isa. 5:1-7. [11] Acts 9:5; 26:14. [12] Deut. 4:1-2; Rev. 22:18-19. [13] Jer. 31:33-34.
[14] Col. 2:6-7. [15] Gal. 4:4-7. [16] Rom. 8:13-16. [17] John 4:21-23. [18] Gal. 4:7. [19] Isa.
63:8. [20] Gal. 4:1-6. [21] Rom. 8:14. [22] 1 Cor. 15:34. [23] Eph. 1:12-13. [24] 1 Cor. 5:9-13.

ion, so that we do not misuse the covenant of grace of the great God,[1] secured for us by Christ.[2] For Christ says, "As the Father has sent me, so I send you."[3]

Here we learn two things, namely, how Christ's messengers should be, and what their task is. First, as Christ, before he was sent by the Father, was filled with the Spirit,[4] so he wants his messengers to be.[5] They shall be blameless,[6] and enter into and walk in the power of his Spirit.[7] Second, their task is to gather with or in Christ and be led into the fold of grace, so that Christ's flock may be complete.[8]

When Christ wished to send his disciples, he first commanded them not to leave Jerusalem till they were clothed with power from on high.[9] That shows us what kind of messengers the Lord wants. He does not want those who go their own way to please themselves, as the Lutherans and papists encourage. Such people choose a fat living, with sheep to be shorn. We see how they care for the sheep! No, the Lord's messengers are chosen beforehand, as Aaron was.[10] If anyone is to go out for the Lord, he must be chosen by the Lord[11] and endowed with his power;[12] he must feel that power working in him.[13] Above all, he must let the Lord's power rule over him and lead him.[14]

What he does must be in keeping with the Lord's nature and character;[15] then he will be conformed to his Master in word and life, and give those who follow an example of blessedness.[16] Such a messenger was Paul, who said, "Be imitators of me, as I am of Christ."[17] Everyone who wants to gather with Christ must be of his nature,[18] mind, and spirit.[19] Whoever does not have the Spirit of Christ is none of his.[20] How could such a person gather with Christ? Christ himself said, "If a kingdom is divided against itself, that kingdom cannot stand."[21]

Christ's kingdom would soon have to fall if he did not send out servants who are like him in nature. He says, "Whoever is not for me is against me, and whoever does not gather with me scatters."[22] Christ will not permit a messenger to go out who is not first clothed with the power of his Spirit.[23] Those who feel this power will heed the command of their Lord, who has sent them. They will be able to proclaim to his good pleasure the tidings they bear in his name.[24] Christ won

[1] Jer. 31:31-34; Heb. 8:6-9; 10:8-18. [2] Heb. 9:13-17. [3] John 20:21. [4] Isa. 61:1-2; Luke 4:14-19. [5] Acts 1:1-8. [6] 1 Tim. 3:1-13; Titus 1:5-9. [7] 1 Cor. 15:1-10. [8] Eph. 2:19-22. [9] Luke 24:49; Acts 1:4-5. [10] Exod. 28:1-3; Num. 17:1-8; Heb. 5:8-10. [11] Acts 13:1-3. [12] Acts 1:23-26; 2:4. [13] 1 Pet. 2:1-5. [14] Rom. 8:10-15. [15] Gal. 6:1-9. [16] Rom. 8:1-9. [17] 1 Cor. 4:16; 11:1. [18] 2 Pet. 1:2-4. [19] 1 Cor. 2:14-16. [20] Rom. 8:9. [21] Mark 3:24. [22] Matt. 12:22-30. [23] Luke 24:49; Acts 1:4-5. [24] John 20:21-23.

the victory and through his death took away the devil's power over death. He then received all power from the Father,[1] as his own words declare: "All authority has been given to me in heaven and on earth. Go, therefore, and teach all nations, baptizing them in the name of the Father and of the Son and of the Holy Spirit, teaching them to observe everything I have commanded you."[2]

Let us note carefully what we are commanded. Christ gives us a twofold command. First, we should gather with him as those who have been sent by him.[3] Second, we should do our utmost to keep those who are gathered, so that they do not again become scattered and torn apart by wolves.[4] Christ's sheep are very dear to him, for he has bought them dearly.[5] He wants his shepherds to cherish them; he commits them to none but those who love him.[6]

Christ first commands us to persevere in gathering. He says, "Go and teach all nations." As was already said, the Lord desires a beautiful temple, a holy church without stain or wrinkle,[7] one that truly has Christ's nature and purpose. Therefore, those who are gathered must first have that nature and purpose explained to them and so be led into the covenant of an heir.[8] Where the Word is believed, the Lord will give it life and growth.[9] Those who believe will participate in his nature[10] through the gift of the childlike Spirit, who assures us that we are God's children and heirs of all his possessions.[11]

When such teaching has been given, God commands baptism as a seal of the childlike covenant. That means all who have received and believed the Word are baptized[12] and so accepted into the community of the faithful. God commands that after baptism the believers should continually be taught to keep all the Lord's commands.[13] Thus Christ wishes his servants to be earnest and persevering[14] in caring for his sheep,[15] doing their best to teach them[16] to obey the Lord.[17] All apostles, as true servants of their Master, have done that to the best of their ability[18] and to the exclusion of everything else, as can be seen and learned in the Acts of the Apostles.

This is like the other text, where the Lord says, "Go into all the world, and preach the gospel to the whole creation. Whoever believes and is baptized shall be saved; but whoever does not believe is con-

---

[1] Heb. 2:14-18. [2] Matt. 28:18-20. [3] John 20:21-23. [4] John 10:1-29. [5] Acts 20:28; 1 Pet. 1:18-21. [6] John 21:15-17. [7] Eph. 5:25-27. [8] 1 Cor. 2:14-16. [9] 1 Cor. 3:7. [10] 2 Pet. 1:2-4. [11] Rom. 8:15-17. [12] Acts 2:36-38. [13] Matt. 28:19-20. [14] Ezek. 33:6-9. [15] John 10:1-30. [16] 1 Tim. 4:12-16. [17] Acts 16:4. [18] Acts 4:33-35.

demned."[1] Thus Christ shows that he is one with the nature of his Father. He himself says, "The Son can do nothing by himself; he can only do exactly what he sees the Father doing."[2] Now as the Father created heaven and earth and all that is in them, he does everything in proper order. He did not wish to do everything in one day, though he could well have done so. He created everything in six days,[3] and on the seventh day rested from all his work.[4]

Notice the providence of God in that. When he wanted to make humans, he first created all kinds of cattle and whatever serves people for food. Thus, when people were created, they would suffer no want. He did the same for the creatures; their food was provided for them before they were created. In the same way, before making foliage, grass, and all kinds of green things, he first created the earth from which it would grow. God observes such order in his work.[5]

The Son does what he sees the Father doing.[6] When the Son wished to create a new humanity, or to renew humanity[7] in the likeness of its Creator,[8] he also wanted to do everything in the proper order. Thus we can learn the true, holy, and godly order[9] from him as he had learned it from the Father.[10] He says, "Go into all the world and preach the gospel to every creature. Whoever believes and is baptized shall be saved, but whoever does not believe shall be condemned."[11]

Christ begins by saying, "Go into all the world." The disciples could not carry out his charge before he had commanded them. Without his command, they would have known nothing of mission, and above all, nothing of going into all the world. The story of the disciples murmuring against Peter for entering a Gentile's house[12] is proof of that. Even Peter testified that it was an unusual thing for a Jew to enter the house of a Gentile, but he did it on account of a revelation from the Lord.[13] What Peter says makes it clear that if he had not had a special revelation, he would not have gone to the Gentiles, in spite of the command Christ had already given him. Even less would he have gone there to preach without being commissioned,[14] for Paul says, "How can they preach, if they are not sent?"[15]

Since they cannot preach without first being sent, it is certain that God, in giving them his command to go out, puts his word in his mes-

---

[1] Mark 16:15-16; Matt. 28:19-20. [2] John 5:19. [3] Gen. 1. [4] Gen. 2:1-3.
[5] Gen. 1. [6] John 5:19. [7] Eph. 4:20-24; Col. 3:8-10. [8] Gen. 1:27. [9] 2 Tim. 3:8-17.
[10] John 5:19-20. [11] Mark 16:15-16. [12] Acts 11:1-3. [13] Acts 10:25-29. [14] Matt. 28:19-20; Mark 16:15. [15] Rom. 10:15.

sengers' mouths. The Lord himself testifies to this when he says, "I have put my words in your mouth. I have set you over nations and kingdoms, to uproot, pull down, and destroy, and then to build and plant anew."[1] Therefore, all who have not been sent have no word from God.[2] They only have what they have stolen from the Scriptures or from one another.[3] That is the main reason God's commission is necessary. It was not enough that they were sent; they also had to know the purpose of being sent, and what they had to do. Christ commanded them to do his work, saying, "Teach all nations,"[4] and "Preach the gospel to every creature."[5]

In this command, Christ puts his word into their mouth.[6] In the same way today, when a person sends a messenger, he gives him orders about what to say and do. If the messenger wishes to be faithful to the one who sent him, he will heed his instructions, taking nothing from them and adding nothing to them. That is how Christ commanded to preach. To make sure that they preach nothing but what he intended, he gave them the gospel, which is simply a joyful message from God and Christ!

Christ warned them not to preach whatever they wished. They should neither add to the message nor take away from it; they should do neither too much nor too little; they should not praise where they should rebuke, nor rebuke where they should praise.[7] Christ confirmed this when he said, "It will not be you who speak, but the Spirit of my Father speaking through you."[8] That is why he did not wish them to leave Jerusalem until they had received power from on high and thus were enabled to go in the power of the Lord[9] and speak his word.[10] They then led many to receive the Word in faith,[11] and so brought them into the true fold of grace. Concerning several who were so led, Paul says, "You did not receive it as a human word, but as it is in truth, the word of God."[12] In that way they were renewed to become God's adopted children.

Because they are not able to believe without preaching, Paul says, "How can they believe in whom they have not heard? How can they hear without preaching? How can they preach unless they are sent? So then faith comes from hearing, and what is heard comes through preaching, and preaching comes from the word of God."[13] There-

---

[1] Jer. 1:9-10. [2] Mic. 3:5-12. [3] Jer. 23:20-32. [4] Matt. 28:19-20. [5] Mark 16:15.
[6] Jer. 1:9-19. [7] Deut. 4:1-2; Rev. 22:18-19. [8] Matt. 10:20. [9] Luke 24:49; Acts 1:4-5.
[10] John 3:34. [11] Acts 3:7-16. [12] 1 Thess. 2:13. [13] Rom. 10:14-17.

fore, Jesus speaks of faith after preaching and adds, "Whoever believes."[1] Believing the word that is preached means writing it in one's heart, cherishing it there,[2] and living accordingly.[3] From then on, it means always allowing oneself to be ruled and guided by the Word.[4] Christ says this is blessed. Blessed are they who hear the Word of God and keep it[5] in a good and pure heart. They are all led to become heirs of God.[6]

Those who become heirs are then included in the bond of the promise, through the covenant of grace, as assurance that they are joint heirs of all the grace and gifts the Father has given us in Christ.[7] Therefore, after faith, baptism is commanded; it is a seal on the believing children of God so that a good conscience may be united with God.[8] "But whoever does not believe is condemned."[9] Here it is evident that the act of baptism alone does not save; only faith confirmed by baptism does that. Therefore, it is pure mockery to baptize children before they believe.

All the apostles have adhered to this order of Christ with the greatest diligence, as their history shows. They have baptized none who have not first believed or at least confessed their faith. Let us now look at some examples. First, we see that Peter spoke to the people at great length. He so pierced the hearts of the listening people that they were moved to ask what they should do. He answered them, "Repent and be baptized, every one of you, in the name of Jesus Christ for the forgiveness of your sins, and you shall receive the gift of the Holy Spirit."[10] Here he does not first point to baptism but to repentance and improvement. What is repentance if not putting aside sin and the old self with all its works?[11] Thus repentance means becoming like Christ's death, into which all the faithful are baptized.[12]

After Peter had shown them repentance, he told them they should be baptized into a new life, for it is a bath of new birth. He also promised the benefit that follows from baptism, the gift of the Holy Spirit.[13] He said they should let themselves be turned and led away from their perverse generation.[14] Those who accepted this word gladly were baptized. "Accept gladly" can only mean to consent to God's ordained counsel[15] and to submit to it with one's whole heart.[16] How-

---

[1] Mark 16:16. [2] Deut. 6:4-6; 11:18. [3] Deut. 10:12-16. [4] Ps. 119:1-8. [5] Luke 11:28. [6] Gal. 4:4-7. [7] Rom. 8:17. [8] 1 Pet. 3:21-22. [9] Mark 16:16. [10] Acts 2:14-41. [11] Eph. 4:21-32; Col. 3:5-10. [12] Rom. 6:3-6. [13] Acts 2:38; Titus 3:3-7. [14] Acts 2:40-41. [15] Exod. 20:3-17; Deut. 10:12-13. [16] Exod. 14:32; 2 Chron. 34:30-33.

ever, some rejected the counsel of God and were not baptized.[1] Here again, those who are led by the apostles into the fold, who have accepted their word with joy, are distinguished from the others.

Let us look at how Philip carried out his task when he came to Samaria to preach about Christ. The people with one accord paid careful attention to what Philip said. When they believed what he proclaimed about the kingdom of God and the name of Jesus Christ, they were baptized, both men and women.[2] Note well that here it says once more quite clearly who were baptized, namely, those who believed Philip's preaching. Nothing is added, however, about telling them to bring their children to have them baptized too. Doubtless they had children then as now, but Philip did not engage in any such mockery as our falsely celebrated preachers now do. Perhaps, according to them, the devout apostle did not have enough understanding. Or maybe Christ forgot to command them to do that. When disciples try to teach their Master, and human understanding wants to rule, the same thing happens that happened to Eve in Paradise.[3] The same still happens to us today!

Paul spoke to the elders of Ephesus, testifying powerfully that he was innocent of blood. In effect, he was saying that if evil should arise after he left, or if anything else should break in, "I did not shrink from declaring to you the whole counsel of God."[4] But I do not find one single word about infant baptism, nor does he speak of it in any of his epistles. Therefore, it is either not the counsel of God, or Paul neglected to declare and explain it to everyone. Moreover, he warns faithfully against teaching a gospel different from the one he had proclaimed.[5] We therefore intend to follow Paul's counsel faithfully, with God's help. He was an instrument chosen to proclaim God's name,[6] and we intend to accept no other teaching than what we have learned from him, and to adopt no other ordinances or customs.

We also read that Philip was led by an angel to the eunuch's chariot on the way down from Jerusalem to Gaza. Philip found the eunuch reading the prophet Isaiah:[7] "He was led like a sheep to the slaughter."[8] In response to the eunuch's request, the apostle began with that text and proclaimed Christ to him. While they were speaking with one another, they came to a stream. The eunuch said, "See, here is water; why should I not be baptized?" The apostle, although he had preached long

---

[1] Luke 7:30.   [2] Acts 8:5-12.   [3] Gen. 3:1-6.   [4] Acts 20:26-27.   [5] Gal. 1:6-9.
[6] Acts 9:10-15.   [7] Acts 8:26-28.   [8] Isa. 53:7.

and knew for certain that the Lord had led the eunuch to him, did not baptize him immediately on his request. Because of what the angel had told him, Philip had no misgivings, yet he still observed the right order and first asked the eunuch if he believed. This means that without faith, baptism may not take place.

Then the eunuch began to confess his faith, that he believed Christ was the Son of God. After that, Philip baptized him in the water on his confession of faith. So we repeat that none should be baptized without a confession of faith preceded by preaching. Even our opponents confess this truth in their ungodly baptism. I am not doing wrong to call it that, for what they do is no baptism. When a child is brought to the puddle-bath, or baptism, the preacher does not immediately baptize, but first gives a long sermon to show that preaching comes first.

After that, he proclaims renunciation of the world, sin, and the devil. Finally, he tells them to have faith, of which infants know little or nothing at all. In all that, they are testifying to the truth and rightness of our order, however much they protest against that order. The truth does not come from their own knowledge but arises unwittingly, as with Caiaphas,[1] which makes us the more certain. They see that the apostles baptized believers,[2] and like apes, they want to imitate them, though they have received no command.

We discover the same from [Saul] Paul, who was baptized by Ananias at Damascus. On the way to that city,[3] he saw the Lord, was caught up to the third heaven, and heard words which cannot be put into human speech.[4] Yet he did not receive the seal of sonship till he had heard what Ananias proclaimed; after that, he was baptized. Scripture says, " 'The Lord who appeared to you on the way here has sent me to you, so that you may regain your sight and be filled with the Holy Spirit.' Immediately it was as if scales fell from his eyes, and he recovered his sight. Thereupon he arose and was baptized."[5]

It can be seen here how God honors the order he himself has established and will not break it.[6] He wants us to keep it, too. Although Paul was caught up into heaven[7] and saw Christ,[8] yet his understanding was opened, and the Holy Spirit was given only after Ananias had proclaimed the word of the Lord to him.[9]

The same took place with Cornelius, the centurion.[10] Although

---

[1] John 11:49-52.   [2] Acts 2:41; 8:12-15; 9:17-18; 10:44-48; 16:14-15.   [3] Acts 9:1-18; 1 Cor. 15:8.   [4] 2 Cor. 12:1-4.   [5] Acts 9:17-18.   [6] Matt. 28:18-20.   [7] 2 Cor. 12:1-4.   [8] 1 Cor. 15:3-9.   [9] Acts 9:10-20.   [10] Acts 10:1-8.

his prayers and his almsgiving had risen up to God and were pleasing to him (and such a thing is not possible without faith),[1] yet God sent an angel to tell him about Peter. Cornelius sent for Peter, and when Peter came and spoke some of the Lord's word, the Holy Spirit fell on him. Here again we see how God follows his own order and what he grants to the Word. In this way, Christ will gather his bride. It is his counsel, a counsel that will never waver, but will stand forever. Although Cornelius was pleasing to God and had heard the voice of the angel, yet he was not sealed with the Holy Spirit until he had heard the word from Peter. God then testified to Cornelius's faith with the gift of the Holy Spirit, whereupon he was baptized. We see what great folly it is for a person to oppose God's order and act in any other way than is commanded.[2]

Another example is the jailer of the prison at Philippi, who believed and was baptized with his whole household. Our opponents often quote this as evidence for their abominable practice, as if children were also baptized. The text clearly states that the jailer took them into his house and set food before them. They spoke the word of the Lord to the jailer, and the jailer and his whole household believed and were baptized. He rejoiced greatly that he had come to believe in God.[3] Now, if there were children present who understood the wonder of God, and if, after hearing Christ proclaimed, they believed, then they also were baptized; but if not, they were not. Hence, this does not prove anything.

When passing through the countries mentioned above, Paul found certain men who had been baptized with John's baptism. Perhaps he felt that they were too superficial for men who were supposed to be brothers, and so he asked whether they had received the Holy Spirit. They answered that they had never heard of any Holy Spirit. Upon hearing that, Paul asked into what they had been baptized. They answered, "Into John's baptism."[4] So Paul said, "John baptized with the baptism of repentance,[5] and pointed to Christ."[6] When they heard that, they were baptized in the name of Jesus Christ. When Paul laid his hands on them, they received the Holy Spirit.[7]

Note well that Paul did not consider the baptism of John to be valid, although it was of God, as Christ himself testifies.[8] How much

---

[1] Heb. 11:6. [2] Matt. 28:18-20; Mark 16:15-16. [3] Acts 16:25-34. [4] Acts 19:1-5; 18:23-24. [5] Matt. 3; Mark 1:4; Luke 3:15-18. [6] John 1:19-34. [7] Acts 19:6. [8] Matt. 21:23-32.

less is infant baptism valid for us, for it is not even appointed by God but by humans. "Every plant not planted by my heavenly Father shall be rooted up,"[1] says Christ. Therefore, infant baptism is not valid for any of God's children. What God ordains will stand firm and endure, not what we ourselves ordain.

Someone may say, "Paul says that all our forefathers under Moses were baptized with the cloud and the sea.[2] There were certainly children among them, and since they are included, you must leave them in the picture." Let us look more carefully into this illustration to discover whether children are included or not. When the Israelites left Egypt and arrived at the sea, they saw Pharaoh's men pursuing them, hard on their heels. When they saw they could not escape, they grew sullen and began to complain against God and Moses, saying, "Were there no graves in Egypt that you had to lead us away to die in the wilderness? Why have you done this?[3] Did we not say to you in Egypt, 'Leave us alone; let us serve the Egyptians'? It would have been better to serve the Egyptians than to die in the wilderness."[4]

However, then they saw the salvation of God, how he separated them from the others with the cloud, cutting them off from one another. They saw how the Lord divided the sea,[5] allowing them to pass through on dry land, but drowning all their enemies.[6] They were shocked and frightened that they had complained against the Lord, the mighty God, and against his servant Moses. They recognized their sin, believed in God their Savior, and surrendered themselves to serve him rightly under the hand of his servant Moses.[7] Paul calls that a submission, or a baptism, to which they were driven by the glorious miracles[8] which God performed before their eyes with the cloud and sea.[9]

Now if newly born children grumbled against God and Moses, then they also blushed for shame along with their elders, and they also committed themselves once more to serve God under Moses. If not, they could not have humbled themselves in submission before Moses nor blushed for shame, since they had not grumbled. That is Paul's real meaning in this passage.[10]

The ark gives us another picture of baptism, namely, submersion and the dying of the old nature. Eight souls, who could all see and confess the work of God, were saved,[11] but no children. That is how

---

[1] Matt. 15:13.   [2] 1 Cor. 10:1-4.   [3] Exod. 14:9-11.   [4] Exod. 14:11-12.   [5] Ps. 106:6-12.   [6] Ps. 136:10-26.   [7] Exod. 14:31.   [8] 1 Cor. 10:1-6.   [9] Exod. 14:19-31.   [10] 1 Cor. 10:1-6.   [11] Gen. 7:13.

God wants it to be in his covenant. Each one is to recognize, sense, and discover for oneself God's power at work, and thus know of whom he should think highly. From now on, he will not allow himself to be led astray by any strange teaching.[1] That is what the ark shows us.

Someone may also object, "Children were circumcised on the eighth day,[2] and although they were without understanding, they were accepted into the covenant.[3] Why not today?" In response, I say that circumcision and baptism are two different things. As Christ surpassed Abraham,[4] so does baptism surpass circumcision. Circumcision was commanded for all male children in the house of Abraham, both sons and slaves.[5] In Christ, being an heir is distinguished from bondage; there are no more slaves, but all are sons and daughters.[6] It is evident that baptism was not commanded to those in bondage, but to the children of Christ.[7] Christ's children are not conceived and born of flesh and blood, nor of the human will, but of God,[8] through his Word.[9]

Hence Paul says, "Not all who are descended from Israel belong to Israel, and not all Abraham's descendants are his true children. It is not the children born according to nature who are God's heirs, but the children of the promise who are reckoned as his true offspring."[10] Therefore, the nation that came forth from the loins of Abraham[11] is simply an allegory of the true seed; it is a picture of those who become children through faith in Christ.[12] Paul says of them, "If you belong to Christ, then you are Abraham's descendants and heirs according to the promise."[13]

From those words it is clear who are the seed with whom God has confirmed his covenant, and to what seed his promise applies.[14] They are those who walk in the footsteps of a believing Abraham.[15] It is but an allegory of the true seed which was to be revealed in Christ. Therefore, all children of the promise are included in the covenant.[16] This was the promise, that Christ should be born of them,[17] and that they and all peoples would be blessed through him;[18] not that they had already received the promise,[19] but that they would receive it.[20]

There was no difference between servants and heirs.[21] Instead, they were kept secure by the taskmaster until the time of Christ.[22]

---

[1] Heb. 13:7-9.   [2] Gen. 17:10-12.   [3] Gen. 17:3-12; 26:1-5; 28:10-15; 48:14-16.
[4] Heb. 7.   [5] Gen. 17:10-13.   [6] Gal. 4:4-7.   [7] Matt. 28:19-20; Mark 16:15-16.   [8] John 1:12-13.   [9] 1 Pet. 1:3-5.   [10] Rom. 9:6-8.   [11] Gen. 15:1-5.   [12] Gal. 4:22-28.   [13] Rom. 9:6-9; Gal. 3:16-18.   [14] Luke 1:41-55.   [15] Rom. 4:9-17.   [16] Gal. 3:7-14; 4:22-28.   [17] Rom. 9:1-8.
[18] Gen. 12:1-3; 22:15-18.   [19] Heb. 11:39-40.   [20] Ps. 132:12-18.   [21] Gal. 4:1.   [22] Gal. 4:2.

When Christ comes, however, bondage departs, just as a shadow withdraws when the sun rises. Paul says, "We raise up the law" from semblance to truth.[1] Therefore, circumcision comes to an end in Christ. In him begins the circumcision which is not physical and which receives God's approval rather than human approval.[2] Abraham was commanded to take the covenant of circumcision on himself and on all the males of his family and household. In the same way, the Father ordained that the house of Christ and all his heirs should be baptized.[3] Christ himself gives witness to this in the words he spoke to John: "Let it be so, for it is right for us to do all that God's righteousness requires."[4]

Let us now consider this parable. Within his house, Abraham was commanded to circumcise both heirs by birth and slaves who had been bought.[5] He was not commanded to do it outside his own household. Abraham, however, could not circumcise children that had not yet been born. Likewise, in the house of God, no one can or will be marked with the covenant of grace, meaning baptism, unless that person has first been born to Christ through the Word of truth.[6]

Those who oppose us say that being accepted by God means being reborn and becoming children of God. They also say that God accepts little children as well as old people, as Peter says, "For the promise is to you and to your children."[7] So it is not right to refuse them baptism. In response to that, I say, we do not deny that God accepts children as well as older people. We too have the firm hope that he will look on them with grace and accept them for what they are—children. Nevertheless, God does not weaken his order or take anything from his Word. He who once gave new birth through his Word will not take that power from it.[8] They who believe the Word[9] are born anew[10] and become children of God.[11] Since God himself honors his own order, as we saw in the cases of Saul [Paul][12] and Cornelius,[13] I am therefore compelled to believe that God's acceptance of us is not the same as our becoming completely "reborn"; otherwise, I take something away from the Word of God.[14]

In addition, God's acceptance of each individual is hidden from our eyes until it shows itself in power. It is like the fruit of a woman's womb before she gives birth. Who can truly know what kind of fruit it

---

[1] Rom. 3:31. [2] Rom. 2:17-29. [3] Matt. 28:18-20; Mark 16:15-16. [4] Matt. 3:13-15. [5] Gen. 17:9-12. [6] 1 Pet. 1:22-23. [7] Acts 2:38-41. [8] 1 Pet. 1:3-5. [9] Mark 16:16. [10] Titus 3:4-6. [11] John 1:12. [12] Acts 9:10-18. [13] Acts 10:42-48. [14] 1 Pet. 1:23.

will be, whether male or female, or what stature or shape it will have? Yet despite that, it is a fruit. So it is with God's acceptance of us; no one knows how or why, for the works of the Lord are incomprehensible.[1] Now, as the child before birth is hidden from our eyes in the mother's womb, so too the acceptance of God and his counsel is hidden until it is born through the Word.[2] Therefore, as a boy cannot be circumcised before he is born, so a person may not be baptized without previously hearing the Word proclaimed, and confessing faith.[3]

Abraham had to circumcise boys on the eighth day, however, and not as soon as they were born. They had to grow a little so as to be able to bear the pain. It is like that in the house of Christ. Before someone makes such a covenant with God, that person should grow a little in faith and knowledge so that each person knows what he is doing. Christ shows us that with the following illustration: "No one intends to build a house or a tower without first sitting down and counting the cost to see whether he can complete it. Otherwise, after he has begun, he is not able to finish the building, and all who see it will begin to mock him."[4] Note this well: God first wishes a person to consider, even test himself,[5] to examine his heart, and to see what graces of God he finds in himself. He should consider whether he can rely on his heart and venture to finish the building without giving up and coming to grief.[6]

Jesus shows us the same in another parable when he says, "Suppose a king is about to go to war against another king. Will he not first sit down and consider whether he is able with ten thousand men to meet his enemy with twenty thousand? If he is not able, then while the other is still far in the distance, he sends an envoy and requests peace terms. So too, if anyone cannot give up all he has, that person cannot be my disciple."[7] See how clearly Christ speaks here of "first growing," and that each one shall first test himself well, whether he is able to do all this. In effect, he says, "Whoever cannot forsake all he has and deny himself, should definitely not attempt it, for he cannot be my disciple."[8]

In baptism we deny ourselves and die to sin; we yield our members to God as instruments of righteousness and become Christ's disciples.[9] Christ wants to make it clear to us through the parable that

---

[1] Rom. 11:33-34.   [2] 1 Pet. 1:22-23.   [3] Matt. 28:18-20; Mark 16:15-16.   [4] Luke 14:28-30.   [5] 2 Cor. 13:5.   [6] 1 Cor. 11:28-32.   [7] Luke 14:31-33.   [8] Matt. 10:34-39; 16:24; Luke 14:33; 17:33; John 12:23-26.   [9] Rom. 6:1-13.

each individual should consider well what he does. Once he has put his hand to the plow, he should not look back and thereby be humiliated.[1] That is why each person needs to consider the matter very well and look at the truth in the right way so that he does not use it to his own downfall.[2] The Lord is not pleased with that.[3]

Again, Peter proves it in his epistle where he speaks of the covenant of grace. He says, "It is not the removal of filth from the body, but rather the covenant of a good conscience with God."[4] Now if that is so, the good conscience must first be attained. How can anyone who has not understood what grace is, make a bond of a good conscience with God? Therefore, we see from the parable how true it is that faith and knowledge should be allowed to grow a little, so that each may know how to build on the foundation of truth. A building made with straw and hay can catch fire. Fire will test each person's work.[5]

What is a good conscience toward God? It is knowing that I have a gracious God[6] who has discounted, remitted, and forgiven me all my sins in Christ. In addition, he has freely offered himself to me in Christ as Father,[7] yes, with all his manifold grace and riches.[8] I too may know him as almighty. I too may be moved and stirred with a longing to bind myself in submission to him, to trust him utterly as my beloved Father,[9] who will always seek the good, yes, the very best, for me.[10] Because of all that, I make a covenant with him in which I pledge myself completely to him[11] and give him my members as tools for his holy work. Henceforth, let me be used by the Master as his instrument, for whatever he wants to do.[12] Like an obedient child, I want to do his gracious will tirelessly and eagerly, not turning from it to right or left as long as I live. I accept the pure water as a proof of that and of my longing that God will inspire me to lead a holy life from now on.[13]

Again, God unites himself with humanity and desires to be its God and Father,[14] to care for humanity as a father for his son, yes, to give them everything in Christ.[15] As an assurance of that, God will witness from heaven by giving humanity the grace of his Spirit. The Spirit leads people into all truth, motivating all they do and fulfilling God's will. In that way people begin a new life in the power of God.[16] Paul says, "Whoever is in Christ, is a new creature."[17] Think now: can a

---

[1] Luke 9:57-62. [2] 2 Pet. 3:14-18. [3] Ezek. 33:7-19. [4] 1 Pet. 3:18-22. [5] 1 Cor. 3:10-15. [6] Exod. 20:6. [7] 2 Cor. 6:17-18. [8] Rom. 8:10-17. [9] Rom. 3:23-26. [10] Matt. 6:30-33. [11] Rom. 12:1-2. [12] Rom. 6:12-13. [13] Josh. 1:7; 23:6; Prov. 4:20-27; Deut. 5:32; 17:18-20; 28:11-14. [14] Exod. 29:43-46; Lev. 26:11-13; 2 Cor. 6:17-18. [15] 2 Sam. 7:12-15. [16] John 16:12-13. [17] 2 Cor. 5:17.

baby make such a covenant of a good conscience with God, since the baby knows neither good nor evil?[1] Not knowing either good or evil, how can the baby know the glorious wealth of the grace of the Almighty? Since he does not know it, how can he bind himself to lead his life according to it? Therefore, it is foolish to profess that infant baptism is right. Such thinking really leads away from God and reduces the true order and command of Christ to nothing.

However, where does that knowledge and good conscience come from? It only comes from a heart awakened through the Word of God. God will cause the Word to flourish and to increase in a person.[2] He will uproot all that is carnal and implant what is godly.[3] From that originates the new birth, of which Christ says, "Unless a person is born anew of water and of the Spirit, entrance into the kingdom of God is not possible."[4] The meaning is that whoever is instructed by the Word of God and believes it, will have his faith sealed by the outpouring of the Holy Spirit.[5] Through that one is renewed or born again and led into a holy, godly life. That person may then receive the water of baptism[6] as a sign of the death of the old self.[7]

It may furthermore be said, "But here it speaks of water first. Therefore, one can baptize first, as long as faith comes afterward." So I ask whether water can give new birth. Of course, they will say, "No," and then add, "water does not do it, but the Word that is put into the water has this power." I answer that nowhere is the Word put into water nor bound to it. On the contrary, the water is bound to the Word, since the Word commands the water. The command does not follow the deed, but the deed has to be in accordance with the command. Neither does the command adjust itself to the deed, but the deed to the command.[8] Where that is the case, the command blesses the deed and makes it holy; otherwise, it remains fruitless. Therefore, the Word demands and brings the water, not the water the Word. Thus it becomes clear that the Word must go first and not the water, for the water is demanded by the Word and not the Word by the water.

Then follow the three witnesses of whom John says, "There are three who bear witness in heaven, the Father, the Word, and the Holy Spirit, and these three are one."[9] Thus, whoever lacks one of them has none, but whoever has one has them all.[10] The Word shows us that

---

[1] Deut. 1:39.   [2] 1 Cor. 3:6-7.   [3] 1 Cor. 2:9-13; 2 Pet. 1:21.   [4] John 3:3-6.   [5] Joel 2:28-29; Acts 2:14-18; Eph. 1:13-14.   [6] Titus 3:3-7.   [7] Rom. 6:3-6.   [8] Matt. 28:18-20; Mark 16:15-16.   [9] 1 John 5:7-8.   [10] 1 John 2:20-23; 2 John 1:7-9.

what the Father requires is that the Holy Spirit should carry out with great power what the Word shows. Whoever allows that to take place has proof of God within him and will be discovered to be a son of God[1] if he continues thus.[2]

As there are three who witness in heaven, so too we have three on earth: the Spirit, water, and blood, which serve as one.[3] Now in case anyone wants to quarrel with the previous text in which water is mentioned first, the Spirit has the foremost place here. The Spirit, then, is the first witness of a godly life. The Spirit is the one who must begin to bring about a new, godly life in us and lead us to become children of God. Paul says, "The same Spirit assures us that we are God's children."[4] He does not say that water does that.

Since God wants a people separate from the world, he has laid the following command on his children. All who have grasped hold of being heirs should receive the sign of baptism into the covenant as children of God. In this bond they will have put the old person to death and thus become like the death of Christ. From then on, they will deny the world utterly and completely, and serve Christ alone in a life devoted wholly to him.[5]

When a person has reached the second step, the witness of water, the third will soon follow. As Christ has foretold, he will be hated by everyone. "The time comes when whoever kills one of you will think he does God a service."[6] But whoever endures in all this and is faithful and devout to the end, turning neither to the right nor the left[7] and daunted by nothing, gives witness that God is true.[8] Such a person is loved by God and accepted as an heir with all the saints.[9]

Paul says, "In his mercy he has provided salvation for us by the waters of a new birth and by the renewing of the Holy Spirit. He has poured the Spirit out on us abundantly through Jesus Christ. Being thus justified by his grace, we are made heirs of eternal life."[10] He confirms this: "Christ gave himself for his church, that he might sanctify her and cleanse her through washing in the Word, in order to present her to himself, a glorious church without spot or wrinkle."[11]

Now if that must take place by the Word, the Word must first be proclaimed. Baptism will follow when the gospel has been believed. Thus concludes this matter for now.

---

[1] 2 Cor. 6:17-18.　[2] Wisd. of Sol. 3:1-6.　[3] 1 John 5:7-8.　[4] Rom. 8:16; Gal. 4:6.
[5] Eph. 4:20-32; Col. 3:1-10; Rom. 6:3-8.　[6] John 16:1-4.　[7] Josh. 1:7; 23:6; Prov. 4:20-27.
[8] John 3:33.　[9] John 14:23-26.　[10] Titus 3:4-7.　[11] Eph. 5:25-27.

Concerning the Last Supper of Our Lord Jesus, in Which He Shows Us How His Suffering Provides Our Salvation

We now wish to concern ourselves with the precious mystery the Lord Jesus revealed to us in the Last Supper he celebrated with his disciples.[1] Let us pass over the misuses which so-called Christians practice. Who can recount the many abuses they have practiced to their own harm,[2] obscuring the light so that it becomes darkness?[3] However, I must mention the greatest of their errors. This is not because I want to speak evil of those who commit them, but because they have gone so far astray from what is right that they have turned it into an abomination. Now, unless the misuse is wiped out, anyone who is not taught can hardly understand the right practice.

These errors point to death instead of life and to the creature instead of the Creator.[4] What was given to all believers for their salvation,[5] comfort, and delight has been changed to something that brings death. That shows us how cruel and damaging it is to be led astray and turned away. It is like the example of carnal-minded Israel in the wilderness. They said to Aaron, "We do not know what has happened to Moses on the mountain. Come, make us gods that will go ahead of us!" Aaron answered them, "Strip the golden earrings from your wives, sons, and daughters, and bring them to me!" They did that; he received the gold from them and used it to shape a calf with a graving tool. "These," they said, "are the gods that brought us up from the land of Egypt."[6] In so doing, they took the honor from God, who had redeemed them, and gave it to a molten image, the likeness of an ox, that eats grass.[7]

The Israelites used their most precious ornaments against God, ornaments which had been given them by God. In the same way to-

---

[1] Matt. 26:17-29; Mark 14:22-25; Luke 22:14-21. [2] 2 Pet. 3:3-10. [3] Isa. 5:7-23.
[4] Rom. 1:18-25. [5] Rom. 7:11-16. [6] Exod. 32:1-4. [7] Ps. 106:19-21.

day, these false people misuse their most precious gift, God's Holy Word, and so bring about their own ruin.[1] The Israelites set up a golden calf;[2] these people have now set up a baked loaf and say, "This is Christ, who has redeemed us with his flesh and blood." The loaf has neither flesh nor blood, life nor breath,[3] nor can it be of use to itself,[4] much less of help to anyone else. Yet not one of them considers deeply in his heart whether perhaps there is some deception here.

Some even want to hide their deceit a little. They say, "The bread is not flesh and blood, for it is a simple loaf like any other, but in it we partake of Christ to the comfort of us all." Then, if one asks where that is written, they point to Matthew 26, Mark 14, Luke 22, and 1 Corinthians 11, the passages from which they draw their conclusions. What foolish devices human reasoning can invent! What better game could the devil have started than to twist just this! Even his own servants disagree and are divided about it, as noted above. One says the loaf is the body, the other that it is not, and they all try to prove themselves right by quoting Scripture.

The first says the bread is not bread but the body of Christ, and he supports his statement with the words, "This is my body."[5] Thereby he sets up an abomination in place of the comforting institution of Christ. Then he says, "This is Christ, as sure as he hung on the cross and redeemed us with his flesh and blood." Such people are blind to the fact that bread has neither flesh nor blood, neither breath nor life; it can neither stand nor walk, and the mice might eat and not be aware of it. They have nothing but a dead Christ. How then can he give life to others? In effect, Christ said, "Whatever you eat passes into the stomach and so is discharged from the body."[6] That would have to take place with their Christ, and he would end up with the swine. What kind of honor would that be? They make themselves the laughingstock of Jews, Turks, and everyone else.

They nevertheless say, "The bread passes through the body, but Christ remains in the heart." I say that if Christ once became bread, then he must remain bread eternally, for he cannot leave himself; and what he has become, he must remain. He became human,[7] and he remains true human and true God for ever and ever. Thus, if he once became bread, he would have to remain bread for ever and ever. Moreover, since the words had already been spoken, the bread would have

---

[1] 2 Pet. 3:2-7. [2] Exod. 32:1-4. [3] Ps. 115:4-8; 135:15-18. [4] Bar. 6:7-15.
[5] Matt. 26:26. [6] Matt. 15:17. [7] Matt. 1:18-25; Luke 2:1-7.

had to suffer for us, and not Christ apart from the bread. That would indeed be to deny faith, for it was not bread but Christ who died for us.

Another will say that bread is not Christ but a simple loaf, yet Christ exists within it. He also wants to prove it with the words, "This is my body." Thus human reason deceives, and human wisdom is considered divine wisdom. Scripture does not say his body is in this bread, but "This is my body." They change the words of Christ simply to defend their foolishness. If the words were spoken of bread, as they say, then according to the text, the pope and not Luther, must be right. It says "this" and not "in this." Hence, if the pope's opinion amounts to nothing, as indeed it is nothing, then the same must be said of Luther's word. The apostle proves that both are worth nothing when he says to the Hebrews, "He was found in every way like any other human, sin alone excepted."[1] Now if sin was the only exception, physical presence everywhere at once was not an exception. If sin was the only exception, that means he will certainly not be in every morsel of bread any more than when he walked and taught on the earth. He was not everywhere at once but went from one place to another.[2]

Then some will say, "It is true he was not present everywhere, but now he is transfigured, so he is present everywhere. Isn't that what transfiguration means?" To this question I reply that he was not transfigured when he held the Last Supper with his disciples.[3] If he was not present everywhere before the transfiguration, then he was not in every piece of bread which he gave to his disciples. If at that time he was not in the bread, still less is he in it now. It is therefore clear that was not Christ's meaning, nor did it occur to him to give us his body to eat, for he was not sent for that purpose by his Father.[4] Jesus himself corrected his disciples when they misunderstood his words. They were horrified and said, "This is a hard saying; who can accept it?"[5] It was as though they would say, "Who can eat your flesh? It would be difficult if no one would receive life unless he eats your flesh." He answered them, "It is the Spirit who gives life, and the flesh, understood as eating the flesh, is of no avail."

What does avail is that Christ was born for us, taught us, was scourged, killed, rose, and ascended up into heaven. All that is a wonderful and great benefit to us. That is the purpose for which he was

---

[1] Heb. 2:14-18; 4:14-16.   [2] Matt. 4:1-8; John 11:6-7.   [3] Matt. 26:26-34; Mark 14:27-31; Luke 22:14-23.   [4] John 5:24-40; 1 Pet. 1:18-20.   [5] John 6:60-63.

sent, but not to be food.[1] But as we have already said, let us now pass over the abuse and speak briefly of the truth.

In the night in which our Lord Christ was betrayed, he took bread, thanked God the Father, broke it, and gave it to his disciples, saying, "Take, eat; this is my body, which is broken for you." In the same way, he took the cup and said, "Share it among you, for this cup is the new covenant in my blood. Whenever you drink it, do so in remembrance of me."[2] We thus see that Christ definitely does not profess that he or his body should be eaten. He is concerned with something quite different, something each one of us truly needs to understand well. Christ had been sent by the Father so that the covenant of the promise could be confirmed through him.[3] Now the time appointed by the Father for that to take place had come. Christ was to give the promised grace to everyone who believed in his name.[4] Through that they would be planted into the divine nature.[5] Christ wanted to explain that to his disciples in this meal.

And so, wanting to tell them that, he took the loaf, thanked his Father, broke it, and gave it to his disciples with the words, "Take and eat it; this is my body, which is given for you."[6] Here Christ simply wished to show us how, with his death, he redeems us from sin, hell, the devil, and death. He has now planted us into the true divine nature.[7] We who share the bread with him are one loaf or body with him.[8] He is the head,[9] and we are the members, belonging to one another.[10] Truly, insofar as we become like his death and suffer with him, we shall be raised to glory with him.[11]

Jesus proves this by telling them to eat the broken bread. Then each member of the body, as far as one is able, identifies with the head and takes on himself the suffering of Christ. That is what Paul means when he says, "I complete in my own body what is lacking in the sufferings of Christ for the sake of his body, which is you, the church."[12] Now it was Christ's will that they should become one body, one plant, and one growth with him. Later, when Judas had left them,[13] Jesus showed them this truth in a truly wonderful way in another parable. There he says, "I am the true vine, you are the branches, and the Father is the vinedresser."[14]

---

[1] Isa. 61:1-2; Luke 4:17-19; 1 Pet. 1:10-12. [2] Matt. 26:26-27; Mark 14:22-23; Luke 22:19-20; 1 Cor. 11:23-26. [3] Heb. 9:13-15. [4] Acts 13:32-41. [5] 2 Pet. 1:2-4. [6] Matt. 26:26. [7] 2 Pet. 1:2-4. [8] 1 Cor. 10:17. [9] Col. 1:18; 2:19; Eph. 1:22; 4:15-16. [10] Rom. 12:3-5. [11] Rom. 8:10-11. [12] Col. 1:24; 1 Cor. 12:27. [13] Matt. 26:21-25; Mark 14:17-21; Luke 22:1-23; John 13:21-30. [14] John 15:1-10.

When Christ wished to take leave of his disciples, he saw their sorrow and tried to comfort them with this parable. He wanted them to know what he had given them and to what he had led them. After his departure, they would be able to find comfort in it. Through it, they could rouse their hearts to cherish that grace, not to be negligent, but to continue to remember all the good things the Father has shown us through Christ.[1]

That is why Jesus says, "Whenever you do this, do it in remembrance of me." In effect, he says, "When you remember this divine grace, then bear in mind that you have become grafted into the divine promise and made one with his divine nature[2] and body. You are heirs to all the Father owns." In Christ, God has become ours and we have become his. We have become one loaf and one body with Christ.[3] We are brought together from many and made one, growing together with him as one plant.[4] Let us take to heart that through his death he has obtained all this for us and has paid dearly for it. We should try earnestly to be true to Christ and never forget to be thankful for what he has done.[5]

Now that is the meaning of this matter. To celebrate the Last Supper in any other way makes it idolatry, which it is not. Therefore Paul says, "Let each of you examine yourself well before eating of this bread and drinking from this cup."[6] The Holy Spirit wants a person to test himself well, to look into his own heart, to see whether he shares the nature and grace of Christ, and whether he is a true member of Christ. In partaking of the bread and wine, each one shows the others that he is a member of Christ, sharing his grace and his nature. Each one shows that he is of one heart, mind, and soul with all believers, and one body and one loaf with them, just as one loaf of bread is made from many grains of wheat.[7]

On the other hand, whoever does not find such unity within, eats and drinks judgment to oneself.[8] Paul shows clearly, if one has eyes to see, what Christ's meaning is. Let whoever will deliberately not see, bear their own sentence. Now, enough of this matter.

---

[1] John 16:4-7. [2] 2 Pet. 1:2-4. [3] Rom. 8:16-17. [4] John 15:5-7. [5] 1 Pet. 1:18-23.
[6] 1 Cor. 11:27-32. [7] Acts 2:42-46; 1 Cor. 5:6-8; 10:16-17. [8] 1 Cor. 11:27-29.

Concerning Oaths,
About Which There Is Much Controversy

Nowadays there is much controversy about taking oaths, with everyone asserting their own opinion. They all lack the truth and with their fabricated delusions seek to lead many astray. They cause hearts to be burdened[1] and led into sin. Therefore I feel urged to reveal what is false, deceitful, and senseless, and to point to the truth. I do not want to quarrel with them, for that is not my way, nor the way of the church of God,[2] but I wish to protect devout people from being tainted by those who represent these many false teachings.[3]

They say first that in the Old Testament, God himself commanded his people to swear by his name. Now the Son is not against the Father; what the Father once commanded, the Son has not changed.[4]

To this we say that, truly, we know the Son is not against the Father. Otherwise, his kingdom would fall.[5] Father and Son are one, and for this reason the Son wants us to be one in him.[6] Christ is one with the Father, and Christ is in the Father, and the Father is in Christ.[7] Therefore, it is not Christ but the Father in him who has now established and not annulled his law. He has brought it, as Paul says, from the shadow into the light of truth.[8] Since the veil is taken from Moses' face,[9] the light of God's grace[10] and the brightness of his glory[11] are uncovered and revealed to us in Christ.[12] The shadows flee away.[13] The sun of divine understanding sheds its light on us,[14] for in Christ all the treasures of wisdom and knowledge lie hidden.[15]

Therefore, in the old covenant, all God meant by the command to swear by his name was simple: they should show, through their use of his name, that they have learned to know, fear, and honor him. He

---

[1] 1 Tim. 6:3-5; 2 Tim. 2:14.   [2] 1 Cor. 11:16.   [3] Matt. 16:1-12; Mark 8:10-15.
[4] John 5:36-39; 17:20-23.   [5] Matt. 12:22-28.   [6] John 17:20-23.   [7] John 14:6-11.
[8] Rom. 3:31.   [9] 2 Cor. 3:15-18.   [10] Isa. 49:6-9; Acts 13:16-24.   [11] Heb. 1:1-4.   [12] Eph. 1:15-23.   [13] Song of Sol. 2:16-17.   [14] Wisd. of Sol. 1:1-7.   [15] Eph. 1:15-21.

wanted to draw them away from abominations, so he commanded them not to swear by the names of heathen gods, since they are powerless.[1] God threatened heavy penalties on those who swore by such gods. He said, especially through the prophet Amos, "The days are coming, says the Lord, when I will send a famine through the land, not a hunger for bread nor a thirst for water, but for hearing the words of the Lord. Those will run around from sea to sea, from north to east, searching for the word of the Lord, but they will not find it. On that day fair virgins and young men will faint for thirst. Those who swear by the sin of Samaria will say, 'As truly as your god, O Dan, lives; as truly as your god, O Beersheba, lives.' They shall fall and never rise again."[2]

The sins of Samaria were the idols with which the Israelites committed sin.[3] The idols were all worthless, empty, and would come to nothing.[4] Therefore, anything sworn in their name was not only worthless, empty, and had no value; it was also an abomination to God. Since the idols themselves were a false invention, no one could testify to any truth by them. Truth cannot be confirmed by a lie.[5] Moreover, whoever speaks of them as a god, which they were not,[6] utters an untruth and a lie. In forbidding the Israelites to swear by the idols of the heathen, God forbids all lying, untruth, and idle gossip. Later the apostle expresses this more clearly, for no veil hangs before his face:[7] "Therefore, put away falsehood, and let every one speak truth with the neighbor, for you are all members of one body."[8]

In the Old Testament, the words "swearing in God's name" mean speaking the truth. David testifies to this: "Whoever swears by God shall be honored, but the mouth of liars will be silenced."[9] The light of divine truth shines more brightly in Christ. Christ has revealed to us the real will of the Father.[10] Therefore, he agrees with the Father and is not against the Father.[11] The children of Israel bore the name of the people of God, though more in outward appearance than in power and truth. Yet they had not been able to grasp that glory, for the veil still hung before their eyes.[12] The veil signifies that the way to holiness had not been shown to them,[13] for the time of grace had not yet come. However, now that the way has been revealed in Christ,[14] we can see that the previous knowledge or revelation was nothing compared to

---

[1] Let. Jer.; Bar. 6:49-56. [2] Amos 8:11-14. [3] 1 Kings 12:28-33. [4] Isa. 41:23-29.
[5] Rom. 3:3-8. [6] Let. Jer.; Bar. 6. [7] 2 Cor. 3:18. [8] Eph. 4:25. [9] Ps. 63:11. [10] John 3:16-17.
[11] John 5:17-21; 17:20-26. [12] Exod. 34:27-35; 2 Cor. 3:13-15. [13] Heb. 9:6-10. [14] 2 Cor. 6:2.

the surpassing clarity revealed to us in Christ.[1] The law was given through Moses, but truth came through Christ.[2]

For this reason Paul says he counted all his previous advantages sheer loss and dirt compared to the superabundant gain of knowing Christ.[3] In order not to experience the abominations of the heathen, the people of the old covenant clung to God in hope of what was to come and not because of what they had already received. Therefore, God placed his name in their mouths, although he was not yet known in their hearts.[4] This is confirmed by the words that the Lord spoke to Moses: "All that the people have said to you is good. Oh, that their hearts would be inclined to fear me, and that they would keep my commandments!"[5]

From these words we see that the people had not truly known God in their hearts. Even though there were some, like the prophets, who knew him, there was as yet no difference between heir and servant. That situation continued until the time appointed by the Father,[6] when he sent Christ. Through Christ we have received grace upon grace.[7] Now that the truth has been revealed in Christ, God no longer wants ceremonial show. Because he is Spirit, he should be served in spirit and in truth.[8] Christ, who is himself the light of truth, comes to banish the shadows so that the light may shine upon us.[9]

Christ says to us, "You have heard that our ancestors were told, 'You must not swear a false oath but must keep the oath which you have sworn before God.' But I say to you, do not swear at all, neither by heaven, for it is God's throne, nor by the earth, for it is his footstool, nor by Jerusalem, for it is the city of the great King. Nor shall you swear by your own head, because you cannot make one hair white or black. Let your yes be yes and your no be no, for anything more than this comes from evil"—that is, from the devil.[10]

Some may wish to say that only false and superficial swearing is forbidden, but that swearing out of love or from need or to benefit one's neighbor is good, not wrong. Such thinking happens when human reason is placed above divine knowledge, and when human cleverness wants to rule over the Spirit of God instead of submitting to it. That is how Eve looked at the forbidden fruit. That is why she chose to take it upon the serpent's advice. She followed its counsel in

---

[1] 2 Cor. 3:7-11.   [2] John 1:17.   [3] Phil. 3:7-8.   [4] Gen. 12:1-3; 22:15-18.   [5] Deut. 5:28-29.   [6] Gal. 4:1-3.   [7] John 1:16.   [8] John 4:24.   [9] Song of Sol. 2:16-17; Matt. 4:16-17; Luke 2:32; John 1:1-18; 8:12; 2 Cor. 4:4-6; Eph. 5:14.   [10] Matt. 5:33-37; James 5:12.

preference to God's and was therefore deceived by the devil's cunning, which led to death.[1] It is still true that whoever wants to please people cannot be Christ's servant.[2] Truly here reason should not be allowed to rule, nor should the Scriptures be twisted to suit arrogant human opinions. All that is futile. The honor belongs to God, and we have to leave his command as it stands.

Someone may ask, "Should we understand the Scriptures only literally?" We say no! Here, as in all Scripture, we must let the Holy Spirit, through whom Scripture was inspired, be the judge.[3] But who can judge in this way without having the Holy Spirit? A carnal person understands nothing of the things of the Spirit of God, but the spiritual person judges all things spiritually.[4] Those who have Christ will easily recognize what is meant here about him. They will discover that Christ brings the truth out of the shadow[5] and says, "People were commanded not to swear falsely,[6] but I say to you, Do not swear at all."[7] It is primarily Christ's purpose, as Matthew 5 shows, to lead us to a more perfect righteousness than that to which God's people of old were led.[8] Thus he points to the command, "You shall not murder,"[9] and adds, "But I say to you, you shall also not be angry."[10]

In the same way Christ says, "The people were taught not to commit adultery.[11] But I tell you that anyone who looks at a woman lustfully has already committed adultery with her in his heart."[12] Again, "It was said to the people in the past that they should love their friends and hate their enemies. But I say to you, love your enemies, do good to those who hate you, bless those who curse you, and pray for those who persecute you, so that you may be children of your Father in heaven." To sum it up, "Unless your righteousness surpasses that of the scribes and Pharisees," Christ says, "you will not enter the kingdom of God."[13]

That is one reason Christ forbids swearing. He wants to invite his people, those who have been called by him, to be more faithful to what they have been taught and to live more righteously than the people of the old covenant. Truth is revealed to them; it has come more fully to light in Christ.[14] A second reason is our weakness. In our own strength, we are unable to do either small or great things unless God works in us. This we see from Christ's words: "You shall not swear

---

[1] Gen. 3:4-6.   [2] Gal. 1:10; James 4:1-6.   [3] 2 Pet. 1:19-21.   [4] 1 Cor. 2:10-16; *carnal means unspiritual, sinful.*   [5] Rom. 3:31; Col. 2:17; Heb. 10:1, 26.   [6] Exod. 20:7.
[7] Matt. 5:34-37.   [8] Matt. 5:20, 48.   [9] Lev. 24:17-21; Deut. 5:17.   [10] Matt. 5:22-24.
[11] Exod. 20:14; Sir. 41:20-22.   [12] Matt. 5:28.   [13] Matt. 5:20, 43-48.   [14] John 1:1-18.

by your head, because you cannot cause even one hair to become white or black."[1] In another place he says, "Which of you by being anxious can add one cubit to his height?"[2]

Because we of ourselves have no strength or ability, God wishes us to give the honor to him who can do everything. He is a jealous God and does not give his glory to another.[3] Now whoever swears to do this or that robs God of his rightful honor. Such a person swears to do a certain thing in spite of a lack of ability and without knowing whether God wants to do that thing in him.[4] That is why James says, "You ought to say, 'If it is God's will, I shall do this or that.' "[5] Therefore, all God-fearing persons will beware of such swearing, however much they may be slandered.

The third reason is that since truth has come and is revealed in Christ, we by grace, through faith in his name, have been planted in the truth.[6] Thus now we do not live, but rather the truth lives in us,[7] and Christ is that truth. Christ does and reveals everything in us, yes, even speaks through us, as he says, "It is not you but the Spirit of my Father who speaks in you."[8] That being so, all that a believer says is firmly rooted in God and remains unwavering. He says it in or through God, or God through him. That is why James says, "Let your yes be yes, and your no be no."[9] In effect, he says, "You are not to speak superficially or gossip thoughtlessly, for that grieves the Holy Spirit of God, who dwells in you."[10] Instead, Christ calls you to take note of what the Spirit says in you, or moves you to say, so that the Spirit may follow it up with deeds and give power to your speech.[11] Then you will walk in the truth, and your words will be true; your yes will be yes, and your no will be no. Beyond this, do not swear any oath.[12]

Yet Paul also says, "How good and faithful is God, who has brought it about that our message to you did not mean yes and no at the same time! Among you, we preached Jesus Christ the Son of God, who was not 'yes and no,' but in him was always 'yes.' All the promises of God are 'yes' and 'amen' in him, praised be his name!"[13] Thus he means to say, "Christ has left nothing undone but has brought about all he told you through me. He himself has borne witness to his Word in power and in truth. Christ revealed that what I proclaimed to you was not a human word but God's word."[14]

---

[1] Matt. 5:36. [2] Matt. 6:27. [3] Isa. 42:8; 48:11. [4] Rom. 2:23-24. [5] James 4:15.
[6] John 1:1-18. [7] Gal. 2:20. [8] Matt. 10:19-20. [9] James 5:12. [10] Eph. 4:25-30.
[11] Matt. 10:19-20. [12] James 5:12. [13] 2 Cor. 1:18-20. [14] 1 Thess. 2:13.

Since God tells all believers what to say,[1] it must be true that anyone who will not believe these words without an oath, does not have the same Spirit. Anyone who does not have God's Spirit, does not belong to him.[2] Whoever demands an oath shows that God's truth is not in him. Likewise, whoever swears an oath shows that he does not respect or value God's truth. Whoever knows his words are rooted in God, in whom all things are anchored, will search no more. He will simply stick to what the truth has spoken and testified through him.

Suppose a person who is rooted in truth and has placed his word in the truth, namely, in God himself,[3] seeks to strengthen his word by swearing an oath. That person thereby turns away from the Creator to the creature, and the truth in him is weakened. The truth is weakened because that person wants to certify more strongly through himself what he says than how God has witnessed to the truth in him. That is robbing God of what is his and refusing to give God the honor for what he does and must do.[4] Therefore, James says, "The person sins who knows what is right and does not do it."[5]

Some may wish to say, "Swearing any kind of oath is certainly forbidden,[6] but it is not forbidden to bear witness to the truth along with God, who is truth."[7] My response is that when Israel was allowed to swear, which was in keeping with the Lord's command, that was also truth.[8] This was also truth because Israel was forbidden to swear to a lie and to a falsehood, but to swear to the truth was permitted.[9] If that kind of swearing were allowed us, Christ would have let stand the first command, that it was swearing falsely that was forbidden. Christ said clearly, however, "It used to be said, 'You shall not swear falsely,'[10] but I say to you, 'Do not swear at all.' "[11]

Therefore, weigh Christ's words carefully. He says, "It used to be said, 'You shall not swear falsely,' but I say to you, 'Do not swear at all.' " He also says, "It used to be said, 'You shall hate your enemy,' but I say to you, 'Love your enemies.' "[12] If I now hate my enemy and pay him back evil for evil, curse for curse, and blow for blow, would I be doing right? No indeed, for that would be to reject the command[13] of our Master, and act against his nature.[14] Swearing an oath is simply wrong, even though what is sworn to is in itself truth, for swearing is forbidden.[15] It is enough that the truth testifies for itself, insofar as it is

---

[1] Matt. 10:20. [2] Rom. 8:9. [3] John 14:6. [4] Rom. 2:23. [5] James 4:17.
[6] Matt. 5:34-36. [7] John 14:6-11. [8] Ps. 63:11. [9] Exod. 20:7-16. [10] Exod. 20:7; Deut. 5:11. [11] Matt. 5:33-36. [12] Matt. 5:43-48. [13] Matt. 5:20-48. [14] 1 Pet. 4. [15] Matt. 5:34.

in us. That is better, nobler, and surer than all human testimony.

Because of this, Christ himself says, "I do not receive testimony from humans, for I have a better witness than that of John. What I do is a witness to me, and furthermore, the Father who has sent me testifies to me."[1] God himself will witness in each person to the extent he wishes. That is why it is vain to swear an oath, however it is done, for in so doing a person ignores God's witness in him.

One who still objects may say, "But love does all things;[2] therefore, in order to help a neighbor, it is not wrong to take an oath." We answer that although love will go to any lengths, yet it neither can nor will act against its own nature.[3] Love does not sin; it does only what is right,[4] and it will never fail.[5] So, on the contrary, love will strive for the betterment of one's neighbor. Love tries earnestly to turn the neighbor away from any evil which he is about to do. That is the task of love, that is why God has chosen his people,[6] and that is why he has put his Holy Spirit into our hearts.[7] He wishes to witness through us against sin[8] and so rebuke the world.[9] Whoever gives in to sin and does not testify against it, fails to witness to the Spirit of God that is in him.

To those who say that God himself has sworn,[10] and that therefore it cannot possibly be wrong, we answer that no one denies that God and Christ have sworn. That, however does not prove that people have the right to do so. God, in his own strength and without anyone's help, can perform what he promises. Therefore, he can truly promise something by himself. He has never sworn by anyone higher, for there is no one higher. The apostle bears witness to this: "Because God had no one greater by whom to swear, he swore by himself, saying, 'Surely I will multiply you.' "[11]

Because God is truth, he of himself can really promise to do such a thing. Therefore, if a person wishes to see the truth, it is as if the person would say, "I will do it." The difference is that what God promises, he is able to do by himself, but humans are not able to act alone. Now, since humans can do nothing, they will rightly and dutifully leave the honor to him who must do everything in them.[12] We agree with James when he teaches, "If it is God's will, I shall do it."[13] Whoever does not do this, deprives God of the honor[14] owed him.[15] Since a person can do

---

[1] John 5:34-37. [2] 1 Cor. 13:7. [3] 1 Cor. 13:4-13. [4] Rom. 13:8-9. [5] 1 Cor. 13:6-8.
[6] 1 Pet. 2:1-5. [7] Joel 2:28-29; Acts 2:14-21; Rom. 8:1-4; Gal. 4:4-6. [8] Gal. 5:16-25.
[9] John 16:7-9. [10] Gen. 22:15-16. [11] Heb. 6:13-14; Gen. 22:15-18. [12] John 15:4-5.
[13] James 4:15. [14] Rom. 2:25. [15] Deut. 32:39.

nothing,[1] he has no power to swear by himself,[2] for of himself he cannot keep his oath. Then how should he have power to swear by one who is greater than he? The one who is not able to swear by the very least (oneself) may even less call upon that which is greater (God).[3]

Christ makes this clear to us in these words: "Woe to you, you blind guides, who say, 'If anyone swears by the temple, it is nothing; but if anyone swears by the gold of the temple, he is bound by his oath.' You blind fools! Which is greater, the gold or the temple that sanctifies the gold? You also teach that if anyone swears by the altar, it is nothing; but if he swears by the gift that is on it, he is bound by his oath. You blind fools! Which is greater, the gift or the altar that makes the gift sacred? So the one who swears by the altar, swears by it and by everything on it. The one who swears by the temple, swears by it and by him who dwells in it. Whoever swears by heaven, swears by the throne of God and by him who sits upon it."[4]

On the basis of these words, it is clear that God has even less desire for people to swear by that which is greater than he has for them to swear by that which is smaller. The priests did not think it wrong to swear by the altar, but they did think it wrong to swear by the sacrifice, because it had become a sweet savor to the Lord.[5] Christ shows here how foolish and unreasonable they were. He calls them fools because they do not know that the altar is more than the sacrifice. They should indeed know that, because if swearing by the sacrifice is wrong, swearing by the altar is even a greater wrong. If swearing by the gold of the temple is wrong, swearing by the temple itself is even a greater wrong, because he who does that is actually swearing by God, who dwells there.[6] Christ rebuked them for their blindness of heart because they did not know this and, thinking themselves wise,[7] they presumed to be teachers of others.[8] Yet they were fools with no knowledge of God.[9]

So it is clear that God does not want us to swear by temple, altar, heaven, earth, our own head, or any created thing. Even less should we swear by his name! The words of James confirm this: "Above all, dear brothers, do not swear, neither by heaven, nor by earth, nor by anything else. Let your yes be yes, and your no be no." James wishes that there be no oaths, whether small or large, in order to avoid hy-

---

[1] John 15:4-5.   [2] Matt. 5:36.   [3] John 15:4-5.   [4] Matt. 23:16-22.   [5] Lev. 1:1—2:16.
[6] Matt. 23:16-22.   [7] 1 Cor. 1:20.   [8] Rom. 2:19-20.   [9] 1 Cor. 2:14; 15:34.

pocrisy.[1] Let people twist it, disguise it, and dress it up as much as they will; yet there is nothing good in swearing an oath. Christ says that our way of speaking should be simply yes and no. Whatever is more than that is evil.[2] The evil one is the devil, who tears out the good from the hearts of people, and plants evil.[3]

Those who are devoted to God will live according to his truth. They will allow the truth to rule and guide them, and will obey what it inspires, speaks, and acts through them.[4] They will believe the truth and follow it for its own sake,[5] for God himself is truth[6] and is dwelling in them.[7] Therefore, God's followers do not need or desire an oath.[8] It is not our duty to go along with those who are outside our fellowship. On the contrary, we should testify against their sin, for God has sent his Spirit for the purpose of rebuking the world for its sin.[9] Therefore, let us look a little more carefully at the writings of Paul, the beloved apostle, and not use them as a cloak to cover wickedness. Let us not distort any of them, for that could bring about our own ruin.[10] For the moment we will say no more about the question of swearing.

---

[1] James 5:12. [2] Matt. 5:37. [3] Matt. 13:19. [4] 3 John 1:1-4. [5] Matt. 13:23.
[6] John 14:6-7. [7] Lev. 26:11-13. [8] 2 Cor. 6:14-16. [9] John 16:7-11. [10] 2 Pet. 3:3-16.

Concerning Governmental Authority
and Its Appointed Service

We are frequently attacked on the question of governmental authority, what we think about it, whether it was appointed by God, and whether rulers can be Christians. We have no wish to hold back the truth, nor to present anything but that which is founded on truth. We want others to see that we do not depart from the truth but live and act according to it. Therefore, it is not our wish to say anything to harm anyone, nor to keep silence to oblige anyone, not even ourselves. We want only to bear witness to the truth as God has placed it in us, because the Lord has commanded us, saying, "You shall be my witnesses to the people."[1] We want to speak according to his Word. Whoever has ears to hear, let them hear!

It is quite clear that in his grace, God the Almighty did not want to reject humanity so completely as to never again remember it or have mercy on it. Therefore, even in his wrath he remembered his grace and promised blessing from the offspring of the woman, even though he banished humanity from the garden of Eden.[2] Since God did not completely withdraw his mercy from people, he was himself Ruler over them all, punishing the evildoers but loving the devout. We see this in Abel and Cain. God loved Abel, but when Cain acted wrongly, God punished him, saying, "Cain, what have you done? Hark! Your brother's blood cries out to me from the ground. You are now accursed and driven from the earth, which has opened its mouth to receive your brother's blood from you. When you till the ground, it will no longer yield its wealth for you. You shall be a fugitive and a wanderer on the earth."[3]

That was the order established by the Lord; that is how he punished evildoers, as we also see with Adam and Eve.[4] However, God loved those who did right. When such were hard pressed by the un-

---

[1] Acts 1:8.   [2] Gen. 3:15, 23-24.   [3] Gen. 4:8-12.   [4] Gen. 3:13-24.

just, God judged the oppressors and did not leave innocent blood unavenged.[1] He will continue to do this, as he promised through the mouth of his prophets: "When I forgive people their sins, I will not forgive them the innocent blood they have shed."[2] That is why Christ says, "Judgment will fall on them for the innocent blood they have shed, from Abel to Zacharias."[3] God himself ruled and judged people through his Spirit until they completely ruined themselves. Then each followed his carnal inclination, which had taken the upper hand.[4]

God declared, "My Spirit shall not contend with humans forever, for they are flesh."[5] Observe that what caused God to take away the power of his Spirit from humans was their own corrupt nature and carnal inclination. Because they would no longer obey but allowed themselves to be overcome by sin, the Spirit of God turned away from them.[6] However, God did not want to cast them off forever, and therefore, after the Flood he gave them a government. We read in Ecclesiasticus, "He set a ruler over every people."[7] Paul tells us the same when he says that all government everywhere is established by God.[8] For what purpose? To be his servant for the punishment of evildoers.[9]

God no longer wanted his Spirit to strive with those who were carnally minded,[10] and yet he did not want the earth to be completely bloodstained or the evildoers to remain unpunished. Therefore, he had to have an instrument of punishment.[11] That, as was said above, was the ruling power,[12] to which he gave the command that whoever sheds human blood, shall also have his blood shed.[13] From that we see that power and government have grown from God's wrath and punishment, rather than from his blessing. Moreover, when God gave the rulers power over the people, he still reserved the highest power for himself. From that it is clear that he wants rulers to look to him and obey him;[14] he wants them to do nothing in their own strength or on their own initiative. They should allow themselves to be used as his instruments of punishment, and to be guided by him in accordance with his will and preference.[15]

All this is the long-suffering of the Almighty, who wants no one to perish but rather to repent.[16] Humans have brought such ruin on themselves that God could rightly have destroyed them all. Yet he remem-

---

[1] Gen. 4:4-11. [2] Joel 3:19. [3] Matt. 23:29-35. [4] Gen. 6:5; *carnal* means unspiritual, sinful. [5] Gen. 6:3. [6] Wisd. of Sol. 1:3-5. [7] Sir. 17:12-15. [8] Rom. 13:1.
[9] 1 Pet. 2:13-14; Rom. 13:2-5. [10] Gen. 6:3. [11] Gen. 9:5-6. [12] Rom. 13:1-4; 1 Pet. 2:13-14. [13] Gen. 9:6. [14] Wisd. of Sol. 1:1. [15] Isa. 10:1-19. [16] 2 Pet. 3:9.

bered his mercy and wished for their well-being. He always seeks what is good for people,[1] that in time to come they may recognize it, be converted to him,[2] and be healed.[3] If they do not do that, the Lord will not lie. He will turn about, rend, and destroy his adversaries, and no one shall save them. Those are the words of the Lord.[4]

Therefore, wherever the ruling power presumes to act on its own, the rod rebels against the striker, the ax against the hewer, and the saw scratches the one who saws. In all this we can see clearly that those who govern are simply instruments whom God wishes to use to punish wicked people. Of itself, a tool can do nothing good. It can only allow its master to use it the way he wishes. When tools are used in that way, the work is done; otherwise, work remains undone.[5]

So it is with governments. Even though they may go their own willful way for a long time, they will achieve nothing good, for they do not allow themselves to be used by him who has appointed them to this position. Instead, they want to act according to their own willful ways. Therefore, God punishes those who flog, together with those who are to be flogged,[6] so that the subjects rebel against authority. Since the rulers rebel against the one who should be their guide, it is their just sentence that God should punish them with their own sins and give them such a disobedient people. They will thus become hateful and spiteful to one another if they recognize that they have failed to do their task and failed to give honor to God, who appointed them.[7]

Whenever governments ignore their responsibility to God and turn to exterminate and wipe out nations, the Lord will punish the fruit of their arrogant hearts and eyes. When rulers do that, they ascribe to themselves great power, strength, and ability to achieve things, not only in this world, but also in the world to come.[8] Of such the sage says, "Listen, you who rule over people and raise yourselves over nations. Your power is given to you by the Lord, and sovereignty by the most High. He will ask what you are doing and inquire how you are ruling, since you are God's ministers. You, however, who are administrators of his kingdom, have not fulfilled your task, nor judged aright, nor walked according to the counsel of God. He will come upon you terribly and swiftly, and a harsh judgment will befall those in high places. The lowly ones will experience grace, but the mighty

---

[1] Matt. 5:45. [2] Prov. 1:24-33. [3] 1 Tim. 2:3-6. [4] Ps. 50:17-22. [5] Isa. 10:15.
[6] Isa. 3:4-9. [7] Wisd. of Sol. 16:15-19. [8] Isa. 10:5-15.

shall be punished severely."[1] We have now said enough of the punishment of governmental authority.

As there are none who desire the right with all their heart,[2] it is only just that they should bear the punishment the Lord said he would give them. Their leaders shall be mere children, and they shall be governed by foolish, effeminate rulers.[3] God attempts all of that for the improvement of humanity. But if all of that is not effective, he vents his anger as he said he would. God left all other nations alone and chose for himself one single people,[4] namely Israel, whose God and King he wished to be. This is said clearly in the words of the wise teacher: "Over all lands God has set a ruler, but over Israel he himself is Lord."[5] That is why God himself keeps watch over them as a shepherd over his sheep,[6] and leads them from one place to another, allowing no one to mistreat them.

For his people's sake, God punished kings and mighty nations and said, "Do not touch my anointed, and do not harm my prophets."[7] He also calls them his heirs[8] and his children.[9] Thus he is their Father,[10] Lord, and King, reigning over them and leading them.[11] Though they sinned greatly against him, for his name's sake he did not forsake them until, after committing many sins, they asked for a king, telling Samuel, "Set a king over us to judge us, as other nations have."[12]

When Samuel described to them the rights of a king, to deter them from such an undertaking, they refused to listen or obey his faithful counsel. "No," they said, "a king shall rule over us; then we shall be like other nations, with one to judge us, to lead us out to war, and to fight our battles."[13] However, the Lord's answer to Samuel was this: "Obey the voice of the people in all they say to you, for they have rejected me, not you. They will not have me as their king. They are doing to you as they have always done to me since the day I led them from Egypt, namely, leaving me in order to serve other gods. Therefore, obey their voice."[14]

Time after time they had forsaken the Almighty, and in addition had even wanted to have a king. So Samuel said, "Thus says the Lord, 'I have brought you out of Egypt. I have delivered you from the power of the Egyptians and from all the other kingdoms that oppressed you.' Now you have rejected your God, rejected him who saved you from

---

[1] Wisd. of Sol. 6:2-8.   [2] Rom. 3:10-12.   [3] Isa. 3:4.   [4] Amos 3:1-2.   [5] Sir. 17:17.
[6] Ps. 23:1-2.   [7] Ps. 105:7-15.   [8] Isa. 19:25.   [9] Ps. 28:9.   [10] Lev. 26:12-13.   [11] Lev. 16:34.   [12] 1 Sam. 8:4-5.   [13] 1 Sam. 8:10-20.   [14] 1 Sam. 8:7-9.

all your miseries and distress. You have said to him, 'Set a king over us.' "[1] In effect, God says, "You have already done enough to provoke God's anger. Therefore, his wrath is kindled against you, and he gives you a king. See, there is your king!"[2] The Lord says further, "You said, 'Give us a king and princes,' so in my anger I gave you a king, and in my wrath I took him away."[3]

From all these words it is clear that God has appointed human rulers, not from goodwill but only from wrath. The people had transgressed, forsaken God, and given themselves up to carnal lusts. Only after that happened did God give them an earthly government, so that his Spirit might not continually be at strife with them.[4] To repeat, God did not do this only to heathen nations but also to the Jews, as we have just seen in the words the Lord spoke: "They have rejected me; they do not wish me to be king over them."[5]

Thus, temporal power is a sign, a picture, and a reminder of turning aside from God. It should truly warn all people to look within themselves and consider to what they have come. Then they can turn back all the more quickly to the one from whom they have fallen. But who thinks in these terms? Since there are none who want to take it to heart, that which they deserve will finally happen to them.[6]

We can thus see, first, where temporal power came from, and what caused God to give it. We can also see the reason for temporal power, which is the punishment of evildoers.[7] Since people did not want to let themselves be ruled by the Spirit of the Lord, God had to use a different rod to protect them from harm. This was done so that the land would not be completely polluted with bloodguilty people, and so that he would not have to destroy the whole world on their account.[8] The world could thus be preserved until the time of the promised offspring, in whom all things would be made right.[9]

When the promised one comes to establish a new kingdom, he comes not with great pomp in worldly fashion, but as it is written: "Rejoice greatly, O daughter of Zion! Shout, O daughter of Jerusalem! See, your King comes to you; he is just and a helper; he is poor, riding upon a donkey, upon a colt, the foal of a donkey."[10] He does not come in wrath, nor for vengeance or destruction, but to bring salvation.[11] He calls people to himself and says, "Come and learn of me, for I am

---

[1] 1 Sam. 10:17-19.   [2] 1 Sam. 12:1-2.   [3] Hos. 13:10-11.   [4] Gen. 6:3.   [5] 1 Sam. 8:7.
[6] Rev. 19:17-19.   [7] Rom. 13:1-4; 1 Pet. 2:13-14.   [8] Gen. 9:5-6.   [9] Gen. 3:14-15.
[10] Zech. 9:9; Matt. 21:5; John 12:12-16.   [11] Luke 9:52-56; John 12:47.

meek and humble of heart."[1] Hence, all who wish to come into his kingdom must become like his nature, his mind, and his Spirit.[2]

That is why Christ rebuked his disciples when they wanted to express their vengeance by calling fire to fall from heaven and consume those who would not receive them. He said, "You do not know to what spirit you belong, for the Son of Man did not come to destroy people's souls, but to save them."[3] He means to say, "What are you doing? That is not my purpose! If you want to be my disciples, you must not act in this way, for I have not been sent to practice vengeance."

Note this text well! Here Christ abolishes revenge from his kingdom. He will not use it against people to destroy them. He commands the same for the church of his kingdom, saying, "You have heard that it was said, a hand for a hand, an eye for an eye, and a tooth for a tooth. But I say to you, do not resist evil. Instead, if someone strikes you on your right cheek, turn the other one to him also. If anyone will sue you for your coat, let him have your cloak too."[4] See how Christ infringes on governmental authority! The law of Moses commanded people to shed blood for blood,[5] and to destroy a hand for a hand, an eye for an eye, and a tooth for a tooth.[6]

However, Christ in his kingdom gives us something different. He does not want us to use retaliation. Paul teaches us the same: "Do not avenge yourselves, dear brothers, but leave room for God's wrath."[7] Christ does not want us to resist evil,[8] and he means that not only for subjects but for all people who enter his kingdom. Then also, Christ limits the authority of governments and does not want that authority to be used in his kingdom. He obviously does not speak only to those who previously had no power, but much more to those who have used it. He tells them to set it aside when they enter his kingdom and leave vengeance to God alone. The others he leaves to their own laws and customs.

Christ says, "My kingdom is not of this world; if it were, my servants would fight for me, to save me from being given into the hands of the Jews."[9] Look at the King of heaven and earth! What power, what magnificence and glory he has![10] Note the battle he wages against those who would kill him! See what a powerful army he takes out against them, how he smites the enemy when he says to Pe-

---

[1] Matt. 11:28-29. [2] Rom. 8:9-15. [3] Luke 9:55-56. [4] Matt. 5:38-42. [5] Gen. 9:5-6.
[6] Exod. 21:23-25; Lev. 24:17; Deut. 19:11-13. [7] Rom. 12:19-21. [8] Matt. 5:39.
[9] John 18:36. [10] Matt. 28:18.

ter, "Put your sword back into its sheath.[1] Do you not know that I can pray to the Father to send me several legions of angels to fight for me?"[2] See how he deals with revenge when he takes the ear of Malchus that had been struck off and puts it on again![3]

"Whoever would be my disciple," says Christ, "let him take up his cross and follow me."[4] From this he goes on to command, "Do not resist evil. Do good to those who wrong you, pray for those who persecute you, and bless those who curse you, so that you may be the children of your Father who is in heaven. He causes the sun to rise and the rain to fall on good and evil people alike."[5]

Thus Christ specifically says that his disciples are not children of revenge. So it is clear that in his house or kingdom, Christ will not have people who practice vengeance. On the contrary, he wants those who spread blessing, love, and deeds of kindness, as he himself did.[6] Whoever does not have this spirit, does not belong to him.[7]

Someone may say, "But Paul calls the rulers God's servants.[8] How can that be? They are not Christians, and yet are they servants of God?" We answer that this really can be true, both in the past and in the present. We all certainly know that in times past Israel alone was the Lord's people. The Lord had chosen Israel out of all nations,[9] and all the Gentiles were as nothing before him. Yet he calls Nebuchadnezzar his servant, when he says, "I will send for my servant Nebuchadnezzar, the king of Babylon, and will set his throne on top of these stones."[10] In the same way he calls the king of Assyria a staff or rod of his wrath, whose hand should strike the hypocrites, the people who deserved his anger.[11]

Now these were servants of God, although not Jews. It is the same today. God has two kinds of servants. One kind, the servants of vengeance, carry out God's wrath upon the evildoer,[12] since they themselves were given in wrath.[13] Christ, however, did not come for vengeance but for blessing.[14] Hence, those who are planted in Christ and are his servants must bring blessing, not vengeance. Each one must edify the other,[15] all growing together and increasing in the knowledge of Christ, and each becoming perfect in Christ's perfect maturity.[16] May we be given a blameless and unspotted life[17] and be-

---

[1] Matt. 26:51-52; John 18:10-11.   [2] Matt. 26:53.   [3] Luke 22:49-51.   [4] Mark 8:34.
[5] Matt. 5:39-45.   [6] Luke 9:55-56.   [7] Rom. 8:9.   [8] Rom. 13:4.   [9] Amos 3:1-2.   [10] Jer. 43:10.   [11] Isa. 10:5-6; 45:1.   [12] Rom. 13:4.   [13] Hos. 13:11.   [14] Gal. 3:13-14.   [15] 1 Thess. 5:11   [16] Eph. 4:7-15.   [17] Phil. 2:12-15.

come holy as Christ is holy.[1]

Some may argue, "The Son is not against the Father; therefore, he neither disobeys nor does away with what the Father has once established. The Father has appointed the government,[2] and it must remain in Christ. Otherwise, the Son would be against the Father." It is true that the Son is not against the Father, for they are one.[3] But it does not follow that what the Father has appointed everywhere, must remain so in Christ, for then the grace of Christ would be in vain.

What, then, is the true reason? After the transgression,[4] God appointed death for all people.[5] But Christ has done away with death's power through his own death[6] and has appointed life[7] for all who believe in his name.[8] Therefore, he is not against the Father. Instead, he has fulfilled the Father's promise.

Furthermore, God appointed circumcision and gave this command to Abraham. So strictly was it to be enforced that the soul of any boy who was not circumcised was to be cut off from his people. Yet, circumcision comes to an end in Christ.[9] The Father gave the command to love the friend and hate the enemy.[10] Because Saul did not keep this law but spared the life of his enemy, the king of the Amalekites, he was rejected as king of Israel.[11] In contrast, Christ commands us to love not only friends but also enemies.[12] Thus, there is much that the Father appointed, such as sacrifices, Sabbaths, and other ordinances, which come to an end in Christ, in whom is the reality of these things.[13] One should not be so presumptuous, however, as to say that the Son is therefore against the Father. On the contrary, one must say that what the Father appointed in Christ will remain in him and not become changed, as these examples show: love,[14] peace,[15] unity,[16] and community.[17] But what he has appointed apart from Christ, such as death,[18] wrath,[19] disgrace,[20] curse,[21] malediction,[22] vengeance,[23] and all that belong to them—these have no place in Christ.

Every person can learn and know what is meant. Whoever does not see and heed this distinction will not be able to understand. This is

---

[1] Lev. 11:44-45; 19:2; 1 Pet. 3:15-16.   [2] Rom. 13:1; Sir. 11:12-15.   [3] John 17:21.
[4] Gen. 3:3.   [5] 2 Esd. 3:4-7; Rom. 5:12-14.   [6] Matt. 27:50; Mark 15:37; Luke 23:46;
John 19:30.   [7] Hos. 13:14; 1 Cor. 15:54-57; 2 Tim. 1:8-10; Heb. 2:14.   [8] John 5:24.
[9] Gen. 17:9-14; 1 Cor. 7:18; Gal. 5:2; 6:15.   [10] Matt. 5:43; here *hate* likely means to love less, as in Luke 14:26; see also Luke 10:25-37; Lev. 19:17-18, 33-34; Deut. 23:3-8, 19-20; 25:17-19; Ps. 139:19-22.   [11] 1 Sam. 15:9-11, 26.   [12] Matt. 5:44.   [13] Col. 2:16-20; Heb. 10:1-18.   [14] John 3:16; 4:14; 14:23-31; 15:9-10.   [15] John 14:27; Eph. 2:13-17.   [16] John 17:20-21.   [17] Acts 2:42-44; 4:32.   [18] Rom. 5:12-21; 2 Esd. 3:9-10.   [19] Eph. 2:1-3.
[20] Isa. 10:3-6.   [21] Deut. 27:15-26.   [22] Gal. 3:10.   [23] Rom. 13:1-4; 1 Pet. 2:13-14.

what the whole world lacks. Christ is the full blessing of the Father,[1] and anyone who wants to inherit this blessing must receive it through Christ.[2] The fullness of God's blessing is in Christ.[3] Yes, Christ is himself the blessing[4] promised to our ancestors,[5] but fulfilled and given to us.[6] What was given and appointed in wrath, under a curse, and in disfavor,[7] that cannot have any place in Christ.[8] Because blessing has come,[9] wrath ceases.[10] The authority of the government was given in wrath,[11] and its function appointed in anger,[12] for the people had rejected the Lord and his rule over them.[13] And so the child of blessing[14] cannot be the servant of wrath[15] and vengeance.[16]

Some may say, "David was a ruler and king,[17] yet he was devout and he pleased God. Why should that not be so now?" We agree that David, who was devout and pleasing to God, was indeed a king. That was possible in his time, but it is not possible today. At that time the way to holiness had not yet been revealed.[18] The people of Israel sinned[19] so much that God could rightly have rejected and abandoned them,[20] yet he refrained from doing so for his name's sake.[21] He patiently put up with their ways until the time when Christ was sent.[22] In speaking of that, Paul says, "God has overlooked the days of ignorance, but now he commands all people everywhere to repent."[23]

At that time vengeance had not been abolished, but was permitted by God's people. Christ himself says, "It was said to those of ancient times, 'Love your friend and hate your enemy.' "[24] Although vengeance belonged to God[25] at that time as it does today, God's people were allowed to take part in it.[26] We read in many parts of the Scriptures that they executed vengeance at God's command.[27] Therefore, in ancient times the devout man was more rightfully king over Israel than the godless man. Israel's king prefigured Christ, the true king of God's "holy hill."[28] All those under the yoke of bondage waited for him.[29]

---

[1] John 1:14-18. [2] Gal. 3:7-14. [3] Col. 1:1-19. [4] John 1:14-16. [5] Gen. 12:1-3; 15:1-5; 21:12; 22:12-18; 26:1-5; 49:10; Acts 3:22-26; Gal. 3:6-9. [6] Luke 2:8-11; Acts 13:32-39. [7] Hos. 13:10-11. [8] Luke 9:49-56. [9] John 1:1-12. [10] Eph. 2:1-7. [11] Hos. 13:11. [12] Isa. 10:5-6. [13] 1 Sam. 8:7-8. [14] Rom. 8:10-17; 15-29. [15] Rom. 13:7-10; 1 Pet. 2:9-16. [16] Luke 9:52-56. [17] 2 Sam. 2:4. [18] Heb. 9:1-12. [19] Judg. 2:8-12; 2 Esd. 3:17-22. [20] Jer. 7:24-34; Amos 5:18-27. [21] Deut. 9:11-29. [22] Acts 13:16-23. [23] Acts 17:30-31. [24] Matt. 5:43; *hate,* meaning to love less. [25] Deut. 32:35-36. [26] Rom. 12:19; Heb. 10:30. [27] Num. 21:1-3; 31:1-10; Josh. 8:1-8; 9:17-27; 10:12-14; 11:1-12; Judg. 1:1-2; 4:4-14; 7:2-3; 11:1-40; 20:26-28; 1 Sam. 11:8-11; 15:1-5; 17:22-51; 2 Sam. 5:19-20; 18:31-32; 20:20-22; 2 Chron. 13:6-12; 14:2, 8-12; 20:15-26; 24:22-25; 1 Macc. 2:23-28; 3:13-25; 4:7-15; 5:1-54; 6:55-63. [28] Ps. 2:6. [29] Gal. 3:16-18.

Now Christ has come,[1] the one who has received and prepared the kingdom,[2] and has separated the heirs from the slaves.[3] They have received the freedom promised them.[4] The King has been given us out of the blessing, grace, and love of God,[5] and not in wrath. What was once given in displeasure and anger has come to an end.[6]

After this they say, "According to your words, no ruler can be saved. Yet it is not God's will that any person should be lost, but that all should receive salvation and come to know the truth.[7] That, however, would be closed to the ruler." To this we say with Paul, "God does want all people to receive salvation and to come to know the truth."[8] However, many do not do his will[9] or obey his voice;[10] that is their own fault, for Christ says, "Come to me, all you who are carrying heavy burdens."[11] He makes no exception. He will reject no one who wishes to come to him.[12] Rulers can also come to him. The way is just as free for them as for any of their subjects,[13] although they find it more difficult[14] to allow Christ to work. Where Christ is at work,[15] he does nothing but what is in keeping with his own nature and character, just as the vine yields only grapes, and its branches are vine branches.[16]

So it is with Christ. Whoever is firmly planted and grafted into him[17] will prove to be Christlike in nature.[18] Such a person will lay aside all self and self-glory.[19] Therefore, Christ said to his disciples, "The kings of the nations are called gracious lords, and those in power dominate the people. Among you it should not be so, for the greatest should be the servant of all."[20] Why? Because such was the mind[21] and character[22] of Jesus, and that is how he acted. He did not come to be served but to serve.[23] He has given us an example that we may follow in his footsteps.[24]

Whoever desires to belong to Christ[25] must surrender himself utterly to him[26] so that he can say with Paul, "I do not live now, but Christ lives in me,"[27] and "Christ is my life."[28] If the living force in a person is Christ and not the person himself, even if that person is a

---

[1] John 1:1-18. [2] Rev. 1:5; 5:1-14; 1 Cor. 15:24-28; Matt. 25:34. [3] John 8:39-58; Gal. 4:3-7; Eph. 1:4-5. [4] John 1:12-13; Rom. 8:10-17; Gal. 3:13-14; Eph. 2:1-10. [5] John 3:2-16; Rom. 5:1-2; 1 John 4:10. [6] Hos. 13:11. [7] Ezek. 33:11; 1 Tim. 2:3-4; 2 Pet. 3:9.
[8] 1 Tim. 2:1-6. [9] Isa. 1:1-4; 2 Esd. 1:4-8; Matt. 23:37; Luke 13:34. [10] Isa. 55:2-3; John 7:19. [11] Matt. 11:28. [12] John 6:35-37. [13] Eph. 2:1-5. [14] Matt. 19:23-26; Mark 10:23-27; Luke 18:24-27. [15] John 5:19-20. [16] John 15:1-8. [17] Eph. 2:4-6; John 15:4-5; Rom. 11:24. [18] 1 Cor. 2:14-16; 2 Pet. 1:1-8. [19] Phil. 2:5-8. [20] Matt. 20:25-28; Mark 9:35; 10:23-31; Luke 9:46-48; 22:25-27. [21] 1 Cor. 2:16. [22] Acts 17:29; Phil. 2:1-8. [23] John 13:12-14. [24] John 13:15-17; 1 Pet. 2:21. [25] 1 Cor. 3:23. [26] Rom. 6:3-6. [27] Gal. 2:20. [28] Phil. 1:21.

ruler,[1] Christ will demonstrate in him what he showed in his own life,[2] namely, that his kingdom is not of this world.[3] Christ fled when people wanted to make him a king.[4] Should the members rebel[5] against the head,[6] or the branches against the roots,[7] since truly the servant is not above his Lord?[8] Today, Christ approves worldly splendor in his saints no more than he did at the time of his pilgrimage here on earth.[9] Whoever will be exalted with Christ[10] must first humble himself with him.[11] He must empty himself of everything.[12]

Suppose some ruler gives up his pomp and glory and takes on himself the poor[13] and humble[14] form of a servant,[15] serving all people,[16] and being obedient[17] and subject to all people in Christ.[18] Then entrance into the kingdom of Christ is not closed to him.[19] Such a person can say with Paul, "Although I was free, I have made myself a servant to all for Christ's sake."[20] But as long as that humbling of self does not take place, and he remains unbroken and clings to his glory, he cannot be Christ's disciple.[21]

In summary, because governmental authority was given in wrath,[22] for the punishment of evildoers,[23] whoever incurs its penalty has fallen under the curse.[24] God's anger, fury, and revenge are directed toward such a person through punishment from the ruling authority; that authority is God's servant of anger, fury, and revenge.[25] Christ has saved us from this anger and fury, and set us free.[26] He has made us children of grace,[27] who can no longer serve revenge.[28] Thus a ruler cannot be a Christian, and no Christian can be a ruler, for one alone is our King. Christ has been appointed by his Father and is upon the Father's "holy hill."[29]

What, then, was the task for which Christ was sent? Was it to shed blood? Never! For he says, "The Son of Man has not come to destroy people's lives but to save them."[30] Or did he come to wage war? Yes, a very great war against the world, hell, and the devil, and he has overcome them all[31] without using spear or sword.[32] We also should arm ourselves with God's armor in preparation for this [spiritual]

---

[1] Rom. 13:8-10. [2] Phil. 2:5-8. [3] John 18:36. [4] John 6:15. [5] Rom. 12:4-5; 1 Cor. 12:12-27. [6] John 15:4-6; Rom. 11:17-24. [7] Isa. 10:15. [8] Matt. 10:24; Luke 6:40; John 13:16; 15:20. [9] John 6:15; 18:36-37. [10] 1 Pet. 5:1-4. [11] James 4:7-10. [12] Phil. 2:5-8. [13] 2 Cor. 6:3-10. [14] John 13:12-15. [15] Phil. 2:7. [16] Gal. 6:10; 2 Thess. 3:7-10. [17] Heb. 13:17-21. [18] Ps. 5:5-6. [19] Eph. 2:1-13. [20] 1 Cor. 9:19. [21] Matt. 10:37-39. [22] Hos. 13:11. [23] Rom. 13:1-4; 1 Pet. 2:13-14. [24] Gal. 3:10. [25] Rom. 13:1-4. [26] John 8:24-32; Gal. 3:13. [27] Rom. 8:14-16. [28] Luke 9:54-56. [29] Ps. 2:6. [30] Luke 9:56. [31] John 16:31-33. [32] Matt. 26:51-56; John 18:36; Rev. 1:16; 5:5-10; 12:10-11.

battle,[1] to fight and overcome with him.[2] But Christ condemns the warfare of the world.

Since Christ did not go to war, did not sue in a court of law, and did not shed blood, what then was his task? David tells us when he says, "I will proclaim the law of the Lord, as the Lord has commanded me."[3] Again he says, "I will declare your name to my brothers; I will sing praise to you in the full assembly."[4] In the temple at Jerusalem, Christ showed what his task was when he answered his mother. He said to her, "Did you not know that I must be busy with the affairs of my Father?"[5] That is the purpose for which he was sent by God,[6] and he fulfilled it. Therefore, when Christ appointed helpers and sent them out, he did not command them to go to court or to shed blood.[7] Instead, he said, "As the Father has sent me, so I am sending you."[8]

For what task were they sent? It was to preach the gospel.[9] The Lord gave them a sword [of the Word][10] with which to punish and discipline evildoers. He said, "If your brother sins, discipline him."[11] That is the law that holds sway in the house of Christ or in his kingdom. The members of his kingdom are at the same time subject to the human laws of the ruling authority[12] and ready for any good service they can do.[13] They wait for the glory that shall be revealed in them[14] when they become like him.[15] Meanwhile, as followers of Christ, they willingly lay aside their rights[16] in hope of their salvation, that they may be glorified with him.[17]

So we think enough has been said clearly about governmental authority. It is a sign of turning away from God.[18] Therefore, its function is simply to be the means of God's punishing, as with a rod, those who have deserted him[19] and do evil.[20] This is not for the devout. As Paul says, "If you do not wish to be afraid of those in authority, then do what is good. For rulers are not to be feared by those who do good, but by those who do evil. They are God's servants to execute vengeance and punishment upon those who do evil."[21] God alone in Christ is Lord over the devout,[22] even as the law was given by the Father, and yet is annulled in Christ. Paul says, "Christ ends the law

---

[1] Eph. 6:10-17.   [2] Rev. 2–3; 21:7; 22:1-5.   [3] Ps. 2:7-9.   [4] Ps. 22:22; Heb. 2:12.
[5] Luke 2:49.   [6] Isa. 61:1-2; Luke 4:16-18.   [7] 1 Cor. 3:5.   [8] John 20:21.   [9] Matt. 28:19-20; Mark 16:15-18.   [10] Eph. 6:17; Heb. 4:12; Rev. 1:16; 2:16.   [11] Matt. 18:15-17.
[12] 1 Pet. 2:13-17; Rom. 13:1-6.   [13] Titus 3:1-7.   [14] Rom. 8:10-19.   [15] 1 John 3:1-2.
[16] Matt. 17:24-27; Phil. 2:3-11.   [17] Rom. 5:1-2; 8:17-18; 2 Cor. 3:18; 4:17; Phil. 3:21; Col. 3:4.   [18] 1 Sam. 8:7-18.   [19] Isa. 10:5-6; Jer. 43:10-13.   [20] Rom. 13:3-4; 1 Pet. 2:13-14.
[21] Rom. 13:3-4.   [22] Deut. 32:46-48; 1 Cor. 8:6; 12:2-6; Eph. 4:3-6.

and brings righteousness for everyone who believes."[1] Again, "The law was our teacher and guide until Christ came, so that we might become devout through faith. Now that faith has come, we are no longer under the law, for we are all children of God through faith in Christ."[2] And, "If you live in the Spirit, you are not under the law."[3]

The law, insofar as it is drawn up in writing, is done away with in Christ. Yet someone who ceases to do the work of the Spirit[4] becomes a transgressor of that same law[5] and is again subject to its punishment.[6] We are free from governmental authority, that is, from its punishment, which is God's vengeance,[7] since we are reconciled to God through Christ.[8] But as soon as persons begin to sin again,[9] they come under wrath[10] and under a curse. They will fall into the hands of the ruling power,[11] who will carry out God's punishment upon them.[12] That is the punishment outside of Christ's rule, and all who forsake God[13] are subject to its curse.[14] Outside of Christ's rule, the power of worldly government still has its place as a sure sign that God's wrath against sinners and the ungodly[15] surely continues. Only the devout are reconciled with God through Christ and receive his blessing.[16]

To continue, our faithful God has appointed certain privileges and rights to every office, whether under Christ or outside of his authority, so that the offices may act without being hampered. That is why the government is allowed to impose duties and taxes, which should be given them without reserve or resistance.[17] Whoever does not pay that, resists what God has appointed.[18] Christ himself gave the government its due[19] and commanded others to do the same.[20]

Therefore, we also wish to give the ruler willingly what his position allows him to receive, whether one calls it taxes, revenue, tribute, customs, toll, rent, or compulsory labor. Thereby we want to show ourselves willing subjects,[21] ready for every good work.[22] But if the ruler willfully goes beyond this, he is not carrying out the Lord's office but rather his own. As has been said, the ruling power is a rod, stick, staff, and instrument of God's wrath,[23] through which God himself, in fury, punishes evildoers.[24] Taxes and duties are appointed for such tasks,[25]

---

[1] Rom. 10:4. [2] Gal. 3:24-26. [3] Gal. 5:18. [4] Gal. 5:1-14. [5] Rom. 13:7-10; James 2:8-12. [6] Gal. 3:23-24. [7] Rom. 13:4; 1 Pet. 2:13-14. [8] 1 John 2:1-2. [9] Rom. 6:1-6; 1 John 3:4. [10] Eph. 5:5-6; Col. 3:5-6. [11] Gal. 3:10. [12] Rom. 13:1-5; 1 Pet. 2:13-14. [13] 1 Sam. 10:1-4. [14] Gal. 3:10. [15] Rom. 13:1-5; Titus 3:1. [16] John 17:8-9. [17] 1 Sam. 8:7-17; Rom. 13:6-7. [18] Rom. 13:5. [19] Matt. 17:24-27. [20] Matt. 22:15-21; Mark 12:13-17; Luke 20:20-25. [21] Rom. 13:6-7. [22] Titus 3:1. [23] Rom. 13:3-4. [24] Isa. 10:5. [25] 1 Sam. 8:7-17; Rom. 13:6.

but not for wanton warfare and bloodshed. We are under no obligation, in fact, we are forbidden and commanded not to pay war taxes of any sort. We are not children of vengeance[1] and may no longer yield our members to be weapons of unrighteousness,[2] nor to serve any unrighteousness.

The governments always do wrong when they set out to exterminate nations.[3] Whoever pays them taxes for that, aids them in their wrongdoing and participates in the guilt of their sin. If they try to force us to it, we say with Peter that we must obey God rather than people.[4] We will not obey them in this matter; we will give them nothing that makes us take part in the sins of others.[5] Many governments use Paul's statement to defend their right to these taxes,[6] and support themselves with the words of Christ: "Pay Caesar what is due to Caesar."[7] Yet we fear they do so only to avoid the suffering which the cross of Christ brings. They want the approval of people, which results in the disapproval of God.[8]

However, neither Christ's words nor Paul's words were intended to permit rulers to carry out every whim. Instead, they speak of those powers which God has assigned to rulers, such as compulsory labor, revenue, duties, and so on, for the purpose of allowing them to carry out their offices.[9] Since Christ has not done away with this office, which exists for the unjust, its appointed service must remain. If the rulers are evil, the punishment of the people is even greater.[10]

Paul commands us to give the government its due, that is, the appointed service or tax it demands, because we are also subject to the human order for the Lord's sake.[11] According to this passage from Paul, certain brothers in Rome apparently wanted to be free from the governing authority and neither obey it nor pay tribute.[12] This is similar to our own day, when the Münsterites, deceived by the devil, revolted against authority. Paul here wishes to oppose them, or rather, to lay before them the full and proper Christian order, of which the whole epistle speaks.

However that may be, Paul teaches them that they should pay the taxes, tribute, and revenue, and not rebel against governmental authority, but be obedient to it. He speaks, however, of the taxes due to the state and appointed by God, and not of what is demanded for

---

[1] Luke 9:54-56.   [2] Rom. 6:19.   [3] Isa. 10:1-16.   [4] Acts 5:29.   [5] 1 Tim. 5:22.
[6] Rom. 13:7.   [7] Matt. 22:21; Mark 12:17; Luke 20:25.   [8] Gal. 1:10; James 4:4.
[9] 1 Sam. 8:10-17; Rom. 13:1-6.   [10] Isa. 3:8-11.   [11] 1 Pet. 2:13.   [12] Rom. 13:1-7.

the willful wickedness of the country's warfare. That is shown by the words, "Give them what you owe them." In effect, he says, "Give the yearly appointed tax which their office requires." What is not appointed and commanded by God, one does not give out of duty and obligation, but rather from a spirit of respect, or more often, because one is driven and coerced by the ruling power.

Therefore, the words make a distinction between two things: First, Paul says, "Give what you owe," and "Pay to whom it is due."[1] Second, he does not say, "Give to anyone who wants it, and pay whatever someone wants." Christ also commands us to give to Caesar what is Caesar's.[2] He does not speak at all, as many interpret it, of taxes for warfare and slaughter. The Pharisees asked Christ whether it was right to continue paying an annual tax. History tells us that this annual tax began when Christ was born, during the rule of the emperor Augustus,[3] and there was peace in all the world. Thus this tax was not imposed for war or bloodshed.

Likewise, today a local lord charges fixed yearly sums to those who take wood from his forest. For example, the man who fetches wood by the cartload pays one gulden per year, the man who fetches it by the barrow load pays half a gulden, and the man who carries his wood pays a quarter gulden. Christ says we should give for such purposes, but he does not speak of blood taxes.

Perhaps someone will still say, "In any case, the authorities use the money wrongly. So from that point of view, one should give nothing." We say that if rulers use it for wrong purposes, they will need to bear the consequences.[4] We do not give them taxes to be used for wrong purposes, but rather for the appointed tasks.[5] Since wars and the extermination of nations are more contrary to the office of government than in agreement with it,[6] God allows them nothing for such purposes, and we can give nothing for them. We do wish, however, to serve humanity and its welfare and improvement in every possible way, and to do this as well as we can. But regarding whatever is against God, against the conscience, and against our calling[7]—we want to obey God rather than humans.[8] We await God's will, that he may give us his grace to do this, through Jesus Christ. Amen.

---

[1] Rom. 13:7-8. [2] Matt. 22:21. [3] Luke 2:1-5. [4] Wisd. of Sol. 6:1-10. [5] Rom. 13:1-7. [6] Isa. 10:1-16. [7] Luke 9:54-56. [8] Acts 5:29.

Conclusion of This Book

We have now, through God's grace, presented the truth about those points which are questioned most in this country. They are, first, that God desires to have a separate people,[1] holy,[2] blameless, unblemished,[3] and without stain or wrinkle.[4] Then we see how God himself divides and separates the devout from the wicked,[5] as he will also do at the end-time.[6] We see what the Lord promises to each.[7] Furthermore, we see how the house of God should be built[8] and what kind of messengers are sent to build it.[9] No one is to run in his own strength, but all should be chosen by God,[10] as Aaron[11] was supposed to gather the Lord's people to him.[12]

We have told how God made the covenant of grace[13] with his people, what kind of covenant it is,[14] and what we should do[15] and receive in it.[16] From this it is clear who will receive it.[17] We have spoken of the Lord's Supper,[18] and of taking an oath[19] in such a way that everyone may learn what is right. We have also spoken of governmental authority and its appointed service,[20] and in our opinion have sufficiently shown for what purposes God uses it,[21] what its function is, and to what extent it is a servant of God.[22]

In addition, we have spoken of the rights and privileges of the government, to what extent it may justly impose certain taxes, and how far taxes are to be given and not given.[23] We have done this as briefly as possible, for the comfort of the devout[24] and as a testimony against the ungodly.[25] It is our hope that all this has warned everyone against willfully opposing the truth, and thus being found among

---

[1] 2 Cor. 6:17-18. [2] 1 Pet. 1:14-16. [3] Phil. 2:12-15. [4] Eph. 5:27. [5] Gen. 4:9-16. [6] Matt. 25:31-46. [7] Deut. 28. [8] 1 Pet. 2:4-5. [9] 1 Cor. 3:10-15. [10] Jer. 23:21. [11] Exod. 28:1; Num. 17:2-10. [12] Ps. 50:1-5. [13] Jer. 31:31-40; Matt. 28:18-20; Mark 16:15-16; Heb. 8:8-13; 10:15-18; Gen. 17:1-5. [14] 1 Pet. 3:18-22. [15] Acts 2:38-47. [16] Acts 2:1-4; Rom. 6:1-4. [17] Luke 7:36-50; Acts 2:1, 37-40. [18] 1 Cor. 11:20-27. [19] Matt. 5:33-37. [20] Rom. 13:1-8. [21] Isa. 10:5; Jer. 43:10-12. [22] Rom. 13:1-4; 1 Pet. 2:13-14. [23] Rom. 13:7; Matt. 22:21; Mark 12:17; Luke 20:25; 9:54-56. [24] 2 Cor. 1:3-5. [25] Matt. 10:11-14; Mark 6:10-11; Luke 9:1-5; 10:10-11.

those who fight against God.[1] Such a person heaps one sin upon another, or takes part in other people's sins.[2] Not one sin will remain unpunished.[3] But whoever wants to do evil should know that it will be hard to kick against the goad;[4] it will be a battle one cannot win.[5] The word of Christ will not fail: "What you have done to my people, you have done to me."[6] God the Lord, who has promised to avenge the blood of his faithful, does not lie.[7] If unclean persons continue to defile themselves, they have to bear their sentence. God is judge.[8] Let anyone who has ears to hear, hear![9]

Thus, we have given an account, with enough explanations, of the truth about the points and beliefs which are mostly called into question in the region of Hesse. May God the Almighty help us and all his chosen children to walk in his truth, as we, through his Christ, have already begun to do. May we continue and endure in the truth to the end, to the eternal praise of his holy name. May God allow no tribulation, no tyrannical force, nor any cunning of deceitful preachers to turn us away or shake us. Thus on the day of Christ's coming, may we appear with all the saints in joy before God, holy and unblemished, and receive the promise in Christ Jesus.

Amen, yes, Amen.

Of this Christian church, which was built up by God through Christ and recently gathered by his Holy Spirit in Germany, the following have been appointed servants. They are the ones to whom the church of God is entrusted. They are listed by name without their helpers: Jakob Hutter from the Tirol; Hans Amon from Bavaria; Peter Riedemann from Silesia, the writer of this confession; Leonhard Lanzenstiel from Bavaria, as mentioned above; and Peter Walpot, also from the principality of Tirol. The church of God was entrusted to them and their helpers till the year 1565, when this confession was reprinted by Philips Vollanndt.

Acts 5:34-39.   1 Tim. 5:22.   [3] Sir. 7:1-8.   Acts 9:5.   Job 42:1-3.   Matt. 25:40.   [7] Deut. 32:43; Joel 3:16-21; Matt. 23:34-38.   [8] Rev. 22:11-12.   [9] Matt. 13:16, 43; Rev. 2:7, 11, 17, 29; 3:6, 13, 22.

Notes to the Introduction

1. Robert Friedmann, "Peter Riedemann: Early Anabaptist Leader," *MQR* 49 (Jan. 1970): 5. Friedmann described Riedemann as the very soul and inspiration of the Gemeinde during his years as spiritual leader of the Hutterites from 1542-1556. For *The Chronicle*, see note 2, below. To locate places on maps, see pages 30-31, above; *The Chronicle*, 815-821; maps inside the cover of *Golden Years*, by Gross (note 10, below).

2. A. J. F. Zieglschmid, *Die älteste Chronik der Hutterischen Brüder* (Philadelphia: The Carl Schurz Memorial Foundation, and Ithaca, N.Y.: Cayuga Press, 1943), 102. This edition plus *Geschicht-Buch der Hutterischen Brüder*, ed. Rudolf Wolkan (Vienna, 1923), were used in preparing an English translation: *The Chronicle of the Hutterian Brethren*, vol. 1, trans. and ed. the Hutterian Brethren (Rifton, N.Y.: Plough Publishing House, 1987), to which the following citations of *Chronicle* refer.

3. *Chronicle*, 300.

4. Friedmann, "Peter Riedemann," 6. The *First Confession* has been published in English: *Love Is Like Fire: The Confession of an Anabaptist, Peter Riedemann*, translated and edited by the Hutterian Brethren (Farmington, Pa.: The Plough Publishing House, 1993).

5. *Chronicle*, 199-200; Friedmann, "Peter Riedemann," 6.

6. *Chronicle*, 216.

7. *Chronicle*, 329-330.

8. On this Bruderhof, see *ME*, 4:222-223.

9. Forty-six of Riedemann's songs are printed in *Die Lieder der Hutterischen Brüder* (Scottdale, Pa: Herald Press, 1914), 450-545. See also Rudolf Wolkan, *Die Lieder der Wiedertäufer: Ein Beitrag zur deutschen und niederländischen Literatur- und Kirchengeschichte* (Berlin: B. Behr, 1903). In this study, Wolkan includes Hutterite hymns on pages 165-265 and discusses Riedemann's hymns on pages 185-209.

10. Friedmann, "Peter Riedemann," 6, states that despite his significant role in the Hutterite movement, "Peter Riedemann has never been made the central subject of thorough research." Until recently, that was still the situation, despite the important studies about Hutterite history published by various scholars, including John A. Hostetler, *Hutterite Society* (Baltimore: Johns Hopkins Univ. Press, 1974); Bernd G. Längin, *Die Hutterer: Gefangene der Vergangenheit, Pilger der Gegenwart, Propheten der Zukunft* (Hamburg: Rasch und Rohring, 1986); and Leonard Gross, *The Golden Years of the Hutterites: The Witness and Thought of the Communal Moravian Anabaptists*

During the Walpot Era, 1565-1578 (Scottdale, Pa.: Herald Press, 1980). The recent book by Werner O. Packull, *Hutterite Beginnings: Communitarian Experiments During the Reformation* (Baltimore: Johns Hopkins Univ. Press, 1995), begins to redress the neglect.

11. James M. Stayer's study popularized the view of polygenesis and signaled a change in the interpretation of sixteenth-century Anabaptism: *Anabaptists and the Sword* (Lawrence, Kan.: Coronado Press, 1972).

12. Claus-Peter Clasen, *Anabaptism: A Social History, 1525-1618* (Ithaca, N.Y.: Cornell Univ. Press, 1972), 32-33, argues for six major groups: Swiss Brethren, the followers of Hans Hut, the group around Pilgram Marpeck, Thuringian Anabaptists, the group around Georg Schnabel, and the Hutterites.

13. *Mysticism* is the belief that subjective experience, intuition, or spiritual insight can bring direct knowledge of God, spiritual truth, or ultimate reality. Communion with God counted for more than the written word of Scripture.

14. *Chiliasm* is belief in a coming thousand-year reign of Christ when he returns. This belief is based on Rev. 20, and the term comes from the Greek word *chilia* (thousand) in Rev. 20:4.

15. Zieglschmid, *Chronik*, 90-91.

16. George H. Williams, *The Radical Reformation*, 3d ed. (Kirksville, Mo.: Sixteenth-Century Publishers, 1992), 281, offers a different view. He states that Riedemann "was a convert of Hut, perhaps in Steyr, or possibly of Schlaffer or Schiemer, or more likely of Wolfgang Brandhuber." All following references to Williams are to this third edition unless the first edition of 1962 is specified.

17. R. Emmet McLaughlin, *Casper Schwenckfeld, Reluctant Radical; His Life to 1540* (New Haven, Conn.: Yale University Press, 1986), 7. For additional studies of Schwenckfeld, see: Peter Erb, *Schwen[c]kfeld in His Reformation Setting* (Valley Forge: Judson Press, 1978) and Horst Weigelt, *The Schwenkfelders in Silesia* (Pennsburg, Pa.: Schwenkfelder Library, 1985). Note that *ck* appears in the middle of the man's name, but his followers have dropped that *c* in naming themselves.

18. McLaughlin, *Schwenckfeld*, 4-5.

19. McLaughlin, *Schwenckfeld*, 10-11.

20. Weigelt, *Schwenkfelders*, 1-2; Williams, *Radical Reformation*, 106-107. Williams (in 1992) claimed that Schwenckfeld converted in 1519. In his 1962 first edition, Williams stated that Schwenckfeld had already converted to Lutheranism in 1518.

21. McLaughlin, *Schwenckfeld*, 28.

22. McLaughlin, *Schwenckfeld*, 17-18.

23. Erb, *Schwen[c]kfeld*, 18.

24. The term *eucharist* comes from the Greek verb *eucharisteĒ*, used for Jesus "giving thanks" as he instituted the Lord's Supper (Matt. 26:27; 1 Cor. 11:24). *Eucharist* was used for the Roman Catholic mass and also by other churches for the communion service.

25. Erb, *Schwen[c]kfeld*, 18.

26. *Luther and Erasmus: Free Will and Salvation*, trans. and ed. E. Gordon Rupp and Philip S. Watson, Library of Christian Classics, 17 (Philadelphia: Westminster, 1969).

27. McLaughlin, *Schwenckfeld*, 57.

28. McLaughlin, *Schwenckfeld*, 59.

29. Erb, *Schwen[c]kfeld*, 18.

30. Zieglschmid, *Chronik*, 250-257, 459.

31. Zieglschmid, *Chronik*, 185, 320, 470. Packull, *Hutterite Beginnings*, 101, lists additional Anabaptists who originated in Silesia but had to flee because of persecution. They played significant roles in the communal groups in Moravia.

32. Packull, *Hutterite Beginnings*, 317. Braitmichel may have done most of his writing late in life, since he explained that he quit because of physical weakness and a problem with his eyes. Other chroniclers continued the account to 1665. *Chronicle*, LXXIV; Williams, 1076.

33. *Balthasar Hubmaier*, trans. and ed. H. Wayne Pipkin and John H. Yoder (Scottdale, Pa.: Herald Press, 1989), 449-491. For a further discussion of this, see Werner O. Packull, "Clemens Adler. A Swiss Connection to Silesian Anabaptism?" *Conrad Grebel Review* 9 (Fall 1991): 245.

34. For a discussion on whether Hut was in Silesia, see G. Seebass, *Müntzer's Erbe: Werk, Leben, und Theologie des Hans Hut* (Erlangen, 1972), 279-280. Also see Daniel Liechty, *Andreas Fischer and the Sabbatarian Anabaptists* (Scottdale, Pa.: Herald Press, 1988), 44.

35. Weigelt, *Schwenkfelders*, 61-62.

36. Liechty, *Fischer*, 31-32. Liechty notes a variety of places where Fischer's name, or at least a similar name, appears in the records of towns and schools. None of these records, however, conclusively prove that any of those names refer to Andreas Fischer, the Sabbatarian Anabaptist.

37. Liechty, *Fischer*, 93.

38. Liechty, *Fischer*, 94-96.

39. Liechty, *Fischer*, 96-98.

40. *Eschatological* or *eschatology* means discussion of things relating to the end of the world, the end-time, or the last days. The term is based on the Greek word *eschatos* (last), which appears frequently in the New Testament (e.g., John 6:39-40; 11:24; Acts 2:17; 1 Cor. 15:52; Heb. 1:2; 2 Pet. 3:3; Rev. 22:12-13).

41. Liechty, *Fischer*, 62, 101.

42. Weigelt, *Schwenkfelders*, 62. Liechty, *Fischer*, 40-66, has a lengthy section on the Sabbath controversy in Silesia.

43. Liechty, *Fischer*, 52.

44. See Erb, *Schwen[c]kfeld*, 136, for a discussion of this controversy from the standpoint of a study of Schwenckfeld.

45. Liechty, *Fischer*, 59.

46. See Liechty, *Fischer*, 61-62, and Werner O. Packull, *Mysticism and the Early South German-Austrian Anabaptist Movement, 1525-1531* (Scottdale, Pa.: Herald Press, 1977), 78. Both argue that Glaidt's Sabbatarian thinking may have been dependent upon Hut because of Hut's interest in the number seven. Further research is likely necessary to establish the origin for Sabbatarian thinking.

47. Gerald Knox Zeman, *The Anabaptists and the Czech Brethren in Moravia, 1526-1628: A Study of Origins and Contacts* (The Hague: Mouton, 1969), 225.

48. Williams, *Radical Reformation*, 628-629; Weigelt, *Schwenkfelders*, 67.

49. Packull, "Clemens Adler," 243-250.

50. Packull, "Clemens Adler," 245-246. For a map of the area, see Horst Weigelt, *Spiritualistische Tradition im Protestantismus: Die Geschichte des Schwenkfeldertums in Schlesien* (Berlin: De Gruyter, 1973), 182, 196.

51. See Adler's article, "Das Urteil von dem Schwert," 1529; in Geiser Codex at Mennonite Historical Library, Goshen, Ind. In a context in which apocalyptic thought was prevalent, his article has remarkably little reference to the end-time. Packull, "Clemens Adler," 247, argues that Adler's thinking is strongly influenced by apocalyptic thinking. This article by Adler does not support that conclusion.

52. Packull, "Clemens Adler," 246-247. Packull notes that this story is contained in "Eind Newe Geschichte Nemlich beschehen zue Glatz in der Schlesig"; in Cod. Hab. 5 (alt Cod. 235), 1571, 168-170ff., at Archiv mesta Bratislavy.

53. Clemens Adler, "Das Urteil," 17: "Die Gebott sollen nicht allein euesserliches wesen in dem Buchstaben, wie die Juden Thäden, sonder zuvor inerlich in dem Geist und warheit gehalten werden, wie ein sölches Christus lehrt."

54. Clemens Adler, "Das Urteil," 21-22.

55. Clemens Adler, "Das Urteil," 28: "Die leiblichen gütter bey den wahren fromen Christen seynd alle gemain vnd niemands soll vnder yhnen erfunden werden der sines guts ein einiger Herr sein wollt. . . ."

56. Clemens Adler, "Das Urteil," 31: "Jch aber sag eüch, yhr solt nicht

schweren, gar mit nicht, weder bey dem Himmel Dan er ist ein stull Gottes, auch nicht bei der Erden. . . ."

57. Clemens Adler, "Das Urteil," 42.

58. Clemens Adler, "Das Urteil," 5.

59. Clemens Adler, "Das Urteil," 30. In the context of a discussion of people making a covenant with God, he says, "Alls mit dem wasertauff bestatt, das er will nach sinem Göttlichen Willen Läben, vnd von sinem wortt von sinem Gesetz niemermehr nicht abwichen, biss in den Todt vnd das verspricht vnd zusagt in der Krafft Gottes vnd in dem Nahmen des Vatters, des Sohns, vnd des Heilligen Geist."

60. Packull, "Clemens Adler," 246.

61. Williams, *Radical Reformation*, 625-626. Williams, in his 1962 first edition, 411, identified this discussion as Judaizing. For the interpretation that Silesian Sabbatarianism is evidence of a Hans Hut kind of spiritualism, see Werner Packull, "Melchior Hoffman's Experience in the Livonian Reformation: The Dynamics of Sect Formation," *MQR* 59 (Apr. 1985): 130-146.

62. Weigelt, *Schwenkfelders*, 49.

63. Packull, *Hutterite Beginnings*, 100.

64. Weigelt, *Schwenkfelders*, 67. Williams, *Radical Reformation*, 628-629. Jarold Knox Zeman, *Anabaptists and Czech Brethren*, 225, suggests that the emigration of Silesian Anabaptists may have been caused by local peasant uprisings rather than by the decree of Emperor Ferdinand I.

65. Weigelt, *Schwenkfelders*, 67.

66. Weigelt, *Schwenkfelders*, 67.

67. Williams, *Radical Reformation*, 647; Zieglschmid, *Chronik*, 102. "Servant of the Word" means one "chosen by the whole church to care for the inner and outer well-being of the community as a whole and of the individual members. . . . His tasks include preaching the Gospel and teaching the assembled brotherhood, counseling, acting as spokesman for the brotherhood, and undertaking mission journeys by unanimous decision of the members." *Chronicle*, Glossary, 835.

68. *Chronicle*, 94.

69. Lydia Müller and Robert Friedmann, *Glaubenszeugnisse oberdeutscher Taufgesinnter*, Band 2, *Quellen zur Geschichte der Täufer*, 12, (Heidelberg: Verein für Reformationsgeschichte, 1967), 1, credits Hans Hut with having introduced Riedemann to Anabaptism. Müller says that it was likely Hut or one of his disciples who converted Riedemann between the years 1527-29.

70. Three men who mediated some of Hut's ideas in Upper Austria, and shaped them based on their own theological insight, were the former Franciscan friar Leonhard Schiemer, the former priest Hans Schlaffer, and Ambrose Spittelmaier, who had a university education. See Williams, *Radical Reformation*, 269-282.

71. Williams, *Radical Reformation*, 269-170.

72. "Brandhuber, Wolfgang," *ME*, 1:404-405.

73. Liechty, *Fischer*, 36.

74. "Und also alle Ding, so zum Preiss Gottes dienen, soll man gemain halten"; Josef Beck, *Die Geschichts-Bücher der Wiedertäufer in (tm)sterreich-Ungarn in der Zeit von 1526 bis 1785* (Nieuwkoop: B. de Graaf, 1967), 89.

75. Beck, *Geschichts-Bücher*, 89. James Stayer, *Anabaptists and the Sword*, 166, argues, "Neither Hut nor his immediate following were nonresistant Anabaptists. They were 'peaceful' Anabaptists, but not adherents of the teaching of nonresistance. In Anabaptist sects where nonresistance was part of the faith, it was affirmed by rank-and-file believers. Among Hut's followers this was not the case." On this issue, Brandhuber seems not to have been a follower of Hut. Stayer, in his more recent study *The German Peasants' War and Anabaptist Community of Goods* (Montreal: McGill-Queen's Univ. Press, 1991), 122, argues that Brandhuber's view of communalism represented a continuation of Thomas Müntzer's view of *Gelassenheit* (yieldedness). He adds that the Hutterites "were right in particularly preserving the testimonies of the Hut Anabap-

tism tendency as sources of their communist spirituality." On both of these issues, the connection with Hut seems somewhat tenuous and probably requires further study.

76. For the text of this *First Confession*, see Lydia Müller and Robert Friedmann, *Glaubenszeugnisse oberdeutscher Taufgesinnter*, 2:4-47. The title is listed as "Ein Rechenschafft und Bekanndtnus des Glaubens vom Peter Ridemann." In the publication it is referred to as "Erste Rechenschaft."

77. Müller and Friedmann, *Glaubenszeugnisse oberdeutscher Taufgesinnter*, 2:34.

78. Müller and Friedmann, *Glaubenszeugnisse Oberdeutscher Taufgesinnter*, 2:43-47.

79. Beck, *Geschichts-Bücher*, 88-89.

80. Zieglschmid, *Chronik*, 102.

81. Zieglschmid, *Chronik*, 86-87.

82. Zieglschmid, *Chronik*, 86.

83. *Chronicle*, 81.

84. Zieglschmid, *Chronik*, 88.

85. Robert Friedmann, "The Oldest Church Discipline of the Anabaptists," *MQR* 29 (Apr. 1955): 162-166, argues that the communal order likely originated with Schlaffer. Williams, *Radical Reformation*, 232, argues that it could have originated with either Schiemer or Schlaffer, but he thinks that the earliest order in Austerlitz was based on a 1527 order in Rattenberg in the Inn Valley. Packull, *Hutterite Beginnings*, 303-315, lists three early Anabaptist church orders in parallel columns. None of them advocated community of goods.

86. Zieglschmid, *Chronik*, 89; Williams, *Radical Reformation*, 639.

87. *Chronicle*, 84.

88. Williams, *Radical Reformation*, 638.

89. Zieglschmid, *Chronik*, 86.

90. Zieglschmid, *Chronik*, 86; Williams, *Radical Reformation*, 638. Philip Plener was also called Blauärmel and Weber.

91. Claus-Peter Clasen, *The Anabaptists in South and Central Germany, Switzerland, and Austria, 1525-1618* (Ann Arbor, Mich.: Univ. Microfilms Intl., 1978), 17.

92. *Chronicle*, 89; Williams, *Radical Reformation*, 638-639.

93. Williams, *Radical Reformation*, 640; Zieglschmid, *Chronik*, 92-95. Reublin summarized the conflict in a letter to Marpeck in a document in C. A. Cornelius, *Geschichte des münsterischen Aufruhrs*, Band 2 (Leipzig, 1855), Beilage, 5:253-259. J. C. Wenger, "Letter from Wilhelm Reublin to Pilgram Marpeck, 1531," *MQR* 23 (Apr. 1949): 67-75.

94. Williams, *Radical Reformation*, 640. Zieglschmid, *Chronik*, 95, says 150 persons left.

95. *Chronicle*, 91; Williams, *Radical Reformation*, 640.

96. Williams, *Radical Reformation*, 641.

97. Zieglschmid, *Chronik*, 99.

98. Zieglschmid, *Chronik*, 100-101; Williams, *Radical Reformation*, 641.

99. Zieglschmid, *Chronik*, 101.

100. Williams, *Radical Reformation*, 641.

101. Zieglschmid, *Chronik*, 102.

102. Robert Friedmann, "Peter Riedemann," 9; "Riedemann, Peter," *ME*, 4:327.

103. Walter Klaassen, *Michael Gaismair: Revolutionary and Reformer* (Leiden: E. J. Brill, 1978).

104. Klaassen, *Gaismair*, 32-34.

105. Klaassen, *Gaismair*, 35-36; Williams, *Radical Reformation*, 169.

106. Klaassen, *Gaismair*, 38.

107. Klaassen, *Gaismair*, 57.

108. Williams, *Radical Reformation*, 170. The text of the *Landesordnung* is in Lowell Zuck, *Christianity and Revolution: Radical Christian Testimonies, 1520-1650*

(Philadelphia: Temple Univ. Press, 1975), 20-24.
   109. Klaassen, *Gaismair*, 63-64.
   110. Klaassen, *Gaismair*, 69.
   111. Packull, *Hutterite Beginnings*, 169.
   112. Hans Fischer, *Jacob Huter: Leben, Frömmigkeit, und Briefe* (Newton, Kan.: Mennonite Publication office, 1956), 14-15.
   113. Grete Mecenseffy, *Quellen zur Geschichte der Täufer, Österreich*, Teil 2 (Gütersloh: Gerd Mohn, 1972), 1.
   114. Mecenseffy, *Österreich*, 2:2.
   115. Mecenseffy, *Österreich*, 2:2.
   116. Mecenseffy, *Österreich*, 2:3-4.
   117. Williams, *Radical Reformation*, 272-273.
   118. "Ein Bekenntnis von Leonhard Schiemer," written at Rattenberg, January 14, 1528; in *Die Hutterischen Episteln, 1527-1763* [1767], vol. 3 (Elie, Man.: James Valley Book Centre, 1988), 37-39.
   119. *Die Hutterischen Episteln*, 3:37-38.
   120. Williams, *Radical Reformation*, 272-273; *ME*, 4:452; Robert Friedmann, "Leonhard Schiemer and Hans Schlaffer: Two Martyr Apostles of 1528," *MQR* 33 (Jan. 1959): 31-41; Thieleman J. van Braght, *Martyrs Mirror*, trans. of 1660 original Dutch ed. by Joseph F. Sohm (Scottdale, Pa.: Herald Press, 1938), 424-425, Schiemer called Schoener in error; *The Writings of Pilgram Marpeck*, trans. and ed. William Klassen and Walter Klaassen, Classics of the Radical Reformation, 2 (Scottdale, Pa.: Herald Press, 1978), 18.
   121. For a recent discussion of the life and theology of Hans Schlaffer, see Stephen B. Boyd, "Community as Sacrament in the Theology of Hans Schlaffer," in Walter Klaassen, *Anabaptism Revisited* (Scottdale, Pa.: Herald Press, 1992), 50-64. For information about Schlaffer's life, see Lydia Müller, ed. *Glaubenszeugnisse oberdeutscher Taufgesinnter*, Teil 1 (Leipzig: M. Heinsius Nachfolger, 1938), 119.
   122. "Schlaffer, Hans," *ME*, 4:457.
   123. Williams, *Radical Reformation*, 273-274. Friedmann, "Leonhard Schiemer," 31; *ME*, 4:458.
   124. Five of Schiemer's letters and articles are contained in *Die Hutterischen Episteln, 1527-1763* [1767], vols. 2-3 (Elie, Man.: James Valley Book Centre, 1987-88).
   125. Hans Schlaffer, in *Die Hutterischen Episteln*, 3:42-50, 66.
   126. *Die Hutterischen Episteln*, 3:52.
   127. *Die Hutterischen Episteln*, 3:55-66.
   128. Boyd, "Community as Sacrament in the Theology of Hans Schlaffer," in Klaassen, *Anabaptism Revisited*, 55.
   129. *Die Hutterischen Episteln*, 3:53, 56.
   130. *Die Hutterischen Episteln*, 3:58-59.
   131. Packull, *Hutterite Beginnings*, 182.
   132. Packull, *Hutterite Beginnings*, 182; Williams, *Radical Reformation*, 639, 1073.
   133. Packull, *Hutterite Beginnings*, 184-185.
   134. Klassen and Klaassen, *Pilgram Marpeck*, 15-16.
   135. Klassen and Klaassen, *Pilgram Marpeck*, 18; *ME*, 3:492, likely because he refused to help catch Anabaptists; 4:452, 458.
   136. Klassen and Klaassen, *Pilgram Marpeck*, 23.
   137. Williams, *Radical Reformation*, 681-721.
   138. Klassen and Klaassen, *Pilgram Marpeck*, 362-368, 498-506.
   139. Klassen and Klaassen, *Pilgram Marpeck*, 36.
   140. See Stayer, *Hutterite Beginnings*, 199, for a detailed discussion of Hutter in Welsburg. See also *Chronicle*, 83, note 1.
   141. Stayer, *Anabaptists and the Sword*, 173; Williams, *Radical Reformation*, 817.
   142. Fischer, *Jacob Huter*, 19; Williams, *Radical Reformation*, 639; *Chronicle*, 83.

143. Stayer, *Peasants' War*, 92, comments that the revolt by Gaismair may have "shaped the indispensable preconditions" for Hutter's reform. A note in *Chronicle*, 83, says that "shortly before Gaismair's assassination, a warrant for Hutter's arrest was issued, dated March 10, 1532, with the following details: 'Jakob Hutter of Welsburg, a person with a black beard, who wears a black woolen military coat, a blue doublet, white trousers, and a hat.' " This warrant may suggest that at some point Hutter was associated with Gaismair.

144. Fischer, *Jacob Huter*, 121-122.

145. Fischer, *Jacob Huter*, includes nine of his letters. See also Robert Friedmann, "Jacob Hutter's Epistle Concerning the Schism in Moravia in 1533," *MQR* 38 (Oct. 1964): 329-343.

146. Friedmann, "Hutter's Epistle," *MQR* 38 (Oct. 1964): 340-342.

147. See Hutter's letters in Fischer, *Jacob Huter*, Teil 3.

148. Fischer, *Jacob Huter*, Teil 3, "Jacob Huters Epistel nach Austerlitz und Bucovic," no page numbers.

149. Zieglschmid, *Chronik*, 101-102. See also "Zaunring, Georg," *ME* 4:1018-1019; "Bamberg," *ME*, 1:219.

150. Zieglschmid, *Chronik*, 103.

151. On July 14, 1528, the Nuremberg city council issued an edict: "All who recant their error of Anabaptism shall be accepted in mercy; those who persist in it shall be expelled beyond a distance of ten miles from the city." "Nürnberg," *ME*, 3:927.

152. Günther Bauer, *Anfänge täuferische Gemeindebildungen in Franken* (Nürnberg: Selbstverlag des Vereins für bayerische Kirchengeschichte, 1966), 1; Clarence Bauman, *The Spiritual Legacy of Hans Denck: Interpretation and Translation of Key Texts* (Leiden: E. J. Brill, 1991), 8; E. J. Furcha, *Selected Writings of Hans Denck, 1500-1527*, Texts and Studies in Religion, 44 (Queenston, Ont.: Edwin Mellen Press, 1989), x-xi; "Nürnberg," *ML*, 3:279-282.

153. "Nürnberg," *ME*, 3:926.

154. Williams, *Radical Reformation*, 486, note 118.

155. See Claus-Peter Clasen, *Anabaptists in Germany*, 188-198, for a list of Anabaptists brought to trial in the various regions in Franconia, including Nuremberg. Clasen lists the occupations of the Anabaptists. See also Bauer, *Anfänge*, 176.

156. See Gottfried Seebass, "Peasants' War and Anabaptism in Franconia," in James M. Stayer and Werner O. Packull, *The Anabaptists and Thomas Müntzer* (Toronto: Kendall-Hunt Publishing Company, 1980), 154-159.

157. For recent discussions of Thomas Müntzer, see Abraham Friesen, *Thomas Müntzer, a Destroyer of the Godless: A Making of a Sixteenth-Century Religious Revolutionary* (Berkeley, Calif.: Univ. of California Press, 1990). For a discussion of the mystical influence upon Thomas Müntzer, see Hans-Jürgen Goertz, *Innere und äussere Ordnung in der Theologie Thomas Müntzer* (Leyden, 1967). See also Hans-Jürgen Goertz, *Thomas Müntzer, Mystiker-Apokalyptiker-Revolutionär* (München: C. H. Beck, 1989); as well as Peter Matteson, *The Collected Works of Thomas Müntzer* (Edinburgh: T. & T. Clark, 1988).

158. Bauer, *Anfänge*, 3.

159. *Apocalypticism* teaches the nearness of the end of the world, a general resurrection, and a final judgment. It is based on Jewish and Christian writings, such as Daniel and Revelation, marked by symbolic imagery which purports to *uncover* God's workings and the future. It expects God to destroy the ruling powers of evil and raise the righteous to life in a messianic kingdom.

160. Williams, *Radical Reformation*, 150, claims that Denck was influenced by the mysticism of Tauler (*ME*, 4:687), as mediated by Müntzer. Bauman, *Spiritual Legacy*, 35, in contrast, argues that Denck was influenced more strongly by Meister Eckhart (*ME*, 2:141-143), the *Theologia Deutsch* (booklet by Berthold Pirstinger, ca. 1500; *ME*, 2:43-44; 4:704), and Erasmus (*ME*, 2:239-240). Packull, *Mysticism*, 34, makes the case that Denck was influenced by a popularized medieval mystical tradition.

161. There is continuing debate about the influence of Müntzer on Denck. Williams, *Radical Reformation*, 151, contends that Müntzer even stayed at Denck's house in the fall of 1524. Bauman, *Spiritual Legacy*, argues that there is no evidence that the two actually met. In *Mysticism*, 39, Packull argues that Denck was influenced by the spiritualism of the Müntzer circle, but he leaves unanswered the question whether Denck and Müntzer met.

162. Cf. Walter Klaassen, ed., *Anabaptism in Outline: Selected Primary Sources*, Classics of the Radical Reformation, 3 (Scottdale, Pa.: Herald Press, 1981), 87.

163. Bauer, *Anfänge*, 149-150.

164. *Chronicle*, 163; Williams, *Radical Reformation*, 426.

165. Zieglschmid, *Chronik*, 175; Williams, *Radical Reformation*, 425.

166. Zieglschmid, *Chronik*, 175.

167. *Chronicle*, 162.

168. Williams, *Radical Reformation*, 422.

169. Zieglschmid, *Chronik*, 105-107.

170. Zieglschmid, *Chronik*, 99-109.

171. Zieglschmid, *Chronik*, 109, indicates that none of the supporters of either Ascherham or Plener left them to join the Tiroleans and Hutter. Williams, *Radical Reformation*, 422, suggests that portions of each of the two groups joined the Hutterites. Perhaps the two writers refer to different time periods, since during the 1540s numerous followers of both Ascherham and Plener joined the Hutterites.

172. *Chronicle*, 110-126.

173. Hutter expressed his views in a lengthy letter to the churches in Tirol. An English translation of the letter is provided by Robert Friedmann and the Society of Brothers, "Jacob Hutter's Epistle Concerning the Schism in Moravia in 1533," *MQR* 38 (Oct. 1964): 329-343.

174. Williams, *Radical Reformation*, 423.

175. Williams, *Radical Reformation*, 423-424. Shortly after Hutter returned to the Tirol, he was captured and then executed February 25, 1536.

176. Williams, *Radical Reformation*, 425.

177. *Chronicle*, 135-136.

178. Friedmann, "Peter Riedemann," 9.

179. Friedmann, "Peter Riedemann," 9; *Chronicle*, 135-136.

180. "Ascherham, Gabriel," *ME*, 1:174-176.

181. Williams, *Radical Reformation*, 674-676, points out that in addition to the main communal group in Moravia, there continued to exist various, much-smaller Anabaptist groups in Moravia, some communal and some not.

182. Zieglschmid, *Chronik*, 176-181.

183. Zieglschmid, *Chronik*, 180.

184. Zieglschmid, *Chronik*, 181.

185. Zieglschmid, *Chronik*, 194. There is a major difference of views concerning the date when Peter Riedemann left Moravia for Hesse. In contrast to *Chronik*, Williams in *Radical Reformation*, 647, states that Riedemann was in prison in Nuremberg for only two years, coming back to Moravia in 1535. According to him, Riedemann left for Hesse in the same year, in the midst of the terrible persecution. Williams says that Riedemann was sent to Hesse to straighten out John Bott. After some time Riedemann returned to Moravia. According to Williams, Riedemann was sent to Hesse a second time, but he does not indicate the date. Since Williams does not note the source for his claims, it is difficult to evaluate them. Thus, in the absence of any other documented evidence, I have followed the dates of the *Chronik*.

186. Zieglschmid, *Chronik*, 195; Claus-Peter Clasen, "The Anabaptists at Lauingen: A Forgotten Congregation," *MQR* 42 (Apr. 1968): 144-148.

187. Zieglschmid, *Chronik*, 195-196.

188. *Chronicle*, 182-186.

189. Zieglschmid, *Chronik*, 197.

190. Zieglschmid, *Chronik*, 137.

191. Stayer, *Peasants' War*, 91.

192. Werner O. Packull, "Peter Tasch: From Melchiorite to Bankrupt Wine Merchant," *MQR* 62 (Jul. 1988): 276-295.

193. *Polygamy* means having more than one wife or husband, as practiced by the Münsterites.

194. Walter Klaassen, ed., Frank Friesen, trans., *Sixteenth-Century Anabaptism: Defenses, Confessions, Refutations* (Waterloo, Ont.: Conrad Grebel College, 1981), 82-108.

195. For the proceedings of the disputation organized by Philip of Hesse in which he made this pledge to introduce church discipline, see Günther Franz, *Wiedertäuferakten, 1527-1626*, vol. 4 of *Urkundliche Quellen zur hessischen Reformationsgeschichte* (Marburg, 1951), 213-237. For a discussion of this event, see Williams, *Radical Reformation*, 676. On the decline of the Melchiorite Anabaptists in Hesse, see Klaus Deppermann, *Melchior Hoffmann: Social Unrest and Apocalyptic Visions in the Age of the Reformation*, trans. Malcolm Wren (Edinburgh: T. & T. Clark, 1987), 379-380.

196. *Chronicle*, 187-188.

197. *Chronicle*, 188-196; they received ill treatment, and many later were marched to Trieste to be galley slaves, but most escaped or disappeared.

198. *Chronicle*, 197.

199. Williams, *Radical Reformation*, 647.

200. *Chronicle*, 197, note 1. Franz, *Wiedertäuferakten*, 276-277.

201. *Chronicle*, 199-200; Williams, *Radical Reformation*, 647.

202. Williams, *Radical Reformation*, 647.

203. The letters are preserved in *Die Hutterischen Episteln 1527 bis 1763* [1767], vols. 1, 3, and 4 (Elie, Man.: James Valley Book Centre, 1986, 1988, 1991). Almost half of Hutter's extant letters were written from Hesse.

204. Williams, *Radical Reformation*, 647-648.

205. *Die Hutterischen Episteln*, 1:175, Peter Riedemann's letter sent to Hansen (Hans Amon) and Leonharden (Leonard Lanzenstiel).

206. Williams, *Radical Reformation*, 648.

207. Klaassen and Friesen, *Sixteenth-Century Anabaptism*, 98.

208. *Chronicle*, 214-216; Williams, *Radical Reformation*, 1064.

209. Williams, *Radical Reformation*, 1066.

210. There is some disagreement about the dating of these eras. Williams, *Radical Reformation*, 1065-1066, states that the persecution lasted from 1545 to 1551. *Chronicle*, 295, claims that "The Second Great Persecution" lasted from 1547 to 1553. On *The Golden Years*, see Gross.

211. Some economic restrictions were placed on them during this time. In 1544 the "Moravian estates issued an order prohibiting the purchase of wool anywhere but in the royal cities, or in the baronial estates"; Williams, *Radical Reformation*, 1065.

212. See *Chronicle*, 240-249, for accounts of capture, interrogation, torture, and execution of a number of Hutterites from 1545 to 1547.

213. Williams, *Radical Reformation*, 630. Some of the Gabrielites also joined the Schwenkfelders.

214. *Chronicle*, 296.

215. Williams, *Radical Reformation*, 1066; *Chronicle*, 296-297.

216. *Chronicle*, 298.

217. *Chronicle*, 300.

218. *Chronicle*, 299-302.

219. *Chronicle*, 302-303.

220. *Chronicle*, 303, 306 with note 1.

221. *Chronicle*, 304-305.

222. *Chronicle*, 304-311.

223. *Chronicle,* 304.

224. *Chronicle,* 304.

225. Williams, *Radical Reformation,* 1006; see note 7 for a list of the communities which were established.

226. *Chronicle,* 319-320.

227. *Chronicle,* 330.

228. *Chronicle,* 329-330.

229. "Rechenschaft," *ME,* 4:259-261. See also Robert Friedmann, "Book Review of *Account of Our Religion, Doctrine, and Faith, Given By Peter Riedemann of the Brothers Whom We Call Hutterians,*" *MQR* 26 (Apr. 1952): 164; as well as *ML,* 3:501.

230. J. Ten Doornkaat Koolman, "The First Edition of Peter Riedemann's Rechenschaft," *MQR* 36 (Apr. 1962): 169-170; on the page facing 169, Koolman includes a photocopy of the title page from the Vienna copy of the *Rechenschaft* in the first edition, ca. 1545.

231. Koolman, "The First Edition," 169-170; on the page facing 169, the facsimile shows the quotation from 1 Pet. 3:15.

232. Koolman, "The First Edition," 170.

233. Friedmann, "Peter Riedemann," 31.

234. Koolman, "The First Edition," 169. Koolman's discussion and his facsimile are not in agreement. This makes it difficult to determine whether he is claiming that the Vienna copy is a copy of the 1545 edition, or whether he thinks it is a copy of the 1565 edition. The cut line to the facsimile clearly identifies the copy as from ca. 1545. But in his discussion he concludes that the Zurich copy is from the first edition, thereby implying that the Vienna copy is of the 1565 edition. Checking the three originals would be necessary to sort out this discrepancy.

235. Friedmann, "Peter Riedemann," 31.

236. Friedmann, "Peter Riedemann," 31-32. Four other copies seem to have disappeared. In 1887 there was a copy of the 1565 edition in the library of the Lutheran Gymnasium of Kronstadt (Brasov), Romania, but it is no longer there. In 1870 there was a copy of this edition in a bookshop in Berlin, but there is no record of what happened to it. The *ML,* 3:504-505, lists a copy in the Landesmuseum in Brünn, Moravia (now Brno, in the Czech Republic), but it is no longer there. C. Sachsse, *Balthasar Hubmaier* (Berlin, 1914), xiv, indicates that there was also a copy in the Bavarian Staatsbibliothek in Munich, but it seems to have disappeared in World War II. For this study a copy of the volume in the British Museum was used: P. Ryedememan, *Rechenschaffe,* 1565 (B.M. REF. NO. 3908 a.8.).

237. Friedmann, "Peter Riedemann," 32 with note; *ME,* 4:261.

238. Vol. 2 (1870): 254-417.

239. It does not appear that Riedemann used the Froschauer Bible for writing his *Confession of Faith.* Even though Froschauer published his Bible in 1536, and the translation could have been available to Riedemann, the text of the 1565 edition of the *Confession* does not indicate use of it. In comparison with the Froschauer Bible, Riedemann's biblical quotations have a different word order, different spelling of the same words, and frequently quite different words.

240. Arianism was a fourth-century heresy which rejected Christ's full divinity and taught that Christ was created by God, albeit before the creation of the world. In the sixteenth century, certain groups drew special attention to Christ's ethical teachings and looked to Christ as an ethical example. Others, thinking such groups overemphasized Christ's humanity, frequently accused them of being Arian.

241. In 1524 Erasmus wrote *On the Freedom of the Will.* In the following year, Luther responded with *On the Bondage of the Will.* For the texts of these two treatises, see E. Gordon Rupp and Philip S. Watson, trans. and eds., *Luther and Erasmus: Free Will and Salvation.*

Bibliography

PRIMARY SOURCES, SIXTEENTH CENTURY
Älteste Chronik der Hutterischen Brüder, Die . Ed. A. J. F. Zieglschmid. Philadelphia: The Carl Schurz Memorial Foundation, and Ithaca, N.Y.: Cayuga Press, 1947.

Bauman, Clarence. *The Spiritual Legacy of Hans Denck: Interpretation and Translation of Key Texts.* Leiden: E. J. Brill, 1991.

Beck, Josef. *Die Geschichts-Bücher der Wiedertäufer in Österreich-Ungarn in der Zeit von 1526 bis 1785.* Nieuwkoop: B. de Graaf, 1967.

Chronicle of the Hutterian Brethren, The. Vol. 1. Trans. and ed. Hutterian Brethren. Rifton, N.Y.: Plough Publishing, 1987. From "Das grosse Geschicht-Buch der Hutterischen Brüder," in codices of 1580 and 1581, and records to 1665.

Denck, Hans. *Selected Writings of Hans Denck, 1500-1527.* Ed. E. J. Furcha. Texts and Studies in Religion, 44. Queenston, Ont.: Edwin Mellen Press, 1989.

Ehrenpreis, Andreas, and Claus Felbringer. *Brotherly Community the Highest Command of Love: Two Anabaptist Documents of 1650 and 1560.* Rifton, N.Y.: Plough Publishing, 1978.

Fischer, Hans. *Jacob Huter: Leben, Frömmigkeit, und Briefe,* Newton, Kan.: Mennonite Publication Office, 1956.

Geschicht-Buch der Hutterischen Brüder. Ed. Rudolf Wolkan. Vienna, 1923. Macleod, Alta.: Hutterian Brethren.

Hubmaier, Balthasar. *Balthasar Hubmaier: Theologian of Anabaptism.* Trans. and ed. H. Wayne Pipkin and John H. Yoder. Classics of the Radical Reformation, 5. Herald Press, 1989.

Hutter, Jakob. *Brotherly Faithfulness: Epistles from a Time of Persecution.* 3d printing. Farmington, Pa.: Plough Publishing, 1986.

Hutterischen Episteln, Die, 1527-1763. Vols. 1-4. Elie, Man.: James Valley Book Centre, 1986, 1987, 1988, 1991 (respectively).

Klaassen, Walter, ed. *Anabaptism in Outline: Selected Primary Sources.* Classics of the Radical Reformation, 3. Herald Press, 1981.

Klein Geschichtbuch der Hutterischen Brüder, Das. ed. A. F. J. Zieglschmid. Philadelphia: Carl Schurz Memorial Foundation, 1947.

Lieder der Hutterischen Brüder, Die. Herald Press, 1914.

Luther, Martin, and Desiderius Erasmus. *Luther and Erasmus: Free Will and Salvation.* Trans and ed. E. Gordon Rupp and Philip S. Watson. Library of Christian Classics, 17. Philadelphia: Westminster, 1969.

Marpeck, Pilgram. *The Writings of Pilgram Marpeck.* Trans. and ed. William Klassen and Walter Klaassen. Classics of the Radical Reformation, 2. Herald Press, 1978.

Mecenseffy, Grete. *Quellen zur Geschichte der Täufer, Österreich, Teil 2.* Gütersloh: Gerd Mohn, 1972.

Müller, Lydia, ed. *Glaubenszeugnisse oberdeutscher Taufgesinnter,* Band 1. *Quellen zur Geschichte der Wiedertäufer,* 3. Leipzig: M. Heinsius Nachfolger, 1938.

Müller, Lydia, and Robert Friedmann. *Glaubenszeugnisse oberdeutscher Taufgesinnter.* Band 2. *Quellen zur Geschichte der Täufer,* 12. Heidelberg: Verein für Reformationsgeschichte, 1967.

Müntzer, Thomas. *The Collected Works of Thomas Müntzer.* Ed. Peter Matteson. Edinburgh: T. & T. Clark, 1988.

Riedemann, Peter. *Love Is Like Fire: The Confession of an Anabaptist, Peter Riedemann.* Trans. and ed. Hutterian Brethren. Farmington, Pa.: Plough Publishing, 1993.

_____. *Rechenschafft unserer Religion, Leer [Lehre], und Glaubens, von den Brüdern, so man die Hutterischen nennt, aussgangen.* 1565. Trans. by Kathleen E. E. Hasenberg as *Confession of Faith: Account of Our Religion, Doctrine and Faith, Given by Peter Rideman of the Brothers Whom Men Call Hutterians.* England: Houghton and Stoughton, and Plough Publishing, 1950; reprinted, Rifton, N.Y.: Plough Publishing, 1970, 1974.

Schiemer, Leonhard. "Ein Bekenntnis von Leonhard Schiemer." Written at Rattenberg, Jan. 14, 1528. In *Die Hutterischen Episteln, 1527-1763,* vol. 3. Elie, Man.: James Valley Book Centre, 1988.

Wolkan, Rudolf. *Die Lieder der Wiedertäufer: Ein Beitrag zur deutschen und niederländischen Literatur- und Kirchengeschichte.* Berlin: B. Behr, 1903.

Zieglschmid, A. F. J. See above: *Älteste Chronik;* and *Klein Geschichtsbuch.*

SECONDARY LITERATURE

Adler, Clemens. "Das Urteil von dem Schwert," 1529. Mennonite Historical Library, Goshen, Ind. Geiser Codex.

"Ascherham, Gabriel." *ME,* 1:174-176.

"Bamberg." *ME,* 1:219.

Bauer, Günther. *Anfänge täuferische Gemeindebildungen in Franken.* Nürnberg: Selbstverlag des Vereins für bayerische Kirchengeschichte, 1966.

"Brandhuber, Wolfgang." *ME,* 1:404-405.

Clasen, Claus-Peter. *Anabaptism: A Social History, 1525-1618.* Ithaca, N.Y.: Cornell Univ. Press, 1972.

_____. "The Anabaptists at Lauingen: A Forgotten Congregation." *MQR* 42 (Apr. 1968): 144-148.

_____. *The Anabaptists in South and Central Germany, Switzerland, and Austria, 1525-1618.* Ann Arbor, Mich.: Univ. Microfilms International, 1978.

Cornelius, C. A. *Geschichte des münsterischen Aufruhrs,* Band 2. Beilage, 5. Leipzig, 1855.

Deppermann, Klaus. *Melchior Hoffmann: Social Unrest and Apocalyptic Visions in the Age of the Reformation.* Trans. Malcolm Wren. Edinburgh: T. & T. Clark, 1987.

Erb, Peter. *Schwen[c]kfeld in His Reformation Setting.* Valley Forge: Judson Press, 1978.

Franz, Günther. *Wiedertäuferakten, 1527-1626. Urkundliche Quellen zur hessischen Reformationsgeschichte,* 4. Marburg, 1951.

Friedmann, Robert. "Book Review of *Account of Our Religion, Doctrine, and Faith, Given by Peter Riedemann of the Brothers Whom We Call Hutterians.*" *MQR* 26 (Apr. 1952): 164.

_____. "Leonhard Schiemer and Hans Schlaffer: Two Martyr Apostles of 1528." *MQR* 38 (Jan. 1959): 31-41.

_____. "The Oldest Church Discipline of the Anabaptists." *MQR* 29 (Apr. 1955): 162-166.

_____. "Peter Riedemann: Early Anabaptist Leader." *MQR* 49 (Jan. 1970): 5-44.

Friedmann, Robert, intro., and the Society of Brothers, trans. "Jacob Hutter's Epistle Concerning the Schism in Moravia in 1533." *MQR* 38 (Oct. 1964): 329-343.

Friesen, Abraham. *Thomas Müntzer, a Destroyer of the Godless: A Making of a Sixteenth-Century Religious Revolutionary.* Berkeley, Calif.: Univ. of California Press, 1990.

Goertz, Hans-Jürgen. *Innere und äussere Ordnung in der Theologie Thomas Müntzer.* Leyden, 1967.

———. *Thomas Müntzer, Mystiker-Apokalyptiker-Revolutionär.* München: C. H. Beck, 1989.

Gross, Leonard. *The Golden Years of the Hutterites: The Witness and Thought of the Communal Moravian Anabaptists During the Walpot Era, 1565-1578.* Herald Press, 1980.

Harrison, Wes. *Andreas Ehrenpreis and Hutterite Faith and Practice.* Studies in Anabaptist and Mennonite History, 36. Kitchener, Ont.: Pandora Press, and Herald Press, 1997.

Hofer, John. *The History of the Hutterites.* Altona, Man.: D. W. Friesen & Sons, 1998.

Hostetler, John A. *Hutterite Society.* Baltimore: Johns Hopkins Univ. Press, 1974.

Klaassen, Walter. *Anabaptism Revisited.* Herald Press, 1992.

———. *Michael Gaismair: Revolutionary and Reformer.* Leiden: E. J. Brill, 1978.

Klaassen, Walter, ed., and Frank Friesen, trans. *Sixteenth-Century Anabaptism: Defense, Confessions, Refutations.* Waterloo, Ont.: Conrad Grebel College, 1981.

Koolman, J. Ten Doornkaat. "The First Edition of Peter Riedemann's Rechenschaft." *MQR* 36 (Apr. 1962): 169-170, plus facsimiles on page facing 169.

Längin, Bernd G. *Die Hutterer: Gefangene der Vergangenheit, Pilger der Gegenwart, Propheten der Zukunft.* Hamburg: Rasch und Rohring, 1986.

Liechty, Daniel. *Andreas Fischer and the Sabbatarian Anabaptists.* Herald Press, 1988.

McLaughlin, R. Emmet. *Casper Schwenckfeld, Reluctant Radical: His Life to 1540.* New Haven, Conn.: Yale Univ. Press, 1986.

"Nürnberg." *ME,* 3:926-927.

"Nürnberg." *ML,* 3:279-282.

Packull, Werner O. "Clemens Adler: A Swiss Connection to Silesian Anabaptism?" *Conrad Grebel Review* 9 (Fall 1991): 245.

———. *Hutterite Beginnings: Communitarian Experiments During the Reformation.* Baltimore: Johns Hopkins Univ. Press, 1995.

———. "Melchior Hoffman's Experience in the Livonian Reformation: The Dynamics of Sect Formation." *MQR* 59 (Apr. 1985): 130-146.

———. *Mysticism and the Early South German-Austrian Anabaptist Movement, 1525-1531.* Herald Press, 1977.

———. "Peter Tasch: From Melchiorite to Bankrupt Wine Merchant." *MQR* 62 (Jul. 1988): 276-295.

"*Rechenschafft* unserer Religion, Leer [Lehre], und Glaubens." *ME,* 4:259-261.

Seebass, G. *Müntzer's Erbe: Werk, Leben, und Theologie des Hans Hut.* Erlangen, 1981.

Stayer, James M. *Anabaptists and the Sword.* Lawrence, Kan.: Coronado Press, 1972.

———. *The German Peasants' War and Anabaptist Community of Goods.* Montreal: McGill-Queen's Univ. Press, 1991.

Stayer, James M., and Werner O. Packull. *The Anabaptists and Thomas Müntzer.* Toronto: Kendall-Hunt Publishing Co., 1980.

Weigelt, Horst. *The Schwenkfelders in Silesia.* Trans. Peter C. Erb. Pennsburg, Pa.: Schwenkfelder Library, 1985.

———. *Spiritualistiche Tradition im Protestantismus: Die Geschichte des Schwenk-feldertums in Schlesien.* Berlin: De Gruyter, 1973.

Wenger, J. C. "Letter from Wilhelm Reublin to Pilgram Marpeck, 1531." *MQR* 23 (Apr. 1949): 67-75.

Williams, George H. *The Radical Reformation.* First ed., 1962. 3d ed., Kirksville, Mo.: Sixteenth-Century Publishers, 1992.

"Zaunring, Georg." *ME,* 4:1018-1019.

Zeman, Gerald Knox. *The Anabaptists and the Czech Brethren in Moravia, 1525-1628: A Study of Origins and Contacts.* The Hague: Mouton, 1969.

Zuck, Lowell. *Christianity and Revolution: Radical Christian Testimonies, 1520-1650.* Philadelphia: Temple Univ. Press, 1975.

Index of Names and Places

Scripture Index

The Translator and Editor

John J. Friesen, a native of southern Manitoba, is professor of history and theology at the Canadian Mennonite Bible College in Winnipeg. He has been teaching at CMBC since 1970 and was appointed dean in 1997.

Throughout his career, John has been interested in helping the Anabaptist-Mennonite heritage come alive for people today. He has done this through his classes at CMBC, in short courses in congregations, through a permanent historical display at the Mennonite Heritage Village Museum in Steinbach, Manitoba, and through various historical societies and committees.

Friesen holds a Ph.D. in historical theology from Northwestern University, Evanston, Illinois. He is also a graduate of Mennonite Collegiate Institute, Gretna, Manitoba; CMBC; Bethel College, North Newton, Kansas; and Mennonite Biblical Seminary, Elkhart, Indiana. John's research interests have included the Reformation, early church, and Mennonite history. He served on the board of the Associated Mennonite Biblical Seminary, Elkhart, Indiana, from 1989 to 1997, and four years as chair.

During his graduate studies, John and his wife, Dorothy, were members of Reba Place Fellowship, Evanston, Illinois, for three years. Now they are members of Fort Garry Mennonite Fellowship, Winnipeg, and both have held numerous responsibilities in that church. John has served the congregation as chair and as lay minister. John and Dorothy have three children and three grandchildren.

Endorsements

"This book, composed by Peter Riedemann, the 'Second Founder of the Hutterites,' is the only known volume published by the Hutterites during the whole of the sixteenth century. Part two is pro ably the most perfectly balanced expression of biblical theology emerging from an Anabaptist perspective. This *Confession* continues to fill a truly unique and central role in defining the Hutterian way. It deserves even greater scholarly attention than it has received. Here Riedemann's thoughts come to us in a fine, modern English translation, thanks to the scholarly efforts of John J. Friesen."
—*Leonard Gross, Goshen, Indiana; Author,* The Golden Years of the Hutterites

"Peter Riedemann's *Confession of Faith* marked a defining moment in the history of the Hutterite community and is, without question, the most substantial statement of faith and practice of that community. Since its influence is evident on subsequent Hutterite confessional statements, it is foundational. But its significance reaches beyond the confines of the Hutterite community.

"This remarkable theological statement by a shoemaker gives potent testimony to lay enlightenment during the Reformation. Luther's notion of the priesthood of all believers was more than rhetoric in Riedemann's community.Riedemann revealed not only a grasp of doctrinal issues; he also knew the cost of discipleship.

"Professor John J. Friesen deserves our gratitude for his labor of love which made this modern, easy-to-read but accurate translation available. Especially welcome is the historical context provided in the introduction, the organization of the text, and the scholarly apparatus with its biblical references."
—*Werner O. Packull, Professor of History, Conrad Grebel College, Waterloo, Ontario; Author,* Hutterite Beginnings

"This volume by the foremost Hutterite leader and thinker of the sixteenth century is a comprehensive guide to daily life in the Hutterite community. Riedemann's *Confession* has served as the basic charter for Hutterites from the sixteenth century to the present day."
—*John A. Hostetler, Author,* Hutterite Society

"We are pleased that *Peter Riedemann's Hutterite Confession of Faith,* an account of our historical beliefs and practices, is available in contemporary English. Both young and old may now read and understand this spiritual message that Riedemann wrote in his dark cell so many years ago.

"We are thankful for the excellent work and effort that John J. Friesen has exerted in translating this vital document. It is one of the confessions that has become the very center of our Hutterian teachings and practices."
—*Paul S. Gross, Hutterian Minister and Historian*
  Author of The Hutterite Way *and several pamphlets*
  Spokane Colony, Reardon, Washington
  (Endorsement received a week before Paul S. Gross passed away on April 8, 1998.)